Globalisation
& the Changing Role of the State

Issues and Impacts

Globalisation
& the Changing Role of the State

Issues and Impacts

Edited by
Rumki Basu

NEW DAWN PRESS, INC.
USA• UK• INDIA

NEW DAWN PRESS GROUP

Published by New Dawn Press Group
New Dawn Press, Inc., 244 South Randall Rd # 90, Elgin, IL 60123
e-mail: sales@newdawnpress.com

New Dawn Press, 2 Tintern Close, Slough, Berkshire, SL1-2TB, UK
e-mail: sterlingdis@yahoo.co.uk

New Dawn Press (An Imprint of Sterling Publishers (P) Ltd.)
A-59, Okhla Industrial Area, Phase-II, New Delhi-110020
e-mail: sterlingpublishers@airtelbroadband.in
www.sterlingpublishers.com

Globalisation and the Changing Role of the State: Issues and Impacts
© 2008, Department of Political Science, Jamia Millia Islamia, New Delhi
ISBN 978 1 932705 79 9

All rights are reserved.
No part of this publication may be reproduced, stored in a retrieval system or transmitted, in any form or by any means, mechanical, photocopying, recording or otherwise, without prior written permission of the original publisher.

PRINTED IN INDIA

TO OUR STUDENTS
IN THE DEPARTMENT OF POLITICAL SCIENCE
JAMIA MILLIA ISLAMIA

Foreword

I am happy to learn that the Department of Political Science has decided to publish a Prelude Volume to their national seminar on "Globalisation and the State Revisited: Issues and Impacts" scheduled for 4th-6th December 2007. The four sections of the book comprising sixteen articles and an introduction explores the multiple faces of globalisation and its contested terrain in theory and practice.

In the book, the globalisation-political economy interface and resultant transformations in society and politics is a major theme of investigation. The evolving idea of a New World Order, issues of global conflict and cooperation, besides other specific impacts of globalisation on human rights, cultural identities, democracy and development have been included for study in the sixteen articles of the book.

The seminar theme is of great contemporary relevance and the department of Political Science has made a pioneering attempt to bring out a Prelude Volume which is exclusively and inclusively an intradepartmental project – it includes articles by all the fifteen members of the department of political science of Jamia Millia Islamia.

The Department of Political Science is the largest in the social science school in Jamia in terms of student strength and courses offered. I take this opportunity to congratulate the faculty and students of the department and wish them good luck in all their future endeavours. I hope their first departmental publication is only a beginning of an ongoing journey to scale newer academic heights and challenges.

Mushirul Hasan
Vice Chancellor, Jamia Millia Islamia

Preface

For more than two decades globalisation has been bringing about changes in the 'rules of the game' for the use of state power, role of multilateral agencies and relations among and between states. The role of the state – as a controller of national economy, as the principal provider of goods and services to citizens and as the engine of national development – has largely been delimited in the face of increasing inability of states to exercise sovereign control over intrinsic economic activities and cross-border economic transactions. The emerging rules of the game for globalisation are inequitable (both interstate as well as intra state) in terms of outcomes, a fact not surprising in a world divided by inequality within and among states. The developed nations, as ever, have the power to make the 'global' rules and the authority to implement them. Such rules are bound to significantly eat into the autonomy of developing countries in the formulation of economic policies in their pursuit of development.

This seminar also brings into sharp focus the changing roles of the state in promoting and supporting an effective human rights regime and the impact it has cast on the capabilities of citizens at all levels to capitalise on these opportunities for self development and eking out livelihood for sustenance. It dwells upon the forces driving globalisation, the factors that contribute or impede the state's capacity to promote economic and human development besides the policies and institutions essential for even a post-globalised state to carry out its delimited core or optional functions of governance.

The basic object of the seminar is to address these questions: is the global multinational governance framework and international institutions created in 1945 adequate for the economy and polity of a globalising state and society at present? Second, what are the issues thrown up by globalisation? What are its positive and negative impacts? In the post-globalised world, is there any need to redefine the role of, or adopt the existing institutions to meet the needs of our age?

As we are marching ahead on the turf of the 21st Century, it is time to reflect on the possibility of evolving a new global ideology and searching for a new consensus on global coexistence, which can only be based on a futuristic vision of the economy, polity and society. In this world view, the concern for efficiency in economic growth calls for a certain degree of balancing with the concern for social equity: for efficiency and growth are means rather than ends by themselves. The list of worthy ends is long including a host of issues and concerns: democratisation, poverty eradication, reduced inequality, rights based human development and sustainable growth. It is also time to evolve a new consensus on development in which the focus should be on human development based on environmentally sustainable economic growth.

This Prelude/Introductory Volume is our Department's humble attempt to place on record, every individual faculty member's views on a chosen theme of Globalisation. This book also attempts a few firsts:

- Seminar proceedings are generally brought out after the seminar. We have decided to publish a Prelude Volume to the seminar. The former will follow.
- This is perhaps the first intra-departmental publication of Jamia Millia Islamia for which all fifteen members of the Department have contributed articles to the present volume.

This edited collection of articles is our departmental collage and preparatory offering for a seminar whose technical sessions will be truly representative of the three different specialisations offered by our department at the post graduate level, viz.; Political Science, Human Rights and Public Administration.

By offering this Prelude Volume (17 articles), we now invite the national fraternity of Political Science teachers and scholars to ponder over these issues as well as impacts of globalisation in our seminar to help evolve a holistic perspective on what has truly emerged as the overarching phenomenon of our times.

I thank all my colleagues in the Department for their devoted cooperation and enthusiastic support in making this book possible and ready on time to meet publishing deadlines. It has been an intellectual endeavour and labour of love of the department, we all collectively care for. We did finally overcome varied obstacles to meet the publisher's deadlines. I would also like to thank Prof. Mushirul Hasan, our Vice Chancellor for all his encouragement, intellectual guidance and logistical support for whatever we have tried to do in our department from time to time.

Finally, I express my sincere gratitude to my publisher, Shri S.K. Ghai for agreeing to publish this book in the shortest possible time. As always, the articles in the book reflect the opinions and views of their individual authors alone, and cannot be attributed to the editor of the volume.

RUMKI BASU

Contents

Foreword vii
Preface ix
Introduction 1

Globalisation and the State/Ideology/Political Economy

1. Globalisation and the State: A Contested Terrain
   – AMIR ALI 19
2. Globalisation and Changing Role of the
   Nation-State
   - S.R.T.P. SUGUNAKARARAJU 33
3. Globalisation and Islamism: Rethinking
   Some Reigning Paradigms
   - S.A.M. PASHA 46
4. Globalisation: Towards a New Perspective
   on Political Economy
   - NISAR-UL-HAQ 78
5. Globalisation and Good Governance: Redefining
   the State Precincts
   - BULBUL DHAR-JAMES 92

Globalisation and the New World Order/Area Studies

6. Globalised Trend Towards Nuclear Proliferation:
   A Case Study of India and Pakistan as Glocalisation
   - MOHAMMED BADRUL ALAM 119

7. Conflict and Development in the Age of
   Globalisation: A Case of Rwanda
   - M. Muslim Khan 140
8. Impact of Globalisation on the GCC States:
   Cultural Dimension
   - Farah Naaz 156

Globalisation and Human Rights

9. Implementing International Human Rights
   Standards in a Globalising World
   - K. Savitri 171
10. Human Rights Discourse in a Globalised World:
    Mumbai Metropolis
    - Naved Jamal 193
11. The Impact of Globalisation on Human Rights:
    A Case of India
    - Mehtab Manzar 209
12. Human Rights Education in the Age of
    Globalisation: Role of UGC
    - Syed Mehartaj Begum 221

Globalisation and Indian Politics/Administration

13. Power Sharing in the Federal Project in Post
    Globalised India: Governance and Fiscal Reforms
    - Rumki Basu 233
14. Democracy and Development: The Indian Experience
    - Furqan Ahmed 265
15. Public Administration in the Age of Globalisation:
    An Alternative Paradigm
    - Rumki Basu 275
16. Role of Non-governmental Organisations
    in Public Policy in the Era of Globalisation
    - S. Ramudu 284

    Contributors 295

Introduction

Despite persisting debates on what globalisation truly implies, there cannot be any doubt about the fact that globalisation is the 'umbrella paradigm' or what is called the 'overarching phenomenon' of our era, which has thrown significant impacts on the economy, society and politics of our times. National economies have become closely integrated through cross-border flows of trade, technology, investment, labour and finance. The revolution in transport and communications has eroded barriers in time and distance, shaping a new era of interaction and interdependence among nations and peoples in the twenty-first century.

Globalisation not only provides unforeseen opportunities for economic and social development through trade liberalisation, foreign investment, capital-labour mobility and information exchange, but it also leads to inequitable benefits thereby pushing to the fringe, the poor and the non-privileged, who become non-beneficiaries of the dominant forces of globalisation in the market. What this book addresses is the complexity of globalisation, its issues, impacts and lastly, its relation with the state and political power. Globalisation is contestable in several ways and the counter movements that we have seen over the last decade bear testimony to the dialectics of emerging alternative models of human society and civilisation.

A period of more than two decades has seen globalisation change the 'rules of the game' for the use of state power, role of multilateral agencies and relations among and between states. The state's role – as controller of the national economy, as the principal provider of goods and services to citizens and as the engine of national development – has largely been delimited in the face of increasing inability of states to exercise sovereign control over internal economic activities as also cross border economic transactions. The emerging rules of the game for globalisation are inequitable (both interstate as well as intra state) in terms of outcomes, a fact not surprising in a world divided by inequality within and among states. As it has always happened, the developed nations possess the power and privilege to make the 'global' rules and the authority to execute them. These rules are bound to significantly reduce the autonomy of developing countries in the formulation of economic policies in their pursuit of development.

During the second half of the twentieth century, the United Nations and the Bretton Woods institutions were created with altogether different concerns. The then industrialised countries were still haunted by the memories of the Great Depression, which had created a desire for the conceptualisation of a welfare state, for putting an end to colonialism and for making the world safe for democracy and peace. This also coincided with the aspirations of the newly independent countries to bring about rapid national progress and economic development, in the pursuit of which the role of the nation state was conceived as crucial on all counts.

At present, perspectives on economic growth in the industrialised world and developmental strategies in the developing world significantly stand apart from each other. The world of competing political ideologies which marked the cold war era has yielded place to a world where due to the collapse of communism, capitalism has received a fresh lease of life. Development thinking has also changed from unilinear trajectories of development to diverse approaches in the contemporary multipolar era. In the industrialised countries, the rise of monetarism and neo-liberal ideologies have meant the retreat of the state from the economy and the advance of the market. In the erstwhile Third World Countries, the development consensus (from the 50's to the 80's of the last century) was in favour of a conscious attempt to delimit the extent of integration of the national economy with the world economy in pursuit of a more autonomous, self-reliant, public sector-led development because the market by itself was not considered adequate to meet the developmental aspirations of latecomers to industrialisation. Four decades later, by the early 1990's, partly as a consequence of intrinsic crisis situations in the political economy of certain states and the collapse of planned economies in most parts of the globe, several countries of the developing world began to reshape their domestic economic agenda to integrate much more into the world economy and to expand the market's purview vis-à-vis the state. The widespread acceptance of this new thinking on development came to be known as the Washington Consensus, since these perspectives on 'development' and 'good governance' came to be disseminated by the IMF and World Bank which exercised enormous influence on economies in crisis.

Since the early 1980's, national economies have been globalising rapidly – markets for goods and services have been expanding internationally, countries have been forming regional and global partnerships, and corporations have been expanding their regional networking to conduct global business. In this age of global interdependence, few governments seeking economic and social development can remain isolated or afford to overlook the challenges of a globalising society.

Although the concept of World Order is not new, it was introduced into the academic vocabulary only after World War-II. With the emergence of the Soviet reformist leader Mikhail Gorbachev, who called for global restructuring, openness, a new way of global thinking, peace for all, super power cooperation and an end to the cold war, the concept of a new world order reemerged. Following the Helsinki Summit in September 1990, US President George Bush increasingly used the concepts of a new world order and globalism. It will be appropriate to raise a question here that what has it come to mean today? This could be another point of investigation.

In the sphere of globalisation, characterised by the dominance of certain key concepts such as market economy, privatisation and liberalisation, two main sets of economic actors exercise major influence on the world stage – transnational corporations which occupy the driver's seat in investment, production and trade in the world economy; and international banks and funding agencies which hegemonise the world of finance. The nation states remain important political actors in the international political system but have retreated considerably in the international economic arena. Globalisation may bring new economic opportunities but also new political, social, technological and institutional complexities for poorer countries as well. In a globalising society, governments must work in tandem with the private sector, civil society organisations and public interest groups to develop institutions that support and sustain economic and social development that is equitable, sustainable and poverty alleviating. However, issues of accountability and control often become problematic in such public private partnerships. Governments in countries seeking to participate in and benefit from globalisation must increasingly assume new roles – as catalysts for economic and social development through better infrastructure support to the market players, enablers of productivity and efficiency, regulators ensuring that economies remain open and equitable, and stimulators of human resource development.

This book also endeavors to offer an insight into the changing roles of the state in promoting and supporting an effective human rights regime and its impact on the capabilities of citizens at all levels to capitalise on these opportunities for self-development and livelihood for sustenance. It describes the forces driving globalisation, the factors that contribute to the state's capacity to promote economic and human development and the policies and institutions essential for an 'effective and nurturing' state to carry out its tasks in the present era of globalisation.

If globalisation is the overarching phenomenon of our age, so is the irreversible (though slow and steady) global movement towards democratisation. All rights for all people everywhere in the globe should be the goal of the 21st Century. There is enough global awareness, resources and capacity to achieve this goal on a worldwide scale. As in earlier times, advances in the 21st Century will be won by human struggle against competing and divisive ideologies and against the opposition of entrenched political and economic structures which are inherently non-egalitarian. People's movements and civil society groups are poised to play the vanguard's role, raising public awareness of rights violations and pressing for changes in law and policy. Today's technologies and relatively open societies present great opportunities for networking and integration to forge alliances for human rights and democracy. Every country is getting alive to the need of strengthening its social arrangements so as to secure human freedoms with standardised norms, institutions, legal frameworks and an enabling economic environment with steady economic growth. Over as many as a hundred countries ended rule by military dictatorships or single parties in the past two decades but that by itself is never enough – a decent standard of living, adequate nutrition, health care, education, sustainable work are not just development goals, they are also human rights. Poverty eradication is not only a development goal; it is a central challenge for human rights in the 21st Century (UNDP Human Development Reports – 2000-2005). Global integration is shrinking time, space and eroding national borders. The state's autonomy is being delimited by new global rules of trade and new global actors wielding great influence. As privatisation goes on at an inexorable pace, private enterprises and corporations have begun to throw more impact on people's lives and economic opportunities. Global corporations can have enormous impact on human rights in their employment practices, in their environmental impact as also in their trade practices. Many of them still fail to meet human rights, or implementation standards and independent audits.

In the contemporary era of globalisation, we need stronger commitments to universalism combined with respect for cultural diversity. This will require shifts in the ideological backdrop and mindsets of states in the following patterns:

- From the state-centred approaches to pluralist, multi-actor approaches with accountability not only for the state but for the media, corporations, educational institutions, society and individuals as well.
- An inclusive approach to rights – the transition should be from civil and political rights to economic, social and cultural rights.
- Strengthening a rights-based approach in development cooperation, without laying conditionalities.

- From a thrust on procedural democracy to inclusive models of substantive democracy.
- From poverty eradication as a development goal to poverty eradication as a human rights goal.

II

Globalisation has brought about a spate of changes in the global political, economic and social landscape thus rapidly opening up unparalleled new opportunities as well as new threats to human security and human freedom. Transition to democracy in state after state brought advances in human rights to many citizens, whereas for several others, globalisation threw up constant threats to human rights as a result of a host of problems such as ethnic conflict, rising poverty, growing inequality and social fissures. Transition and economic collapse in the erstwhile communist states dismantled the universal economic and social assurances given to their citizens. Volatile state structures in 'failed and soft states' in the developing bloc also pose serious threat to human rights and legal guarantees to citizens continually as do intra- or inter state inequalities.

Most research on globalisation impacts have concluded that a shift towards a more competitive world economy that began to surface during the early 1990's, benefited not only richer nations but also liberalising developing countries that moved from closed controlled economies to open ones. The organisation for Economic Cooperation and Development (OECD) concluded that countries which opened their markets to international trade and investment have achieved double the average economic growth from those that did not *(Open Markets Matter: The benefits of Trade and Investment Liberalization,* Paris, OECD, 1998). As per the report, open market economies have higher investment ratios, better macroeconomic balance and stronger private sector roles in economic development than non-market economies.

Criticisms that globalisation rewards economic competitiveness at the cost of social progress often tend to ignore or belittle the substantial improvements in social conditions around the world over the last two decades. Overall, social conditions and quality of life indicators improved in much of the developing world during this period. The UNDP Human

Development Report informs that since 1990, 800 million people obtained improved water supplies and 750 million gained access to improved sanitation. Primary school enrolments worldwide increased from 80 per cent in 1990 to 84 per cent in 1998. Countries, where half of the world's population live, have reduced hunger by 50 per cent, or are on the right track towards achieving that target. About eighty countries have moved significantly toward democracy and more countries than ever before – 140 of the world's nearly 200 nations – hold multi party elections. (Human Development Report 2004, New York, OUP). A globalising economy is subject to cyclical spurts of growth and periodic recessions: regional recession in Latin America in the 1980's, Africa in the 1980's and 1990's and in Asia in the late 1990's and the worldwide recession beginning in 2000 – temporarily dampened its pace but globalisation drove world economic growth by 140 per cent (in US dollars) between 1970 and 2000 to nearly $40 trillion in annual output of goods and services. (World Development Indicators 2004, World Bank, Washington).

With globalisation, some old asymmetries continue while some new ones have been added. Poverty, inequality and deprivation are old problems that still persist. One-eighth of the people in the developed world live in poverty, while approximately 1.5 billion do in the developing world, in terms of absolute deprivation of basic needs. 580 million suffer from malnutrition and 1 billion do not have access to clean water or sanitation. More than 250 million children are out of school and 800 million adults remain illiterate globally even in the 21st Century.

Some popular myths about globalisation (rich become richer, and poor poorer!) however need to be seriously investigated. From 1990 to 2000, during the worldwide shift from centrally planned to competitive market economies, the number of people living in absolute poverty on less than $1 a day actually fell from 1.3 billion to 1.1 billion or, in percentage terms, from 29 per cent to 23 per cent of the population in developing countries during the same period when the world's population was growing rapidly. The deepest dent in poverty was made in regions of East Asia and the Pacific, South Asia, Latin America and the Caribbean where the globalisation process was well underway. In India also, between 1993-2000, when economic growth averaged 6% per annum, poverty declined from 36% to 26%. Thus, a 10 per cent drop was evidenced during the first decade of globalisation. Absolute poverty declined the least or worsened in countries in the Middle East, North Africa, Sub-Saharan Africa and Eastern Europe which were the greatest laggards in economic growth during the period (World Development Indicators, Washington DC, World Bank).

Even the claims of those, who call into question the efficacy of globalisation, that it has virtually resulted in the demise of the nation state, can be taken more in a spiritual sense, than the empirical one. To refute these charges, many scholars argue that even today the global economy is more multinational than global because most production and consumption in most states remain restricted to national frontiers. In most states (developed and developing) though MNC's may control a substantive share of the world's private sector productive assets, the bulk of goods, capital and jobs remain home based. The share of trade in GDP is still minimal in all but the smallest countries. Exports account for 12 per cent of GDP or less for the U.S, Japan and Single Unit Europe and the Asian and Latin American averages are well below 10 per cent. This reinforces the view that even now, a larger bulk of production and consumption in a majority of states cater to the domestic market (World Investment Report 1993 – New York, UN Publications). For example, the sharp increase in India and China's economic growth predates the rise in their foreign trade. Again, the decision to classify many poor countries as non-globalised despite the fact that much of their gross domestic product derives from the export of raw materials, is anomalous. Besides, even India, China and other countries which have benefited the most from globalisation, first engaged themselves in widespread economic regulation and state promotion and protection of their home industries before reducing tariffs and other barriers to foreign trade.

Globalisation is a contested terrain – which accounts for the drastically divergent descriptions and analyses of its impacts on poverty and inequality presented by Robert Wade, Joseph Stiglitz, Branko Milanovic and Vandana Shiva on the one hand, and Thomas Friedman, David Dollar, Aart Kraay and Martin Wolf on the other. Can the contentious issues be reconciled? These are worth probing for in serious studies of globalisation as some recent studies have shown that among the subset of countries with low and middle levels of average income in purchasing power terms and higher levels of trade, openness is associated with more inequality, while among higher income countries more openness precedes more equality.

In the literature on globalisation, the word 'governance' has at least four separate usages in the present context. As such, they are used a) as the minimal state, b) as the new public management, c) as good governance and d) as self-organising networks.

In the agenda of globalisation, the key theme is delimiting the functions of government and of public intervention. The loss of functions by government departments meant expanding the functional domain of private and voluntary organisations as alternative delivery systems. Limits were also set to the discretion of public servants through the new public management paradigm with its stress on managerial accountability and clearer political control through a sharper distinction between politics and administration. Government reform became one of the worldwide trends of globalisation and good governance as spelt out by the World Bank (1992).

For the World Bank, good governance served as a package, which included an efficient public service, an independent judicial system and legal framework to enforce contracts, accountable administration of public funds, responsibility to a representative legislature, respect for the law and human rights at all levels of government, a pluralistic institutional structure and a free press. In order to achieve efficiency in the public services, the New Public Management protagonists sought to encourage competition and markets, privatisation of public enterprises, reform of the civil service by cutting down over staffing and introducing budgetary discipline, decentralising administration and making greater use of non-governmental organisations. Governance also refers to governing by self organising inter organisational networks, public/private partnerships and transnational groups. Governance is broader than government, covering non-state actors. An alternative interpretation suggests more space for civil society and citizenry in public policy making and implementation. Citizens could be regaining control of government through their participation in networks as users and governors, thereby creating a post-modern public administration where citizens as users of goods and services remain ultimately in control. However, governance as self-organising networks can pose a challenge to governability because the autonomous networks may resist accountability to any central authority. Thus, governance may degenerate into becoming governing without government. A decentred theory of governance not only aggravates the problem the state encounters in regulating markets and networks but also the possibilities and dangers markets and networks pose for democracy. So, the post-globalised decades were a challenge and search for patterns of devolution, participation, control and accountability reflecting on our capacity to redefine the parameters of democracy.

Finally, as we are moving through the first quarter of the 21st Century, both qualitative and quantitative changes in the global economic, social and political scenario are all being clubbed together in the single defining umbrella of globalisation. Huntington (1996) spoke of the 'clash of civilisations'. Prior to him, Fukuyama (1992) had prophesied 'the end of history of man'. Globalisation wears many hats and means differently to different people. Economists consider globalisation as a step toward a fully integrated world market. Political Scientists view it as a move towards an inclusive concept of governance, with the state and non-state actors included. All discussions of globalisation deal with the question of 'borders' and associated issues of state jurisdiction, economy, identity, markets and civil society. However what needs to be stated unambiguously is that globalisation (following its current practice) will not necessarily mean the demise of the state or its bureaucracy, but may mandate their functions and role to be redefined and reinvented. It is now ultimately the citizens (whether viewed as 'clients' or 'user-groups') who will and must strive to be in control directly or indirectly to spread out the benefits of globalisation for a new world order. At last, it is 'global justice' – that can be the only worthy end of globalisation in whichever local avatar it manifests itself in any state. (World Commission on the Social Dimension of Globalisation, 2004, A fair globalisation: Creating opportunities for all, Geneva ILO)

III

On the issue whether globalisation should be replaced by some innovative and new system or it should be reformed is also an open question. No amount of tinkering can resolve problems associated with the current global brand of capitalist production and exchange processes, including the economic costs and environmental damage due to transporting goods across long distances, assaults on local autonomy, and North-South inequalities inherent in global exchanges.

The anti-globalisation movement has also rendered its focus substantially broad-based. Those opposing neo-liberalism today are more likely to use the term 'movement for global justice' to signify their efforts to offset the negative impacts of globalisation. The change took place a few years after the 1999 demostration at Seattle, when activists decided that they should not simply try to stop neoliberal globalisation but also achieve a more ambitious and positive goal. The content of what should be included in the concept of global justice is of course highly complex and contentious differing on the principal target of opposition. Should they target the global financial institutions or affluent nation states? TNC's? Or, should they 'think globally and act locally' – which directs activists to mount protests around local or national manifestations of globalisation, such as privatisation of public services or large dam projects? The harbingers of 'deglobalisation' suggest an alternative vision: that deeply flawed bodies like IMF, World Bank and WTO should be decommissioned. After this process of deconstruction, globalisation should be reconstructed and checked by other international organisational agreements and regional groupings. This strategy would include democratising global economic government by strengthening democratic regional economic institutions from the ground up.

The major objects of the book is to address these issues: Is the multinational governance framework and the Brettonwoods institutions created in 1945, adequate for the economy and the polity of a globalising state and society today? What are the issues thrown up by globalisation? What are its positive and negative impacts? In the post globalised world, do we need to redefine the role of or adopt the existing institutions to meet the needs of our age?

The need to improve governance and public administration and to enhance the state's capacity to carry out new functions and roles is now recognised globally. The UN Millennium Declaration categorically calls for respect for human rights, the promotion of democracy, and good governance. Good governance is not the only instrument, changes in deep-rooted and unequal structures in the developing world are also a necessary condition to achieve each of the Millennium Development Goals, eradicating extreme poverty and hunger, achieving primary education, promoting gender equality, reducing child mortality, combating disease, ensuring environmental sustainability and promoting global partnerships for development.

Certain major roles can be identified in strengthening the capacity of public institutions to promote socially equitable economic growth, combat poverty and create an enabling environment for participation in globalisation. Strengthening public power and institutional capacity can be directed towards the following:

- democratising, decentralising and improving government efficiency, accountability and responsiveness.
- mobilising financial resources for infrastructure development and human development.
- protecting the natural environment.
- protecting the economically vulnerable.
- evolving partnerships and collaborations with the private sector and NGOs for efficient service delivery systems.
- building social capital by strengthening civil society and other voluntary associations of citizens.

States that redefine their roles and functions can play a positive role in helping citizens participate more effectively to claim a share in the benefits of globalisation. A proactive state needs to continually reinvent government through innovation, strengthen its relationship with citizens, and organisations of civil society. During the 21st Century, it is imperative for 'the reinvented state' to be efficient, effective, participative honest, transparent, professional, responsive and collaborative if it is genuinely poised to achieve the goals of socially equitable economic growth and sustainable human development.

In the international arena, the prevalent institutional arrangements for global governance are quite unrepresentative and inequitable. Developing countries account for more than 80 per cent of world population and contribute almost 50 per cent of world output. Nonetheless, it is a stark reality that their influence in multilateral institutions that govern the world economy is at best limited and at worst symbolic. The problem, however, is not confined to unequal weights in representation in institutions like the World Bank or IMF but it extends to exclusion from representation in arrangements such as the P-5 or the G-8, or even the OECD, which deliberates on decisions which have profound importance for global governance. The right of veto in the Security Council of the UN is glaringly undemocratic. But decision making by consensus, as in the WTO, can also be undemocratic, if a consensus is reached among a small group of powerful states, while most others remain passive spectators or at the receiving end. The vital pre-requisite then, is to create institutional mechanisms that give the marginalised states a voice in the process of global governance.

It is time that countries like Russia, China, India and Brazil (likely to be among the largest economies by 2050) have a bigger say in the decision making of the IMF and World Bank. IMF's voting rights do not reflect the changes in the power equations and positions in the new world economic order. Emerging countries today account for 43 per cent of World exports against 20 per cent in 1970. At purchasing power parity rates, their share in global GDP has inched ahead of that of the developed world, as against a contribution of 40 per cent to world output in 1950. The change in the case of China and India is an eye-opener. In PPP terms, the two make up 17% of world output and account for a third of global GDP growth. Even in market exchange terms, China and India make up 7 per cent of World GDP and 10 per cent of World GDP growth, but their votes at IMF jointly account for only 5.5 per cent of all votes. Organisations like G-8 are out of step with a multipolar world, where the old divide between the developed and the developing world has blurred and fast growing economies are emerging as centres of strategic power. In terms of the evolving global system, the choices and decisions that the group makes may probably determine to a substantial degree, the future course of world affairs. India, for example, is not just an emerging economy of over a $1 trillion; it is also the world's most populous democracy. India has arrived in the world stage in more ways than one – its voice need to count in matters of climate change, poverty eradication, human rights, terrorism and as a leader of developing nations in WTO negotiations.

Any desirable strategy of development in a world of globalisation should aim at creating economic and political space for the pursuit of national interest and development goals. In this regard, there is a major role for the nation state not only in the domestic economic sphere but in the international sphere as well. In the national arena, the state must attempt to create the pre-conditions for a more equitable national developmental strategy, practice fiscal prudence in the macro management of the economy, intervene more proactively on behalf of the marginalised and the market excluded to achieve truly egalitarian patterns of growth and development.

Both 'market failure' and 'public policy failure' need to be avoided in the 21st Century, wisdom lies in introducing correctives against both. My own submission is that what are often called 'market failures' may truly be 'policy failures'. The problems persist from the unwillingness or inability of governments to enact and implement policies that moves towards a greater level playing field for all citizens in terms of social opportunity, rights and entitlements. If unequal social structures are resistant to policy changes then the 'entitlement' approach to human development is a sound policy option. In fact, markets and governments can provide some mutual checks and balances vis-à-vis each other. For it is only democratic political systems with supportive institutions and practices, that can provide these checks and balances. If market economy is the current buzz word of globalisation, then democracy has been a time tested ideal of good governance as well. The role of the nation state continues to be a crucial input for both development and democracy in the world. In a national context, the globalisation belief that markets know best and that less government is better government is open to serious debate. Governments are morally accountable to the people (at least in democracies) whereas markets are not obliged to be. In the international arena, where the distribution of economic and political power is grossly unequal, the nation-state is perhaps the only institutional medium through which countries can attempt to influence policies and institutions in the global sphere.

After two decades of globalisation, rhetorical statements and polemical debates surrounding economic reforms or the role of the state have mobilised enormous acrimony and energy, leading to well known arguments on either side. Time has now come to review and re-appraise the entire process and effects of globalisation – its gains and losses, imagined and real. Its also the appropriate time for a more dispassionate analysis of the entire spectrum of globalisation based on empirical evidence of the last two decades. There is need to revisit the role of the state, which has nowhere withered away under the impact of transnationalism, but whose existence still remains crucial and non-negotiable as the only real guarantor of citizen rights and entitlements. Widespread deprivation, economic stagnation and social inequality have been a bane of human rights and development in developing countries the world over and in our attempts to operationalise and successfully achieve the Millennium Development Goals (MDGs), accepted as a benchmark by all nations, we have to understand that state, the market and civil society all have significant roles to play. This book is certainly not merely about pro or anti state/market debates or even about governance – which embraces multiple actors in community problem solving, but it seeks to seriously investigate the cumulative as well as independent effects of the roles of the state, market and civil society in enhancing people's capabilities – the sine qua non of substantive democracies based on inclusive growth. If after liberalisation, we target a growth rate of 10% and continue to be one of the largest growing economies of the world, there is absolutely no reason why this should not and cannot be mobilised for an equitable and capability enhancing growth and human development. For this to happen, the state will remain the most important agency and the autonomy or powers of such a state should never be underestimated: e.g. if power is measured today in both economic and nuclear capability terms, then in India's case neither get disparaged by globalisation. The debates on globalisation are no longer confined to simple pro- or anti-advocates of the phenomenon, but has probably moved to another level of discourse – where two conflicting paradigms are visible. The first paradigm accepts the reality of working within the system of globalisation with the awareness that there is inequality in the rules of the game, (especially for the poor, the weak and the underprivileged) due to the absence of a level playing field. Therefore we may fight for the inequalities and double standards within that paradigm for fairer terms of exchange between the haves and the have-nots. Even while working within the first paradigm we may still be acutely aware of the ecological limits of high growth, however equitably that growth may be shared. We would then move to the second paradigm where de-globalisation in every form would be considered the only way to remedy global inequalities and attain global justice. With that belief then, one may start advocating de-industrialisation and local small scale production as only alternatives to the high growth model. Ultimately in the long run, if we can devise a social system that can move towards environmental sustainability in a socially equitable manner resulting in enhanced human capabilities, then it would have met the greatest development challenge of our age.

As we march ahead in the 21st Century, it is time to reflect on a new global ideology and search for a new consensus on global coexistence, which can only be based on a futuristic vision of the economy, polity and society. In this worldview, the concern for efficiency in economic growth needs to be balanced with the concern for social equity: for efficiency and growth are means, not ends by themselves. The list of worthy ends is exhaustive: democratisation, poverty eradication, reduced inequality, rights based human development and sustainable growth. It is also time to evolve a new consensus on development in which the focus is on human development based on environmentally sustainable economic growth.

In all these blueprints of the future the respective roles of the state, market and civil society needs to be clearly identified, amplified and delimited through functional boundaries.

GLOBALISATION AND THE STATE/IDEOLOGY/POLITICAL ECONOMY

1

Globalisation and the State: A Contested Terrain

AMIR ALI

This article makes an attempt to develop a comprehensive insight into the concept of the state in the specific context of flux caused by the winds of globalisation blowing across all spheres of human thought and practice. It starts with taking a retrospective look at the authoritarian and absolutist roots of the state brought to the fore by Thomas Hobbes centuries ago and argue in the light of the Hobbesian proposition that states have a general tendency to manifest their coercive sides. It argues that the nation-state may be totally eclipsed by numerous processes of globalisation which can be noticed in the response to the fast-spreading menace of international terrorism, where they have only reflected a jingoistic frenzy instead of making any genuine endeavour to evolve an international system of jurisprudence and justice of cosmopolitan nature.

The present essay aims to develop a comprehensive conceptual understanding of the state, in an era dominated by the idioms of globalisation. There is no gainsaying the fact that developing such a conceptual understanding has become an extremely difficult task to accomplish in the present age precisely due to the fact that the strong currents of globalisation have given rise to such an unpredictable situation that, to a considerable extent, problematising the concept has been rendered quite difficult.

It might be both useful and necessary to consider the rise of the modern state to be an abstract idea as also a category of analysis in both social and political theory. Undoubtedly, the modern state is radically different from its medieval predecessor, the feudal state and there has been a complex set of forces that have served as drivers in bringing about the emergence of this significant idea. These precisely include the disappearance of feudalism, the rise of capitalism, the reformation, and the conflict involving the church and the state. These developments together resulted in the coming into being of the idea of the state by the end of the 16th century. In this regard, the name of Thomas Hobbes immediately comes to our mind as probably the most important theorist who expatiated upon the concept of the state in elaborate detail. The state that was taken into consideration by Hobbes for his exhaustive effort was almost equated with a monster, dubbed as the Leviathan. It was an absolutist state, one endowed with absolute and unquestionable sovereignty. Evidently, the theoretical foundations of the modern state were laid on a glaringly absolutist grounds. While the superstructure of the modern state shows an unmistakable divergence from such blatantly absolutist foundations, every modern state makes no bones about its intolerant and coercive side at one point of time or the other, and the clue to this can be probably found deep down in the absolutist foundations of the state.

While Hobbes evolved his idea around a state that was absolute and intimidating, the effort to build a holistic theoretical foundation marked a change in more liberal directions subsequently. As David Held clearly pinpoints, Hobbes 'marks a point of transition between a commitment to the absolutist state and the struggle of liberalism against tyranny'. In Held's opinion, Hobbes's idea is both 'profoundly liberal and illiberal' at the same time. It is liberal since it is rooted in the idea of individuals coming together and unequivocally agreeing to a contract or covenant which, in turn, gives birth to the Leviathan. Simultaneously, it is illiberal because when this Leviathan is brought into existence, it commands total conformity to itself from those very same individuals who had earlier consented to create it.[1]

The state was to make steady movement in a more liberal direction with the writings of John Locke, who was also a social contract theorist like Thomas Hobbes, but unlike his distinguished predecessor, made use of the device of a contract to create a state that was more amenable to the will of those who created it. Apparently, Locke's state as well as the social contract theory from which his ideas have been drawn are more advanced. It is so because, in Hobbes, the contract is merely a one stage contract. Individuals, when they decide to sign the contract, create the Leviathan and exit the dreaded Hobbesian state of nature, where life was eminently nasty, savage and brief. In Locke's more advanced social contract theory, there appears a distinction between state and government and further between the state and society. In precise terms, Locke's state is more amenable to the influence of society, and the government is also more accountable as there is a feasibility of withdrawal of consent, which will not result in society sliding back into the state of nature.

The idea of the modern state was to be further developed following a spate of efforts made by the 19th century utilitarians which led to the creation of the liberal-democratic state. The crucial democratic component was then to be assigned to the idea of the state propounded by utilitarian thinkers, rather reluctantly at the outset as utilitarians like Jeremy Bentham and James Mill were not so enthusiastic about democracy and have been billed as 'reluctant democrats'. The concept of democracy received a boost in the more enthusiastic response of a later utilitarian thinker, John Stuart Mill.[2] However, it is only after the development of Marxism that new insights regarding the state began to be noticed. The state is delineated as an institution pervaded by the influence of class. It is an institution that in classical Marxist thought will wither away.

In a bid to come to terms with the concept of the state, it might be useful to put forward three different conceptions of the state. Of these, the first is the classical Marxist conception regarding the state. As per this conception, the state is referred to famously in the following terms that can be found in the *Communist Manifesto*: 'The executive of the modern state is but a committee for managing the common affairs of the whole bourgeoisie'. The state is thus a blatantly partisan institution.

In stark contrast to this conception, we have the liberal understanding of the state which looks upon it as a neutral umpire or referee, ensuring fair play on a level playing field, blowing the whistle when there is something amiss, but otherwise allowing the game to proceed in a smooth and unhindered fashion. Such a simplistic liberal understanding is unable to factor in the very real consideration that fair play and level playing fields can be endangered by a politically biased umpire or referee, which constitutes the quintessence of the Marxist view of the state that since it has conceded property rights it has sold out to the bourgeoisie and hence works in its interests.

There is a third conception of the state which is also found in the writings of Marx, in the *Eighteenth Brumaire of Napoleon Bonaparte*. It is distinct from the first Marxist conception of the state described above in the sense that it may factor in the various agencies of the state being deeply rooted in the complex class layering of society. Hence, it is susceptible to being influenced by the different cross-currents and trends of society. The striking point that this other Marxist conception makes is that the state is 'relatively autonomous' from society. Both these Marxist conceptions of the state offer interesting insights about the state. The first conception would view the state as being only part of the superstructure, catering to the interests of the dominant class. The second conception of the state views it as being comparatively independent of the society. It is primarily this aspect of the 'relative autonomy' of the state that has motivated the social democratic tradition to argue that it was likely to influence and regulate the state machinery in ways that make it function to the advantage of the poor working classes. In contrast to this are the more radical strands of socialism bearing the influence of the previous Marxist conception, where the state was looked upon as an instrument of class domination, and must therefore be demolished. It is interesting to note then that these two distinct Marxist conceptions of the state, inspired by and drawn from a diverse range of texts authored by Marx have yielded place to two different kinds of socialism. Of these, one is revolutionary and impatient with the state, seeing in it no possibility of progressive social change, while the other one is evolutionary, which sees in the state the possibility of being harnessed for gradual progressive social change.[3]

Bringing the state back in and rolling it back: The juxtaposition of perspectives

In the arena of political and social theory, theorisation regarding the state had come to a halt to such extent that in the late seventies one group of theorists had to talk about 'bringing the state back in'. No doubt, the idea of bringing the state back in was commendable in itself, but the state was brought back into theoretical consideration only to be eclipsed by two developments. One of these was political and economic while the other one was theoretical. The political and economic development that started from the late seventies triggered a massive swing in the global political pendulum to the right accompanied by and appertained to the rise of economic neo-liberalism. These political and economic developments argued that the state had to be rolled back and that the activities of the welfare state had to be curtailed.

The theoretical development referred to resulted in the emergence of a particular concept from the decade of the eighties, namely, the concept of civil society, which, as Neera Chandhoke puts it, went on to become a 'hurrah' concept,[4] keeping in view the fact that almost everyone from socialists, to liberals, to economic neo-liberals were praising and acclaiming the term immeasurably. Civil society, in its theoretical elaborations, definitely did use the state as a point of reference but their purpose was only to negate it and serve the political purpose of further rolling it back. That way, the state was certainly brought back in briefly before the 'rolling back' discourse started.

What has actually happened is that instead of the state just being rolled back, something more interesting and contradictory has been taking place. The global swing of the political pendulum to the right has ensured without an iota of doubt that certain activities of the state be rolled back. However, what it has rolled back and curtailed has been the welfare activities of the state. The welfare state was that component of the state which was created with a view to taking care of citizens by providing them with cheap, reasonable and subsidised housing; it was meant to ensure a decent education as well as a cheap and efficient public transportation system, especially in the advanced first world. The welfare state was also meant to help citizens in times of unemployment, sickness, and most crucially, in times of emergencies and calamities. Several activities of the welfare state were scaled back. Simultaneously, as this welfare arm of the state was being withdrawn, something else was being extended. This was the repressive arm of the state. In many countries, which have witnessed economic neo-liberalism in full swing, the repressive arm of the state has been getting heftier, with greater and more repressive policing, mass imprisonment of people belonging to certain delinquent sections of the society, and ever greater expenditure on defence. This is the more accurate picture of what the rolling back of the state actually signifies.

What is being argued here is that with the concept of civil society becoming popular in the arena of political theory, which views the state as its reference point, the concept of the state has been eclipsed.[5] It almost seems as though civil society, which is construed as a tool for promoting democracy by acting as an arena beyond the purview of the state, thus facilitating the likelihood of democratic dissent and debate, is locked in a zero sum struggle with the state. So, as the frontiers of the state are expanded, this is understood as encroaching upon freedom and democracy, while, on the other hand , civil society, pushing back the frontiers of the state, is understood in terms of the promotion of democracy. Gurpreet Mahajan , in a paper on 'Civil Society and Its Avtars', makes a very pertinent observation in this regard as she says: 'Instead of ensuring that the state provides equal rights to all citizens, its retreat from the public arena is presented as being a condition necessary for strengthening and reinventing democracy'. She then goes on to pose the question: 'And why should civil society be placed outside the state?'[6]

The distinction made on theoretical lines between the state and civil society has led to the promotion of the civil society at the expense of the state. Instead of looking upon this phenomenon as one's gain at the expense of the other as it can be seen in a zero sum game, it appears to be more reasonable to view the state and civil society as working together and in tandem with each other in order to promote democracy and freedom. Nonetheless, the point that this essay aims to lay emphasis on is that the tendency of theorisation on civil society has emerged precisely at that time when disillusionment with the state has grown. Disillusionment with the delivery systems of the state has increased, along with exacerbating state authoritarianism hell-bent on curbing civil liberties and rights of citizens. This increasing state authoritarianism, it is argued in this regard, results from the impact of the absolutist foundations upon which the theoretical edifice of the modern state was constructed by Thomas Hobbes. To reiterate then, the increasing state authoritarianism arises from their absolutist foundations that were referred to at the beginning of this essay. This essay will touch upon the absolutist foundations of the state again at the end of the next section.

The State of the Nation[7]

There is yet another dimension of the state that has to be taken into consideration with a view to comprehending the state in a better way. This is the stark fact that the modern state has been tied to a specific ethnic group or nation. So, the modern global system is one of nation states in which one dominant nationality has its own state system. In the hyphenated concept of the nation-state, we can notice that two extremely significant and richly theorised strands of social and political theory are married. While on the one hand there are the twin concepts of nation and nationalism with a theoretically rich bulk of literature which has expanded considerably since the 1980s, we have, on the other hand, the political theory of the state as well with a host of advocates.

Interestingly, the literature on nationalism has got increasingly enriched since the last three decades with many people associated with the field feeling that some closure or some sort of an end is glaringly visible with respect to the phenomena of nationalism.[8] This has been effectively brought to the fore in the observation at the end of the British Marxist historian Eric Hobsbawm's book *Nations and Nationalism since 1780*, which undoubtedly adds to the rich theorisation on nationalism that has emerged since the decade of the 1980s: 'After all, the very fact that historians are at least beginning to make some progress in the study and analysis of nations and nationalism suggests that, as so often, the *phenomenon is past its peak*. The owl of Minerva which brings wisdom said Hegel, flies out at dusk. It is a good sign that it is now circling round nations and nationalism' (emphasis mine).[9]

This view leads to the consequence that nationalism is now approaching its end; many have argued that the nation state will collapse, disintegrate and eventually disappear while the concept will fall into abeyance. This view is advocated by many but also contested by many others. That notwithstanding, there is hardly any doubt about the fact that recent developments do suggest quite categorically the nation state reaching a point of termination. Here, one can single out globalisation as being the process which might well bring about the demise of the nation-state. Inherent in the process of globalisation are the tides of change that will lead to the undermining and surpassing of the nation state. That precisely is the reason why the title of this essay is 'State against Globalisation'.

Globalisation as a phenomenon is difficult to understand and this is not the place to launch into a full blown discussion of the concept. However, there is one aspect of globalisation that will be picked up here to argue that the nation state will gradually collapse and fade into oblivion. Globalisation, as a process, is one that rejects and obliterates boundaries. In fact, it is a process that has encouraged unprecedented increase in investment flows and trade across state borders. In contrast, the nation-state is an entity that prides itself on creating and maintaining boundaries and borders. Juxtaposed in this manner, the process of globalisation understood as one which denies and undermines borders and the nation-state as an entity which is indeed premised upon the creation and continued maintenance of such borders,[10] one can understand what the state is up against. Many have argued that the nation state will continue to flourish and that they are not being obliterated.[11] Despite that, it should not be lost sight of that the nation-state is a phenomenon which is at least two hundred years old. It is an entity that emerged as the fallout of certain historical contingencies. It is definitely past its prime. So, it seems to be a doubtful proposition that it will be able to grapple with the powerful forces unleashed by globalisation, which are bound to wash away and obliterate the carefully guarded boundaries of the nation-state.

If the nation-state is facing impending termination, then what type of political entity is likely to replace it? It is difficult to speculate as to what a future global political order will look like. Of late, especially in the aftermath of the US global war on terrorism and assertion of the military supremacy of the US, terms such as empire and imperialism have made a return. Could this imply that the system of sovereign nation states will be subsumed under another future imperial dispensation? It is not the task and objective of this essay to indulge in such speculation as to what the future will look like. Suffice it to say that the present international order of sovereign nation-states rose on the crumbles and remnants of former empires[12]. Should they come together and re-unite to provide the building blocks of another future imperial world order, it would certainly amount to a turning of the wheel full circle.

The question that this essay proposes to deal with here is the efficacy of the nation-state in tackling the problems that are of a trans-national character and which demand a truly international or global response. In short they are problems that do not stop at, and respect national borders, and are so, truly global ones. There are numerous such problems that instantly come to light. The environment, for example, is one international issue which it seems, simply cannot be addressed by nation-states acting as independent units, each trying to maximise its own interests.

However, the issue that this essay aims to bring into focus is not the environment, but another phenomenon, that has assumed the proportions of a global problem which again, it is unlikely that nation-states acting individually will be able to solve. This is the problem of international terrorism. There are a number of reasons why this problem is being taken into consideration. First, international terrorism counterpoises the problem of the nation-state being confronted by non-state actors that threaten it with violence in order to attain and extract political benefits. In the classical sociological definition of the state given by Max Weber, the state is considered to be the only legitimate repository of legal violence. While confronting terrorist non-state actors, the state tries to quell, most often with a heavy hand, the illegitimate claims to violence of such entities.[13] Secondly, international terrorism is a problem that has attained menacing proportions in the wake of the advance of globalisation. Thirdly, terrorism is a global problem and by way of a solution, calls for the establishment of an architecture of international jurisprudence, a genuinely cosmopolitan and global rule of law.[14] Fourthly— and this is a point that links up with a point made at the very beginning of this essay—in its bid to take on and put down terrorism, nation-states have brought to light their own absolutist foundations in that they have often tended to use extremely coercive methods that have come down too heavily, often not on terrorist outfits but ordinary citizens whose civil liberties and individual freedoms have been subjected to blatant violation. The fifth and last point that this essay proposes to make is that the establishment of an international architecture of jurisprudence grounded into a global rule of law as a response to terrorism has to be comprehensive, all inclusive and cosmopolitan. It must therefore be able to transcend the narrow confines of nation-states. The reason why this is so significant is that an inability to do so in the context of the ongoing global war on terrorism will give rise to a global situation that increasingly bears resemblance with a Hobbesian state of nature. Such a situation is extremely dangerous as even the weakest and lowliest of actors will be able to cause considerable harm and damage to even the most powerful states. Obviously this will be not prove to be a viable solution to the problem of international terrorism and will only go on to create a situation that spawns and creates more of the same problem.

Danielle Archibugi and Iris Marion Young have noted that the 9/11 terror attacks can appear in two distinctively dissimilar frames of interpretation. While the first one sees them as attacks on the United States and its people, the second looks upon them as crimes against humanity. Archibugi and Young go on to attack the 'statist' response to the 9/11 terror attacks. While recommending a response to international terrorism that is truly cosmopolitan and grounded into a global rule of law, they bewail the fact that 'Aspirations to a global society governed by fair rules should be counted among the casualties of September 11'. They further go on to 'propose two premises for reasoning about what an alternative response' to the September incidents 'might have been and still could be'. To begin with, the situation should be first conceptualised in people-to-people and not state to state terms. The reason for this is that those who were identified as attackers did not represent any particular state and the victims themselves belonged to as many as seventy different countries. Secondly, that the terrorist attacks should be conceptualised as crimes against humanity that can be met by proper legal investigations and judicial proceedings instead of the so called 'just war' response that we have witnessed.[15]

Rather than a cosmopolitan response rooted in a global rule of law, it is interesting and indeed somewhat paradoxical that in the era of globalisation, the response of nation states to international terrorism has been a retrogressive patriotism that easily descends into jingoism. Indeed, this appears to be an interesting paradox with the process of globalisation which we construe as a phenomenon that seems to move so rapidly, at an almost break neck speed. In spite of its hectic speed, some of the vehicles that it makes use of are the most retrograde and conservative. To underline and further explain this point, it may be worthwhile to take into account what globalisation has done to television. In this regard, it merits consideration that with the onset of cable television, which is celebrated as something of a revolution in India, channels like Star TV telecast soap operas and serials depict and celebrate some of the most obnoxious and reprehensible aspects of Indian family life.

To reiterate, the point is that a tendency to promote some of the most retrograde social tendencies is inherent in the process of globalisation. It is very much noticeable in the case of 'statist' responses to global terrorism, which, far from being cosmopolitan, are actually pervaded by the most thoroughgoing, retrogressive patriotism that easily degenerates into jingoism as it has been mentioned earlier.[16]

What has been the outcome of this whipped up patriotic frenzy? The answer is something very interesting if one considers this in the light of globalisation. Apart from the increasing authoritarianism of states leading to violations of individual freedoms, which has already been alluded to, there has been a systematic tightening of immigration rules.[17] This tightening of immigration rules has severely affected the flow of labour across borders. Again a paradox comes to the fore, which is that in the era of globalisation, the pioneers of the idea have encouraged steps which seek to do away with restrictions on trade and investment. In this respect, it is worthwhile to take into consideration the Trade Related Intellectual Property Rights (TRIPS) of the WTO as also the massive financial flows which take place across international borders. However, there has simultaneously been a restriction on immigration and labour flows. It is perhaps some of these aspects of globalisation that have evoked angry reactions from citizens of the Third World. It is not that most people reject globalisation *per se*. Kok-Chor Tan has captured the point well: 'But much of this popular opposition has been presented as an outright rejection of globalisation, and as such, to my mind, oversimplifies and misses the crux of the problem. What is at issue is not the process of globalisation as such but the *terms* of globalisation, in particular the neo-liberal ideology underpinning and driving it'.[18]

The state is thus placed at a difficult conjuncture. The kind of globalisation that is being triggered across the world bears unmistakable underpinnings of the ideology of economic neo-liberalism, premised on liberalised trade and investment flows. These processes threaten to erode the very existence of the nation state. At the same time, globalisation gives vent to problems that nation-states are just not able to handle, and certainly much less to solve them. In this interface between the state against globalisation, states are not keen to look outwards to create a system of cosmopolitan international justice but have instead started increasingly looking inwards.

End Notes

[1] David Held, 'Central Perspectives on the modern state', in Gregor McLennan, David Held and Stuart Hall (eds.) *The Idea of the Modern State*, Open University Press, 1993.

[2] *Ibid*.

[3] *Ibid*. p 56.

[4] Neera Chandhoke, *The Conceits of Civil Society*, Oxford University Press, Delhi, 2003.

[5] For a useful collection on civil society, see Carolyn M. Elliot (ed.) *Civil Society and Democracy: A Reader*, Oxford University Press, Delhi, 2003.

[6] Gurpreet Mahajan 'Civil Society and Its Avtars: What Happened to Freedom and Democracy?' in Carolyn M. Eliot (ed.) op. cit. p 168.

[7] The title of this section is taken from a collection edited by Stuart Hall, *The State of the Nation: Ernest Gellner and the Theory of Nationalism*, Cambridge University Press, Cambridge, 1998.

[8] The literature on nationalism has proliferated especially since the decade of the 1980s. Without doubt, Benedict Anderson's book *Imagined Communities:*

Globalisation and the State: A Contested Terrain   31

Reflections on the Origins and Spread of Nationalism, first published in 1983, is the most important. Other important works on the development of nationalism are Ernest Gellner's Nations and Nationalism, also published in 1983 and A.D. Smith, Theories of Nationalism.

9 Eric Hobsbawm, Nations and Nationalism since 1780: Programme, Myth, Reality, Cambridge University Press, Cambridge, 1990, p 192.

10 This point has been borrowed from Kok-Chor Tan's book, Justice Without Borders: Cosmopolitanism, Nationalism and Patriotism, Cambridge University Press, Cambridge, 2004, see especially the introduction and chapter 2.

11 See for example the essay by Michael Mann, 'Nation-states in Europe and Other Continents: Diversifying, Developing, Not Dying', in Gopal Balakrishnan (ed.) Mapping the Nation, with an introduction by Benedict Anderson, Verso, published in association with New Left Review, London, 1996.

12 There are some works on nationalism which have looked at nations and nationalism as the product of the tremendous rubble that was produced by the crumbling and break up of large empires such as the Austro-Hungarian, the Russian and the Ottoman. See Hugh Seton-Watson, Nations and States: An Enquiry into the Origins of Nations and the Politics of Nationalism, Methuen, London, 1976 and Rogers Brubaker, Nationalism Reframed: Nationhood and the National Question in the New Europe, Cambridge University Press, Cambridge, 1996.

13 Isabelle Sommier has the following, very pertinent, observation to make regarding terrorism: 'It may be regarded as the civilian "version" of the extreme violence that is in most cases used by states.' She further notes that 'terrorism is the imitation and use of terror methods by those who are not – at least not yet – in state power' p. 473. See Isabelle Sommier ' "Terrorism" as total violence?', International Social Science Journal, 174, December 2002, pp 473-81.

14 See James P. Sterba (ed.) Terrorism and International Justice, Oxford University Press, Oxford, 2003.

15 Danielle Archibugi and Iris Marion Young 'Envisioning a Global Rule of Law', in James P. Sterba (ed.) Terrorism and International Justice, Oxford University Press, Oxford, 2003.

16 The idea of patriotism being backward looking occurred to me when I was reading Karl Popper's famous attack on Plato and his ideas. Commenting on the origin of the term patriot he writes: 'From the slogan of the movement, 'Back to the state of our forefathers', or 'Back to the old paternal state', derives the term 'patriot'. See Karl Popper, The Open Society and Its Enemies. Volume One: The Spell of Plato, Routledge, London and New York, p. 196. For an attempt to reconcile cosmopolitanism with patriotism and nationalism see Kok-Chor Tan, op.cit. See also Alasdair MacIntyre 'Is Patriotism a Virtue?'

17 There is a connection between 'statist' responses to international terror and immigration laws. John Upton writing in the London Review of Books notes: 'This Government has added a further dimension to the UK's anti-terror legislation. Instead of using the criminal law as its basis, it has arrived at the solution of grafting anti-terrorist provisions onto immigration law.' He

further notes: 'The checks to the power of the state in the form of due process, available in the criminal justice system, weakened though they might be in the case of terrorist legislation, do not exist at all under immigration law.' 'In the Streets of Londonistan', *London Review of Books*, 22 January 2004, p. 6.

[18] Kok-Chor Tan, op. cit. p. 32.

2

Globalisation and Changing Role of the Nation-State

S.R.T.P. SUGUNAKARARAJU

Globalisation is, in no way, an entirely new phenomenon but a part of a historically ongoing and continuous process of the evolution and development of global economy as well as world capitalism. The politics of globalisation is driven by the neo-liberal political agenda, which privileges individual liberty over social equality and seeks to maintain strong private property rights. According to both Liberal and Marxist perspectives, the Nation-State has not disappeared nor is it likely to disappear in the face of the seemingly all-powerful phenomenon of globalisation. There has been a clear change in the political ideology of the Nation-State that, under the influence of neo-liberal ideology, prefers to discard its social obligations and actively promotes globalising policies. The process of Globalisation is inherently undemocratic as this leads to the denial of democratic rights to the people. Given that, an imperative need has arisen for the state to play an active and interventionist role, especially in the developing world, to bring about genuine individual freedom and social justice.

In the liberal thinking, the state, with its monopoly right to the legitimate use of physical force, is considered as an institution of common welfare, whereas Marxist thought perceives state as a class institution designed to protect the class interests of the bourgeoisie or the capitalist class. Whatever be the definition and nature of the state, there is no doubt about the fact that state has played a significant role, whether positive or negative, in the historical evolution of human civilisation and at different phases of economic and social development.

Since the beginning of the modern sovereign and territorial state-system, which came into existence as a result of the Peace of Westphalia of 1648, the state has played a dominant role in matters of war and peace and in bringing about economic and social development within the territorial borders of modern nation-states. State has been so prominent an actor, both externally and internally, that state practice in inter-state relations has come to form one of the important foundations of modern international law which regulates international relations, though not always with a considerable measure of success, besides maintaining international peace and order.

Yet another contribution of the state has been the recognition and protection of individual rights, though as a response to the struggles waged by the people, at different phases of human history. In an overall analysis, it appears that the nature and role of the state as an institution has been sovereign and predominantly interventionist encompassing almost all aspects of human life.

Now, with the so-called 'end of history' and the supposed decisive triumph of liberalism as an ideology, all other political ideologies and 'isms' including the likes of communism, billed as "market fundamentalism", have come to threaten the very sovereignty of the nation-state in the form of globalisation. Globalisation signifies a process of free and unbridled flow of trade, investment, technology, information and culture across territorial borders. Globalisation in its current form, though not a novel historical phenomenon by any standard of judgment, is believed to have pushed the nation-state to a corner limiting the latter's role to that of a mere facilitator in the operation of free market forces. In the present era of globalisation, the state is called upon to be a referee in the game of free-market, setting rules and monitoring its functioning.

As a political ideology, Globalisation advocates a minimalist and non-interventionist role for the state, free-market economy and strong private property rights. It strongly opposes any state intervention and advocates individual freedom as the supreme political ideal. It reposes its unconditional faith in the potential of free market forces in bringing about economic prosperity and welfare of all. It is in this context of globalisation and the retreat of the sovereign nation-state that the present paper attempts to examine the changing role of the contemporary nation-state. The fundamental objective of this paper is to see how the liberal and Marxist approaches to politics comprehend the process of globalisation. The implications of globalisation especially for the third-world states and their peoples are also sought to be ascertained here.

In order to come to terms with globalisation in its right perspective, it is of utmost significance to take cognizance of how differing approaches to politics perceive the phenomenon of globalisation. Here, an attempt is made to see how the two divergent perspectives regarding politics, namely Liberal and Marxist, look upon the political phenomenon of globalisation and the role of the nation-state in contemporary context of globalizing times.

To start with, take into consideration the liberal perspective on globalisation and the state's role in this process. Liberalism, for analytical purpose, can be classified into two variants: negative liberalism and positive liberalism. The negative liberal tradition of the 18th century advocated what came to be known as 'Laissez Faire' theory, which expounded non-intervention of the state in the economic affairs of society. This phase of liberalism was characterised, in its economic dimension, by the classical economics of Adam Smith showing tremendous faith in the potential of market forces or what Adam Smith called the 'invisible hand' in the creation of wealth of nations and in bringing about economic development as well as prosperity through 'trickle down' effect. Political liberals of this age advocated absolute individual liberty and setting limits to the state power. They wanted the state to play a minimal role and restrict itself to police functions such as maintenance of law and order and giving protection to people from external aggression. On the other hand, they championed unflinching faith in individual initiative and the potential of 'free market', 'free trade' and open competition in achieving economic development and prosperity. It is worthwhile to note in this regard that the liberal ideology of this phase broadly corresponded to the historical ascendancy of mercantile and industrial capitalist classes. These political ideas, as we all know, led to industrial revolution with its positive and negative consequences on the people and the society as a whole.

However, the gross economic inequalities, poverty, declining living standards of the workers, and the growing social unrest that emanated from the industrial revolution compelled the liberal political thinkers to reconsider their views on individual liberty and role of the state in economic development. The paradigm shift that subsequently came in the political attitude and ideas of liberals blazed the trail for the emergence of "positive liberalism" as a political ideology with its stress on positive individual liberty and 'welfare state' during the late 19th and early 20th centuries. The theory of welfare state advocated a strong and dynamic role for the state not only in regulating the economy but also in taking necessary welfare measures. The state was called upon to assume a proactive role in containing social evils and grappling with economic problems generated by the industrial revolution as also capitalist mode of development. Whatever be the political objectives, the state with its national character, however, re-emerged as a key actor in political and social aspects of national and international life. State sector or Public sector, in fact, had become a leading engine of economic growth assuming commanding heights of the economy. State, indeed, ensured growth of national economies through its protectionist economic policies such as tax concessions, giving protection against foreign competition through maintenance of high tariffs, provision of basic infrastructure facilities etc.

The state during this phase came to be known as "managerial state" because of its pro-active role. The dominant position and interventionist role of the state was justified in the weberian framework of bureaucratisation and rationalisation of state power. In the United States, during the 20th century, for instance, the managerial state played an active role in the economy and society under the influence of 'Fordism'. 'Fordism' referred to the network of political, economic and social relations that dominated managerial states increasingly from the 1930s to the 1970s under which a class-compromise was effected where the worker was seen as a consumer and paid more than subsistence wage so that he could buy more and more and push the aggregate demand upwards. The state, during this phase of managerialism, came to function as the instrumentally rational guarantor of the Fordist class compromise and consumer society.[1] During the first half of the 20th century, the state in the developed world played a significant role in tiding over the economic crises caused by the Great Depression and the Second World War by implementing 'Keynesian' fiscal and monetary policies and focusing on full employment, economic growth and the welfare of its citizens. This phase of liberalism was termed as "embedded Liberalism"[2] by some scholars.

The nation-state played a vital role in structuring various international political and economic institutions for managing global economic and political order. By and large, the nation-state, wherein sovereignty is vested in the nation as an 'imagined community', played a leading role in ordering human society under the liberal ideological framework of individual liberty, rule of law and state intervention in the 20th century.

However, at the beginning of the 1980s, a new variant of liberalism, dubbed as 'neo-liberalism' started casting its overarching influence on economic and political thinking. Having its philosophical roots in the libertarian ideas of thinkers such as F.A.Hayek, Milton Friedman and Karl Popper (belonging to Mont Pelerin society), neo-liberalism wielded unquestionable dominance in the political arena in the U.S.A. and England. This dominance was in the form of Reganism and Thatcherism during the 1980s.

Following the disintegration of the Soviet Union, and the end of cold war politics, neo-liberalism started dominating political and economic thinking, setting a new agenda of globalisation. Neo-liberalism is a theory of political and economic practices which propose that human well-being can best be advanced by liberating individual entrepreneurial freedoms and skills within an institutional framework characterised by strong private property rights, free markets and free trade.[3] Globalisation, advocated by neo-liberals, in its economic dimensions, is defined as the integration of national economies into an international economy through trade, direct foreign investment (by corporations and multinationals), short term capital flows, and international flows of technology.[4] For Malcom waters, Globalisation is a social process in which constraints of geography on social and cultural arrangements recede and people become increasingly aware that those constraints are receding.

As Joseph Stiglitz opines, globalisation has potential to enrich everyone in the world, specifically the poor and, can be a force for good.[5] As a matter of fact, Globalisation is an inevitable and a potentially good phenomenon in neo-liberal thinking. However, as far as the question of state's sovereignty in the era of globalisation is concerned, some liberal scholars argue that while state's power is declining, the power of the markets is on ascendence. Susan Strange, for instance, argued that the state is retreating in the face of superior power of globalisation. She claims: where states were once the masters of the markets, now it is the markets, which, on many crucial issues, are the masters over the governments of the states.[6] Some other scholars believe that the technological changes and liberalisation of international trade, production and finance have dealt a decisive blow to the formerly unchallenged position of the state.[7] The state is loosing its sovereign status in key domains such as military affairs, control over domestic economic and social matters, etc. in the wake of globalisation.

Contrary to the retreat-of-the-state argument, there are scholars who argue that state is assuming a new role: that of a powerful institution capable of promoting economic globalisation. According to Saskia Sassen, the new role of the state aims to "denationalise" the state. This assumption precisely implies that state has changed its policies of protecting national business firms and started actively promoting globalisation policies by opening up the national economy.

For Marxists, globalisation means entirely different things. According to one scholar, globalisation is the term under which imperialism presents itself in its current phase.[8] As Immanuel Wallerstein maintains, globalisation is a misleading concept since what is described as globalisation has been happening for 500 years. What is new in all that is happening today is that we are entering an 'age of transition'...the modern world system is in crisis and has entered into a period of chaotic behavior which will cause a systemic bifurcation and transition to a new structure whose nature is as yet undetermined and, in principle, impossible to predetermine, but one that is open to human intervention and creativity.[9] James Petras and Henry Veltmeyer argue that globalisation is a class project of the emerging class of transnational capitalists seeking to promote their economic interests. They further say that the term 'imperialism' better explains the contemporary global economic and political situation than the term globalisation, which is an ideological veil for economic interests, and which seeks to obfuscate what is going on worldwide presently.[10]

For certain other scholars associated with the Marxist tradition, globalisation represents the response of the global capitalist class to the classical capitalist crisis of over-accumulation, which the contemporary global economy is facing. Walden Bello argues, for instance, that *Reaganism* and *structural adjustment* in the 1980s and *globalisation* in 1990s are attempts to address this problem of over-accumulation.[11] Contrary to the claim that the current phase of globalisation promotes free trade and much greater mobility of productive capital across borders, some Marxist scholars argue that the present era represents the globalisation of financial capital. There has been an enormous increase in the global mobility of capital as finance. It is not capital-in-production but capital-as-finance, which has become immensely mobile in the current epoch and this, certainly constitutes one exceedingly important specificity of the current process of globalisation[12]. Contemporary finance capital, Marxists argue, is an autonomous entity with little interest in production as such and concerned primarily with quick speculative gains through rapid global movements. In global political terms, as Marxists further observe, global finance capital across borders results in the emergence of world imperialist super-state which is being superimposed on, and which would act through the already existing system of nation-states[13]. In other words, the contemporary nation-states do not disappear but continue to exist, serving the interests of the global capital. The structure of the nation-state remains the same but its nature as well as character transformed substantially as it secures the vested interests of the global financial oligarchy.

What are the implications of global finance capital for the contemporary nation-state and its role in economic affairs? Marxists maintain that finance capital is always opposed to an 'activist state' in matters of employment and welfare promotion. But when finance capital is globalised and the state continues to be a nation-state, its position suddenly acquires an effectiveness: any state that dares to be activist, overriding the opposition of the finance capital would find itself confronting a capital flight, with adverse consequences for the economy. To avoid these consequences and hence, to prevent possible capital flight, states make every attempt to ensure that the confidence of the investors in the economy, which is basically a euphemism for the confidence of the speculators, is not undermined. And they do so by eschewing any activist role in employment promotion and subjecting the economy to deflationary process, which reduces the growth rate[14]. Thus, the global finance constraints the freedom of the nation-state, especially in the developing states, in playing any major interventionist role by making substantial use of diverse economic and financial pressure tactics. Not surprisingly, it seems to be particularly difficult for these states to step out of the neo-liberal regime and pursue an alternative agenda.

While the advocates of globalisation assert that globalised free markets lead to the spread of democratic institutions or the democratisation of existing institutions, Marxist scholars perceive a fundamental contradiction between the adoption of neo-liberal policies and the preservation of democratic institutions. The globalisation theorists maintain that liberalisation leads to export of capital from north to south and higher rates of growth in third world economies, whereas Marxists refute this claim and argue that opening up to finance capital actually leads to a retardation of growth or even stagnation and accompanying social problems. In the wake of globalisation, Marxist thinkers argue, the state has been captured or reoriented by the global capital towards its vested interests. The nation-state's role or function has been tailored to accomplish the following tasks with an utterly reductionist approach :(1) to adopt fiscal and monetary policies that ensure macro-economic stability; (2) to provide the basic infrastructure necessary for global economic activity; and (3) to provide social control, order and stability. The role of the state prescribed by these functions has been designed to facilitate accumulation on a global scale and to regulate labour. To assume this role, as Marxists opine, the state has been generally downsized, decentralised and modernised and has had its regulatory and policy-making capacities hollowed out[15].

However, on the other hand, Marxist writers also argue that while state has withdrawn from its social obligations, it is actively promoting the interests of the global capital, in holding down wages, and in bailing out the troubled overseas investors, TNCs and speculators by resorting to international financial institutions. Never before has the nation-state played a more decisive role or intervened with more vigour and consequence in shaping economic exchanges and investment at the local, national and international levels. It is impossible to conceive of the expansion and growth of multinational banks and corporations without the prior political, military and economic intervention by the nation-state.[16]

Marxist scholars subscribe to the view that the nation-state has indeed played an active role in structuring political economic arrangements and institutions that help the globalisation process. The most elementary and important trade agreements such as GATT, WTO, NAFTA, etc. and trading blocks like European Union were formulated, codified and implemented by nation-states. The scale and scope of nation-state activity have grown to such a point that one needs to refer to it as the 'New Statism' rather than the free market. Globalisation is, in the first instance, a product of 'New Statism' and continues to be accompanied and sustained by direct state intervention.[17]

After taking a look at liberal and Marxist perspectives, it becomes evident that globalisation is not an entirely new phenomenon but just another phase of the historically ongoing process of evolution and development of the world economy or world capitalism. If globalisation is to be understood as integration of national economies with the global economy and shrinking of the globe, then there is nothing substantially new about it. The Asian, African and Latin American economies had long been integrated with the world economy when they were colonial economies producing raw materials and cheap labour for the industrial growth of, and serving as profitable markets for, the West. Even after the decolonisation process, a majority of the Third World states developed such kind of economies that were terribly dependent on the Western countries for finance and technology. And this dependency continues even till our times, which is one of the factors that explain the process of globalisation itself. It is also obvious, after surfing through liberal and Marxist perspectives on globalisation, that nation-state has not disappeared, nor is it likely to disappear in near future due to its existence being threatened by the tides of all-powerful globalisation sweeping across the world. Instead, the nation-state is actively promoting and facilitating the globalisation process displaying a change in its political attitude. And this, evidently, is the change in the nature and role of the nation-state.

To understand this change in nation-state's nature and ideology, it is necessary to examine the politics behind the political phenomenon of globalisation. Globalisation is indeed a political theory of the neo-liberal state, a theory which privileges individual liberty over equality and social justice, as also one that prefers strong private property rights to social obligations of the state. The tension and contradiction between liberty and equality has for long been a contested politically issue. Globalisation, however, seems to have decisively resolved this issue in favour of individual liberty, no matter whatever are the accompanying social costs. The neo-liberal globalisation seeks to pit the long-longed political ideal of individual freedom against interventionist and regulatory state practices. The necessary political consent for neo-liberal policies is sought to be constructed through powerful ideological and cultural influences. Neo-liberalism is very much compatible with the present–day dominant cultural trend of 'post-modernism' in so far as it appeals to traditional and cultural practices to justify its policies.

Globalisation, in effect, denies democratic rights not only to the smaller and less developed states but also to the people, at large, to determine their national, economic and social future. The irony of globalisation is that while it advocates political ideals like freedom, democracy, human rights, good governance etc. the very nature and essence of this process is inherently undemocratic. The unfair system of voting rights in the decision-making process of global financial institutions like the IMF, World Bank, etc; the rise of monopoly and oligopolistic practices in trade, investment and technology; unfair competition; bypassing of the democratic and parliamentary institutions in the making of key decisions at the national and international levels; and the rising social costs are some of the indicators that reflect the undemocratic nature of the globalisation process. Many scholars have pointed to this 'Democratic Deficit' in the way globalisation came to be managed[18]. Moreover, globalisation has also led to tremendous surge in inequalities both within and among nations. So, Eric Hobsbawm aptly observes, "The currently fashionable free-market globalisation has brought about a dramatic growth in economic and social inequalities both within states and internationally; there is no sign that this polarisation is not continuing within countries, in spite of a general diminution of extreme poverty"[19].

What is, then, the role of the nation-state in this undemocratic and unequal game of globalisation? As pointed out earlier, the nation-state has not disappeared in political terms in the face of globalisation but has only adapted itself to, and facilitated globalisation, sometimes under economic and political pressure and on some other occasions, with clear political willingness. In other words, the status of the nation-state remained the same but its political nature has drastically changed in that it no longer considers it wise to play an active and interventionist role. Instead, it prefers to lose sight of its social responsibility and relies on the potential of free-market economy in bringing about social welfare and individual freedom. Within nation-states, it appears, the nation is increasingly being bypassed in the key decision making processes and the state, represented by a select few political and bureaucratic elites, takes important decisions regarding integration of nations into the globalisation process and other key decisions of national importance.

It is interesting to note that the state, which tends to withdraw from its social obligations, goes all out in providing good business environment and protection of overseas and domestic investments, sometimes even resorting to militarism and use or threat of force in the name of protection and promotion of freedom. Consequently, the scale and magnitude of violence in international relations have dramatically gone up. The Gulf War, Iraq War and imposition of economic sanctions against certain countries are some of the examples, which point towards this trend. This tendency of resorting to the use or threat of force, violating international law and norms, is particularly true of the developed countries. The states, especially in the developing countries, have developed a tendency to increasingly resort to force to quell various political and social movements, especially those directed against globalising policies of liberalisation, privatisation, etc.

Those governments or regimes which refuse to follow neo-liberal policies of *structural adjustment, liberalisation, privatisation,* etc. are either destabilised or overthrown by sponsoring 'regime change', military coups, economic sanctions, or due to the threat of flight of foreign investments and withholding of loans from international financial institutions like IMF and World Bank. These are some of the many pressure tactics used to force the non-complying states to fall in line with the neo-liberal agenda of globalisation. Human rights, democracy and nuclear non-proliferation are some of the means, which the hegemonic powers selectively use against the developing countries to force them to adopt neo-liberal policies. While the western countries have pushed poor countries to eliminate trade barriers, they themselves retained their own barriers, preventing developing countries from exporting their agricultural products and thereby depriving them of their much desperately needed forex[20]. The nation-state's political intervention in bailing out troubled overseas investors, speculators and TNCs suggests the continuing role of politics in sustaining the crisis-prone globalist perspective[21]. Thus, the nation-state instead of weakening with globalisation has started playing an active role in pushing globalisation policies.

Conclusion

The state has played and can always play a significant role in achieving comprehensive and inclusive growth and economic development. It was with the help and active interventionist and protectionist role of the state that the developed countries of the west achieved the state of development in which they are at present. Whatever be the stage of political and economic development a country is in, government makes a difference. The state can, and has always played an essential role not only in regulating markets but also in ensuring social justice. To deny any role to the state, especially in the developing world in promoting development and social welfare is not only unjust but also ahistorical. Even in the communist countries where the state is supposed to wither away, has not actually withered away and continues to play an interventionist and active role in economic and social life. Without an interventionist state, Third World societies not only cannot make any progress but may also degenerate into social disorder, injustice and anarchy.

Globalisation, however, does not seem to hold much hope for the developing world. An activist state with positive intervention is the imperative need of the hour, which can help in making things better, especially in the underdeveloped south.

End Notes

[1] Walter C Opello,Jr and Stephen J Rosow, *The Nation-State and Global Order*, (New Delhi:Viva Books, 2005) pp.146-147.

[2] David Harvey, *A Brief History of Neo-liberalism*, (oxford: oxford university press, 2005), p.11

[3] *Ibid*, p.3

[4] Jagadish Bhagawati, *In Defence of Globalisation*, (New Delhi: Oxford University Press, 2004) .p.3

[5] Joseph Stiglitz, *Globalisation and its Discontents*, (NewDelhi:Penguin Books, 2002), p.248

[6] Susan Strange, *The Retreat of the State: The Diffusion of Power in the World Economy*, (New York: Cambridge university press,1996), p.4

[7] Mark Kesselman, *The Politics of Globalisation : A Reader*, (New York: Houghton Mifflin Company, 2007), p.210

[8] Prabhat Patnaik, "*The Meaning of Contemporary Globalisation*" Mary John et.al(eds), *Changing Economics and Identities in Contemporary India*, (New Delhi:Tulika Books, 2006), p.3

[9] Immanuel Wallerstein, "*Globalisation or the Age of Transition?*" in Samit Kar (ed), *Globalisation:One World, Many Voices*, (New Delhi:Rawat Publications, 2005),p.47

[10] James Petras and Henry Veltmeyer, *Globalisation :Unmasked:Imperialism in the 21st Century*, (New Delhi: Madhyam Books, 2001), p.8

[11] Bello, Walden, *The Capitalist Conjuncture: Over-accmulation, Financial Crises, and the Retreat from Globalisation*, "Third World Quarterly", vol.27, no.8, 2006, pp.1345-1367.

[12] Prabhat Patnaik, "*Globalisation and the World Politics*", Social Scientist, vol.30, no.11-12, November-December, 2000,p.5

[13] *Ibid*.p.9

[14] Prabhat Patnaik, n.8, p.5

[15] James Petras and Henry Veltmeyer, n.10.,p.24

[16] *Ibid*.p.48

[17] *Ibid*.p.54

[18] Joseph Stiglitz, *Making Globalisation Work: The Next Steps to Global Justice*, (London: Allen Lane, 2006), p.276

[19] Eric Hobsbawm, *Globalisation, Democracy and Terrorism*, (London:Little, Brown;2007),p.3

[20] Joseph Stiglitz, n.5, pp.6-7

[21] James Petras and Henry Veltmeyer, n.10, p.48

3

Globalisation and Islamism: Rethinking Some Reigning Paradigms

S.A.M. PASHA

The global resurgence of religion has, inter alia, awakened the epistemic community the world over, to revisit its hitherto-held paradigms geared towards comprehending social phenomena. The present essay is a modest contribution to such an endeavor, which takes account of Islamic resurgence germane to Muslim societies. The need for such a rethink is primarily directed towards the binary notions of ecclesiasticism and secularism. As an offshoot of the latter, modernisation theory reduced religion to the private domain, thanks to the phenomenon of Enlightenment. In the backdrop of the notions of Umma, Tawhid, Jihad, and others, the re-evaluation of the reigning paradigms is attempted. They provide a Weltanschauung of sorts to the ongoing movements of Islamic resurgence in the Muslim world. Further, the Huntingtonian and the Fukuyaman notions of the 'Clash of Civilisations' and the 'End of History' respectively are subjected to an analytical scrutiny.

The Religion-Politics Syndrome Revisited

A broad consensus exists among scholars and statesmen the world over about 'perniciousness' of the religion-politics mix, particularly in the context of the traditional and transitional societies of Asia, Africa and Latin America.[1] In the 1970s, this notion of perniciousness was further reinforced,[2] with reference to the reactivation of the Islamic forces in the Muslim world and elsewhere. A realisation has dawned among the columnists and academic intelligentsia that the West can no longer neglect the study of Islam as a force affecting people's total behaviour especially in the Muslim world.[3] The Enlightenment thesis that developmental processes, resulting from the impact of science and technology on society, will lead to secularisation of human relations seems to have been belied by developments taking place in the Islamic world. On the contrary, modern means of technology and communications have been effectively employed by the late Ayatollah Ruhollah Khomeini in the 70s, and is being followed dutifully elsewhere in the Muslim world by the Islamic forces.

Secularisation of state institutions was conceived and imposed in many Third World countries by a minuscule minority of westernised ruling elites. It did not involve and promote secularisation of minds and cultures of the masses. This is particularly true of the majority of Muslim populations, which did not internalise a secular outlook and values.[4] For evidence, one may look at the state of secularisation practiced in the so-called modern "secular" states with a predominantly Muslim population like Algeria, Egypt, Turkey, etc., juxtaposing it within the increasing tide of Islamic activism there. Clearly, the state-sponsored secularisation had not found favour with the broad sections of the Muslim populations in these countries. Turkey presents a pathetic case of this reality. Mustafa Kamal Pasha, during the second decade of the present century, ordained a comprehensive programme of modernisation (Westernisation) of the Turkish society in every sphere of life in order to make Turkey a part of Europe. Domestically, such a wholesale imitation of the West gave birth to contradictions, while on the international front, the European Union could not accept it as its full-fledged member. Part of the explanation may lie with the subterranean consciousness that resides among its European members that Turkey does not belong to the Christian civilisational heritage to which they perceive themselves as the rightful legatees. In view of the far reaching effects which these developments may imply, the need has arisen for a closer look at the social science formulations and historiography of the phenomenon, as articulated by Wayne A. Wilcox, and others,[5] because many of the models developed within the Western epistemology have not adequately explained the processes in non-Western societies. Hitherto, the ethos of Enlightenment with the concomitant compartmentalisation of the spiritual and the mundane aspects of human life have informed the sociological perspective on religion. It considered religion as only a sum total of archaic traditions, ritualistic practices and superstitious beliefs, which by themselves do not shape public affairs or policy. Viewing the phenomenon from this angle, positivist Western intellectual thought and its counterpart in the non-Western world categorised, studied and judged religion and its traditions in terms of modern, post-Enlightenment, secular and rationalist criteria, with its separation of religion and state as an accepted axiom. The roots of Enlightenment thus lie in skepticism, iconoclasm, and eclecticism; compared to faith, tradition, and purity which constituted the bedrock of religion.

Theoretically speaking, Islam, a creed whose cardinal principles are contained in the *Holy Quran* and the *Hadith*[6], does not recognise the politics-religion dichotomy, even though, at an empirical level, since the times of the Damascus-based Ummayad dynasty, the de facto separation of religion and politics in Islam has been in vogue.[7] Such a phenomenon ran parallel to the emergence of monarchy as a specific political model with early Muslims' interactions with Sassanid and Byzantine political cultures and institutions. The subsequent Muslim dynastic rulers did not hesitate to seek religious legitimacy for their rule from the *Ulama*. However, the *Madinah State* created by the Prophet and the one carried forward by the *Khulafa-e-Rashidun* (Rightly Guided Caliphs) did not structure itself on the religion-politics dichotomy.[8] The model of the *Madinah* state as provided by the Prophet continues to be a source of inspiration to all those protagonists of political Islam who wishes to infuse the *Madinah* spirit into modern politics.[9] Hence the rationale in their demand for returning to pristine Islam remains central to the ideology of contemporary Islamism. It is also perceived that there is a close nexus between faith and power, which was manifested during the lifetime of the early Islamic community, in the ascendance of

Islam as a dominant world power and civilisation. It was, in fact, the superpower of its time. As a scholar remarked:

> There is unanimity among the Muslims that the Madinah State founded by the Prophet Mohammad (PBUH) and later governed by the Rightly Guided Caliphs *(Khulafa-e-Rashidun)* was the best ideal state ever found on earth and hence provided a normative standard.[10]

The early political successes of Islam were attributed, *inter alia*, to Islam's integrationist perspective on religion and politics (state), unlike the Christian belief, "give unto Caesar that which is Caesar's, and unto God that which is God's". Moreover, the need for "State" in Islam never remained a subject of controversy as, in the first instance, the Prophet, and later, the *Rightly Guided Caliphs*, set the record straight by establishing and running an Islamic State in *Madinah*, though for a brief period, thus setting a role model for subsequent Muslim societies to emulate. Hence, the "State" in Islam was perceived as "divinely ordained necessity";[11] and the notion that there is anything sinful, or even dangerous, about the State did not gain ground in Islamic thought.[12] However, the aforesaid is not intended to promote the perception that the State in Islam entertains theocracy, as the management of the affairs of the State is not the exclusive domain of theologians *(Ulama) per se*.

The secularist ideology as understood in terms of the total bifurcation of the private and public domains, is alien to the spirit and worldview of Islam, for the former is historically in league with forces opposed to sacerdotalism in Europe which have been conspicuous in their absence in the Islamic lands.[13] (In fact, in classical Arabic, there is no equivalent word for secularism. However, in modern Arabic, the word *Almaniyya* conveys the spirit of secularism). Agents of modernisation such as urbanisation and industrialisation emanating from the impact of science and technology did not lead to the secularisation of social processes in the Muslim world as they did in the case of the West. In the contemporary Muslim world, characterised by resurgent Islam, it is not uncommon that 'Secularism, Westernisation,' 'being like the west' or *'Gharbzadegi'* (Weststruckness) as coined by an Iranian intellectual, Jalal Ali Ahmad in his work titled *Occidentosis: A Plague From The West*,[14] and other similar concepts have lost their credibility and attraction,[15] notwithstanding the nationalist/

secularist elites' penchant for them. (Besides Jalal Ahmad, Ali Shariati denounced the evils of *"Gharbzadegi"*: "Come, friends, let us abandon Europe, let us cease this nauseating, apish imitation of Europe. Let us leave behind this Europe that always speaks of humanity, but destroys human beings wherever it finds them").[16] In fact, the Western colonial encounter did not result in secularisation. On the contrary, Muslims' faith in Islam grew stronger than ever before. Islam came to occupy a pivotal role in the wars of national liberation which colonialism had spawned in the Muslim lands. Under the banner of the latter, the partisans of the anti-colonial liberation wars created an overarching national identity in which the 'nation' connoted simply 'the sum of Muslims on a given territory.[17] Thus, the Western colonial encounter coupled with the pre-modern historical experience of crusading Christianity militated against the feasibility of Muslims adopting Western norms and values in their social fabric. Recognising this fact, a prominent Western scholar on Islam says that 'somehow or other, Islam is secularisation-resistant'.[18] Muslims following a scripturalist Islam and fresh attempts at strengthening native ethos further facilitated such a resistance. Thus, viewing the whole argument in its historicity, it may be surmised that the original charismatic community (which was religious in its orientation) had no reason to posit itself against the state. In fact, the community was the state personified from the very beginning.

Notwithstanding this, the post-colonial elites' honeymoon with this European-tempered type of state building had resulted in contradictions that manifest now-a-days in the form of Islamic assertion.

Implicit in this type of state building is the much-touted universal applicability of the notions/models of Western statecraft. Of late, such *a priori* assumptions have lent themselves for critical evaluation in the light of the growing dissatisfaction visible in Muslim societies. As John L. Esposito aptly observed:

....a major obstacle to (the) understanding of (Muslim societies) was the secular presuppositions that informed (social science) disciplines and methodologies or, ...(the) Western Worldview. Acceptance of the "enlightened notion of separation of Church and State .... and of

Western, secular models of development relegated religion to the stockpile of traditional beliefs, (valuable in understanding the past but) regarded as irrelevant or an obstacle to modern development. Neither development theory nor international relations considered religion a significant variable. Those who accept separation of religion and politics overlooked the fact that most religious traditions were established and developed in historical, political, social and economic contexts. (Countries doctrines and laws were conditioned by these contexts). This was certainly true in the history of Islam and even more so in the belief of many Muslims .... The post-enlightenment tendency to define religion as a system of belief rather than a way of life has seriously hampered ability to understand the nature of Islam. It has artificially compartmentalised religion (doing violence to its nature) and reinforced a static, reified conception of religious traditions rather than their inner dynamic nature.[19]

Both Liberal development theory of modernisation and the Neo-Marxist theory of dependency/underdevelopment (which came into vogue in the 70s to ostensibly comprehend the Third World non-Western societies), relegated religion and other forms of culture to the level of epiphenomenona or considered such factors as part of metaphysics. Such an approach hardly considered religion as a way of life; a living entity and a dynamic with its own processes. Besides, western scholarship considered secularisation as the *sine qua non* of modernisation because their understanding of the phenomenon (with its structures and processes) was rooted in the Western experience and history, as they believed that this experience could be replicated elsewhere on a unilinear pattern: a way of looking at the non-Western world in their own image. Contrary to this episteme of modernisation/secularisation, the religion of Islam, as viewed from the *Quranic* perspective, is directly concerned with the life processes which seeks to have a direct impact on life and which also seeks to provide value, meaning and direction to life.[20] Such *a priori* Western understanding of the non-Western Muslim World (with all its concomitant prejudices, misperceptions, inconsistencies, etc.) is further boosted with the notion of the 'End of History' and the 'Triumph of Liberalism', as articulated by Francis Fukuyama, following the collapse of communism in the erstwhile Soviet Union and Eastern Europe. As Fukuyama wrote, in this context:

> What we are witnessing is not just the end of the Cold War, or the passing of a particular period of post-War history, but the end of history as such: that is, the end point of mankind's ideological evolution and the universalisation of Western Liberal democracy as the final form of human government.[21]

The Fukuyaman prognosis might be likened to Karl Marx's prophecy of the 'withering away' of the state with the setting up of a society devoid of class antagonisms or contradictions. In both the prognoses, there was an implied element of certainty as far as the progress of human history was concerned. To Fukuyama, Liberal-Philosophical Order is "the end point of mankind's ideological evolution" and to Karl Marx, progressive development of history ceased with the attainment of a classless society resulting in the disappearance of the State. Fukuyama did not envisage nor advocated the encouragement of political pluralism (the co-existence of liberalism and non-liberal ideologies, for instance). The very absence of such a pluralism and its subtle advocacy which has implicit in the thesis of Fukuyama, smacked of contradictions in the liberal idea if it had not recognised the existence of diverse cultures and systems (including political) inhabiting and endeavouring to shape the world. The convulsions in the Muslim world spearheaded by Islamic groups increasingly defy Fukuyaman thesis. As for Karl Marx, the demise of the Soviet system contributed a blow to his ideas. As regards the potential challenge of Islam as an ideology, Fukuyama dismisses it because he finds the Third World a Wasteland of Ideas: he argues that the "flow of ideas has been from the West to the Third World, and not the other way around", and also asserts that Islamic fundamentalism has "virtually no appeal outside of communities that were not Muslims to begin with". As regards his former viewpoint, it is historically untenable to assert because the Muslim Andalusia (Spain) during the Middle Ages, was the centre of intellectual ferment from whence dispersal of ideas to the rest of medieval Europe took place, resulting in Renaissance, Reformation and Enlightenment. Fukuyama's dismissive attitude towards non-Western cultures as reflected in his two view points cited above, displays a deep-rooted prejudice that blinds the West from understanding non-Western contribution. *Tawhid* visualises human life as a direct relationship between the transcendent Creator and His creation in which life is seen as a test of excellence and worth. The uniqueness and oneness of Allah, the Creator, is replicated in the Unity and equality of man (thus negating distinctions of colour, language, wealth, etc.) as embodied in his role as the Vicegerent and Custodian *(Khalifah)* of Allah on earth, and is required to rule in accordance with Allah's will. *Tawhid*, therefore, endows a Muslim with the psychological make-up and worldview to function as a citizen of the world.[22] Thus, it is not the threat of Islamic fundamentalism *per se*, but the vision of the *organic unity of life* (emphasis supplied), which it represents, that antagonises the West.[23] Such a Muslim worldview and the Muslim movements' on-going endeavours to translate the ideal into reality do bring into sharp focus the relevance and salience of Islam for the contemporary International relations. As Suroosh Irfani writes at length:

> ....the Muslim ideal (life is an organic unity) reflects a counterconsciousness for the materialistically motivated ideal of Western Liberalism. In the Muslim view of history, the ideal is the reconstruction of social life in the light of mankind's common spiritual origin. Muslim ideological movements today are seeking a redefinition of the society on the basis of this transnational belief.... However, Universalisation of this ideal of unity would be a gradual process and depends for its growth on peoples' entry into the mainstream of World politics. in this sense, the politicisation of the Muslims, resulting from their growing awareness of being in a continual state of subordination to Western reality, is accelerating the crystallisation of an ideologically reconstructed Muslim identity. Central to this identity is the belief that the meaning and role of Islam lies in the inevitable march of history towards World unity.[24]

Similarly, nationalism-multiplicity of the system of nation-states finds its ideological and historical moorings in the soil of Europe, having blossomed during the sixteenth and seventeenth centuries. While colonising Islamic lands since the 19th century onwards, European colonialism tried to supplant the *Weltanschauung* of universal Islam with the ideological systems represented by secularism and nationalism, to cite only the two.[25] It has an advantage in one sense in this endeavour: the physical occupation of Muslim lands enabled it to experiment with its own value systems. However, it has to be noted here that they were met with resistance of varying degrees in all occupied lands.[26] As anti-thesis to the ideology of territorial nationalism in particular, Pan-Islamism still continues to have an emotional appeal to Islam's adherents as did Ottomanism till March 3rd 1924 when the Grand National Assembly of Turkey formally voted to disband the institution of Caliphate. Pan-Arabism held its sway over Arabs in the heyday of Gamal Abdel Nasser of Egypt. Libya's Colonel Muammar Gaddafi, Syria's Hafez al Asad and Iraq's Saddam Hussein became its later-day adherents with mixed results. The balance sheet of the Arab League, an institutional expression of Pan-Arabism at governmental level, has been loaded on the liabilities side. Even though the League takes it for granted the Islamic element as part of its Arab heritage, it is nevertheless true to say that the former is subordinated to the latter in its style of functioning. Regionalism forms an essential principle in its activities, whereas it could well have organised itself on the over-arching frame of Islam which also draws into its vortex, the Arab variant of Islam in the region. Retrospectively viewed, the fate of the Al-Quds (Jerusalem) might have been quite different had it been dealt with an Islamic rather than a regional (Arab) framework. To bring the point home, two contrasting styles with which the Arabs fought their two wars with the Israelis in 1967 and 1973 are worthy of note for their equally opposite results. The crushing defeat of the Arabs in the 1967 Arab-Israeli War, leading to the consequent loss of East Jerusalem to Israel, besides other Arab territories, created a pressing urgency for soul-searching among Arabs, both Western-oriented secular elites, as well as the more Islamically committed ones. The search led to the questioning of the relevance of Western statecraft models, which were obviously rooted in the socio-cultural ethos of the Western societies. Positively, for Arabs, the quest confirmed the authenticity and relevance of the familiar, indigenously evolved and nurtured Islamism, thus engendering spiritual rebirth among them. The stark contrast, between the two, in terms of their efficacy to the Arab predicaments is too important to be neglected. The 1967 War was fought in the name of Nasserism (Arab Socialism) and was lost by the Arabs. The shock of defeat made Nasser to philosophise that "precaution is useless against fate",[27] implying that defeat was predestined and realised that reliance on faith was the only road to victory. This being the case, the 1973 Ramadhan War (its code name was *Badr*) was fought under the banner of Islam, which was won by the Arabs. The latter also witnessed the liberal use of idioms and symbols associated with Islam. For instance, the Egyptians named their blitzkreig against Israel as "Operation Saladin", reminding themselves of the victory scored by the Muslims against the crusading Christians during the Middle Ages. Thus, the war of 1967 led to the indictment of Arab nationalism/socialism while the War of 1973 provided a fillip to Islamic resurgence.

In view of the aforecited scenario, it makes sense to view in perspective the ideology of Pan-Islamism as propounded and propagated by the yester-year's widely acclaimed Jamal-al-Din Afghani. The late Ayatollah possessing all the necessary credentials in this regard; i.e., having successfully effected an Islamic revolution and also possessing an Islamised ideological vision which might have swayed the Third World populations in general, and its Muslim segment in particular may be said to be Afghani's rightful successor. It is, of course, necessary to view them in their respective climes and times. Afghani operated in, and his ideas were addressed to, a situation characterised by colonialism under which most of the Muslim societies were languishing then. Whereas the late Ayatollah operated in a politically sovereign international system of nation-states some of which are still subjected to neo-colonial and neo-imperialist stranglehold of the Great powers internationally and to despotic rule internally. Sayyid Ali Khameini, succeeding to the mantle of spiritual leadership of Iran after the demise of Ayatollah Khomeini, is very much cognizant of the precedents left behind by his illustrious, charismatic predecessor and is steadfast in carrying forward the torch lit by the Ayatollah, although the political stature is one of the traits which distinguish the two from each other. Islamic history is replete with examples of *Mujtadeed* (renewers) who influenced, and in turn were influenced by, the destiny of their generation. They provided a direction to their generations and reminded them of the latter's forgotten obligations. The Islamic World is, thus, not without its historical antecedents and precedents for its present state of affairs for purposes of emulation and inspiration from within. Ralph Braibanti ably captured Islam's salience as a propelling force in the present-day world:

No other religion [save Islam] has quite so compelling a doctrinal base for global unity – neither Buddhism, Christianity, Judaism nor Hinduism. There was once a thrust for a universal Christendom and the Holy Roman Empire was its political expression. While the doctrine of Christian unity still exists, it has been eroded by sectarianism, schism, nationalism and secularism. Christianity has lost most of its moral and virtually all of its political dynamism. Islam is, in a different stage of development. Its renewed sense of identity unleashed by the creation of independent states free form colonial rule, have given it a new dynamic force. Even now, that force activates its concern for Muslim minorities living in non-Muslim States ....it is true that Muslims are separated into distinct nations often antagonistic to each other, but this arrangement does not fit comfortably in the Islamic perception of order. Hence, there is a ceaseless dialectic between maintaining national boundaries and yet transcending them.[28]

Disillusionment With the Western Statecraft Models/ Paradigms

The disappointment and the attendant frustrations stemming from the operational/functional inefficacy of the developmental models provided by the West had a salutary effect in so far as it paved the way for a genuine search for indigenous roots of development and identity on the part of these states. The endeavours in this direction did not ceased to exist and instead, are aimed at bringing out a holistic/multi-dimensional perspective germane to their present and future state of affairs.[29] Some of them have already expressed themselves in institutional terms; replacement of the colonial civil and criminal codes by the Islamic ones, regulations in the banking sector (notably the doing away of interest from its operational milieu and the consequent introduction of what are called profit-and-loss schemes) and Islamisation of knowledge, polity and social institutions, to cite only a few.

In the arena of Islamisation of Knowledge, the Virginia-based International Institute of Islamic Thought has been engaged in the endeavor to provide, *inter alia*, an ideological base to Islamic resurgence by means of what Bryan S. Turner calls "methodology of academic Indigenisation. The Institute aims at providing an alternative to the existing Western-dominated epistemology and seeks to make it an equally acceptable methodology.[30] The trend towards indigenisation of diverse phenomena is not, however, confined only to the Muslim segment of the Third World; instead, it manifests itself in the Third World as a whole. As an indication of the growing self-assertion in the field of culture, the Algerian parliament on 26 December 1990, adopted a Bill to the effect that by 1997 "the use of Arabic in all official and work transactions as well as in schools is to be total.[31] Discrediting the politico-economic model provided by the National Liberation Front (FLN) of Algeria which spearheaded the Algerian Liberation against French colonialism and which ruled the state, following Independence, for full three decades, since 1962, the Islamic Salvation Front (FIS) secured 188 seats in the first round of elections conducted to the National Parliament in June 1990. In this elections, it secured 55 percentage votes thus enabling the Front to become the largest Islamic party in the Arab world. Further, it gained control of each and every big city and 32 of Algeria's 48 provinces. FIS-run assemblies soon proceeded to put into practice their plans for e.g., in areas under their domination, they enforced bans on the sale of alcohol schooling, and stopped rock music festivals.[32]

The second round surfaced with wearing of shorts and swimming costumes in the streets, which tried to prevent mixed-sex election process began on 16 January 1992 was subsequently cancelled with the intent to prevent the FIS from capturing power. Western response, particularly from France and the USA, towards the cancellation of the second round elections and the consequent usurpation of power by the armed forces was obviously dictated by the fear that if the FIS was allowed the certain victory, by means of democratic elections, France would be inundated by Algerian refugees allegedly posing a threat to western ways of life.

When the Islamists appeared set to win elections by the time the second round of polls were about to start in January 1992, the state prevented their victory by raising the spectre of 'Islamic fundamentalism' and dealing with it accordingly. It was alleged that 'Islamic fundamentalism' would utilise the electoral system in order to capture power and then outlaw all secular political parties, allowing only like-minded Islamic movements to operate. Such a process of removing the wheels from the democratic vehicle was viewed with a great sense of relief and satisfaction by the west as it thwarted the political aspirations of the ascendent

FIS at that time. Guided by this logic, the West extended its support to the military-backed government under the High State Committee (HSC) which determinedly crushed the FIS during 1992. The role of the West in the Algerian crisis indicated its clear intention of making or breaking regimes as it deemed fit. Egypt and Morocco were among the Arab states which welcomed the state crackdown against the Algerian Islamists, lest the latter should have spillover effect on their restive populations. Even the response of the international human rights organisations was not above board. No such organisation thought it imperative to condemn the cancellation of elections and the taking over of the reigns of power by the Army, nor was the violation of the rule of law and the arbitrary arrests of suspected FIS cadres by the military regime ever denounced.

The Algerian conundrum has thrown open certain issues of fundamental nature which are of relevance not only to political thought but also to the international community. What if the Third World peoples do not seek the road of liberal democracy towards the promised land of politically plural and open societies? What should be the response of the international community to such a situation? Would it allow its constituent members to choose unhindered social, political and economic system of their choice which may not be to the liking of the Great Powers? The answers to these and similar other questions, do significantly determine the nature of the international community and its adherence to the principles of international law.

"THE CLASH OF CIVILISATIONS"?

With the exit of communism as an ideological force in international politics following Soviet Union's demise, a variety of futuristic perspectives are advanced by scholars in relation to the nature of post-Cold War international system. One of such popular perspectives has considered Islam to have already filled the ideological vacuum created by the demise of communism.[33] Such a perception reminds one of a Cold War psyche which refuses to give up the habit of manufacturing an enemy to sustain itself; a tendency to juxtapose itself vis-à-vis the Other. Resurgent Islam is being projected as representing that entire ethos which are at variance with, or said to be in antagonistic relationship with, Western civilisation. The writings of Orientalists lend credence to and reinforce the existing popular stereotypes in the West about Islam. A noted Orientalist scholar, Bernard Lewis stated the "spectre" attributed to Islam poignantly vis-à-vis the West:

> We are facing a mood and a movement far transcending the level of issues and policies and the governments that pursue them. This is no less than a clash of civilisations, the perhaps irritational but surely historic reaction of an ancient rival against our Judeo-Christian heritage, our secular present, and the worldwide expansion of both.[34]

Other Orientalists are also no less emphatic than Lewis in their views. Samuel P. Huntington, a celebrated Harvard author of an article titled "The Clash of Civilisations?"[35] Had given respectability to such views, and following their logic, projected that the future contests among states will be fought on civilisational lines. He went to the extent of prophecying that "the next World War, if there is one, will be a War between civilisations".[36] He further asserted that "the clash of civilisations will dominate global politics" and that "the fault lines between civilisations will be the battle lines of the future."[37] However, his hypothesis that "the fundamental source of conflict in this new world will not be primarily ideological or primarily economic"[38] is difficult to endorse. Under the veneer of civilisations, the salience of ideologies or worldviews cannot be obliterated. Islamic activism, for instance, is not merely "terrorism" or "extremism" as the Western mass media would have us believe, but also a serious endeavour to project an alternative worldview distinct from the existing (hegemonic?) materialistic-consumeristic-hedonistic Worldview. The other name given to this worldview is democratic liberal international order. As contra-distinction to this world order is an alternative normative order based on the Quranic principle of *Tawhid*, which looks at the universe from a holistic/comprehensive perspective combining both the elements of spirit and matter, thus constituting an organic unity. The politics of Islamic activism is, *inter alia*, informed by this integrating principle of *Tawhid*. Thus, ideology may not become obsolete in the future wars as projected by Huntington. Moreover, it may so happen that ideology may find itself absorbed in the vortex of civilisational cleavages.

JIHAD

As a Quranic term, *Jihad* lends itself to a variety of meanings. In generic terms, it refers to the human effort to lead a good life, to make society more moral and just, and to spread Islam through preaching and teaching by means of the heart, tongue and hands. It is of central importance to Muslim self-understanding and mobilisation.

In the heyday of the history of Islamic civilisation, the framework within which foreign relations were conducted, was subsumed under the notions of *Dar al Islam* (Abode of Peace), *Dar al Harb* (Abode of War), and *Dar al Sulh* (Territories under Treaty). In pristine Islam, it was *Siyar* - the law that governed Islam's intercourse with the rest of the world - which held sway. In the early Islamic history, the *Siyar* envisioned a *Pan-Islamica* wherein the *Dar al Harb* would be integrated into the *Dar al Islam*. During the Middle Ages, Islam and Christendom clashed with religious fervour, employing the weapons of Crusades and *Jihad* as their organising principles. The general perception that the spirit and hence the essence, of this conflictual relationship still continues to exist is held by both the contestants. The initial Western support in bringing Israel into existence and their subsequent measures to strengthen Israel in the latter's fight with the Arabs,[39] is cited by Muslims as an example to this effect. In this context, Muslims perceive Israel to be an extension of the West in the heart of holy Islamic lands and that Zionism constitutes a constant threat to the Islamic world.[40] Further, the Jewish state, to borrow an evocative statement of Sheikh Muhammed Hussein Fadlallah, a Shiite leader of *Hizbollah* (Party of Allah) in Lebanon, is "a conglomeration of people who came from all parts of the world to live in Palestine on the ruins of another people".[41] Numerous instances of this genre can be cited.

The Islamic view of international relations has itself been evolutionary.[42] It did not spring all of a sudden. Islamic legal learning made a substantial contribution to the sum total of universal legal scholarship in such areas of international law as the notion of trusteeship of political power, the right of rebellion against unjust rulers, the law of war and peace, etc.[43] In the context of the contemporary world scenario characterised by the system of sovereign nation-states and the proliferation of nuclear weapons and weapons of mass destruction (notwithstanding the efforts to control their spread), the traditional *Jihad*-centric framework of international relations becomes a potential source of perpetual tensions and antagonisms among states. It has to give way to notions of Islamic solidarity, peaceful maintenance of international relations, and the like. In view of this, a need to re-orient Islamic methodology in the arena of external relations has been felt in the contemporary times, in order to enable the Muslim states to conduct their foreign policies on those lines.[44] However, in one sense, the spirit of early times is still evident in the modern age: the frequent calls for *Jihad* (a striving towards a righteous, just cause in all public matters) on the part of the Muslim leaders against the external encroachments on the territorial integrity and independence of Muslim states[45] is a proof of this. In fact, the history of twentieth century Islamic societies acts as a testimony to the fact that *Jihad* had acted as an anti-colonial and anti-imperialist ideology against their subjugation by the West.[46] It performed the function of mobilising an entire population for a national cause. Conscious of this historical function of Jihad, its present day votaries espouse its application to the existing Muslim societies in order to stall Western penetration and influence in various hues. The cultural penetration of the West into the Third World Muslim societies in the form of mass media and the aggressive promotion of consumerism (hedonism) as an antidote to neutralise the affectation of the Third World populace to their own cultural forms has also established the relevance of Islam in international relations.[47] Islamists are cognizant of the dangers emanating from global mass consumerism and they perceive the latter as a further extension of westernisation and a new form of indirect colonial penetration, resulting, albeit, in internal cultural invasion. By offering a variety of possible lifestyles, consumerism does compete with, and in many respects, contradict the holistic lifeworld epitomised in the Islamic concept of *Tawhid*. By seeking to elevate hedonism, to the level of a global culture, consumerism directly cuts through the religious beliefs and values held dear by Muslims. Thus, it is a challenge as well as an opportunity for forces of Islamic resurgence as the latter have a potential to counter the utilitarian ethos represented by consumerism with the latter's emphasis on leisure, gratification, and hedonism.

Besides, in the context of contemporary politics, Islam can still guide international relations if the needs of the present and modern conditions are taken into consideration. John L. Esposito substantiates them as follows:

1. "A human brotherhood with an honoured status among creation.
2. The supremacy of justice: "Be just under all circumstances".
3. Continuous preaching of Islam by peaceful means and if freedom to do so is denied, or the Muslim community is attacked, war must be waged to deter aggression.
4. Contracts and Trusts must be honoured under all circumstances whoever the party may be.
5. Reciprocity in the conduct of relations when no agreements to regulate them exist."[48]

The short and successful swift action of the Western states against the Iraqi occupation of Kuwait has once again brought into public reminiscence the bygone spirit of the crusades, the erstwhile colonial domination and the contemporary neo-colonial tendencies of hegemony buttressed by the post-Cold War international politics manoeuvred by the so-called "unipolar superpowerism" of the USA. "During the crusades, the West attacked Muslims in the Middle East, and during colonialism the West occupied Muslim lands. The present is the same, only the political context and form of operation differ."[49]

Referring to the re-emergence of the West's crusading spirit in modern times,

W M. Watt has this to say:

> Some Muslims today ...see various forms of western aggression against the Islamic world as a recrudescence of the crusading movement. Colonel Qadhafi of Libya goes so far as to speak of Napoleon's invasion of Egypt in 1798 as the Ninth Crusade and the establishment of the state of Israel with American support as the Tenth Crusade.[50]

Among the popular perception of the Muslims, crusades preceded the colonial phase in the evolving historical relationships between the West and Islam and the present-day scenario of Islam's interaction with the West is a continuation of the earlier two historical phases. To quote Watt again:

Many Muslims now see colonialism as a continuation of the aggression of Christians against the Islamic world begun by the crusades. This is in no way a folk memory but it is a new perception based on what Muslims have learnt in the West... Doubtless there is some justification for their seeing the crusades as an early stage of the struggle between the Islamic World and Christian Europe for the southern and eastern shores of the Mediterranean.[51]

Alan Richards and John Waterbury also refer to such Muslim perceptions:

...the nineteenth and twentieth century confrontation of the Middle Easterners as another enactment of an ancient struggle between Christianity and Islam, and European colonialism as an effort to snuff out Islam once and for all.[52]

The end of colonialism in the Muslim World enabled the ruling elites of the latter to engage their entire societies to define afresh their social priorities accordance with their genuine needs and indigenous cultural heritage. This genuine search for indigenisation is virtually evident in the entire Third World. As Braibanti notes:

The emergence of Islamic national identity is part of a larger global trend of developing nations turning to indigenous models of development. Disenchantment with foreign models and growing self-confidence in a national identity encourages.... 'endogeneity'. This search for roots leads inevitably to a reconsideration of Islam.'[53]

Thus, the Muslim endeavour to indigenise their ethos and reorganise their societies within the framework subsumed by those ethos have caught the popular imagination in those societies. Implicit in those endeavours are not merely to stall those outer layers of Western cultural artifacts such as music and other permissive exhibits, but also to prevent politico-ideological penetration in the form of nationalism, secularism, westernisation, etc., An alternative Islamic vision, to enthuse various walks of life, and hence holistic, is touted as an ever-lasting panacea to the sufferings and tribulations being faced by Muslim societies.

In the backdrop of this scenario, it is not fortuitous that Islam still governs a greater part of the world in many aspects, and ... when the European domination of the world system tends to fade out in many respects, it [Islam] is free to come to the surface again, after many centuries under colonial system.[54]

In the last fifty years, the Muslim world has transformed itself from a dominated area to a dynamic force in global affairs. In the words of Bo Johnson Theutenberg again:

> Present evidence has shown that Islam again acts with strength, and naturally the rest of the world asks the question whether this means that some doctrines of the Islamic Shariah law in the long run will influence the corpus of international law with regard to inter-state relations, and in that case what interpretations of the *Shariah* law will be the guiding one.[55]

An important dimension of the West-Islam interaction that borders virtually on confrontation and hostility is exhausted in what is widely known as *Jihad*. For most of the time in the history of Islam's contacts with the Occident, *Jihad* constituted a significant governing principle. In the context of the re-emergence of Islamic forces in contemporary international relations, a serious question regarding Jihad to be a constituent element has to be raised. The frequent calls for *Jihad* that are often made in modern times indicate, on the face of it, an affirmation of its present relevance. During the time of West's colonial domination over the Islamic world, *Jihad* played a progressive role in the form of liberation struggles. In our times, its salience lies in defending the Muslim world's political independence and territorial integrity when encroachments are made upon them, and the Muslims right to adopt socio-economic and political systems of their choice in the light of *Shariah*. In this context, Bo Johnson Theutenberg aptly depicts the changing nature of Jihad in the dynamics of Islam's relationship with the Occident:

> Islam and the Occident have much to talk about, much to inform each other about, *but now on an equal footing* (emphasis added). We must be fully aware of the fact that politico-military circumstances and constellations may 'push' the dogmas towards a clear distortion, and after that much is destroyed. The distorted and misunderstood dogmas will exist as "eternal" barriers to rapproachment between the systems.[56]

Jihad, in the present times, has assumed defensive connotations vis-à-vis the West, in particular, in view of its proclivity to safeguard identity, independence and sovereignty of Muslim lands.[57] "This rightly runs counter to the popular notion of a *"holy war"*: an expression consciously propagated primarily by the western media in the present times and by the Christendom in the medieval ages. As it does to other Quranic concepts, the Western media consciously attributes to *Jihad* a new and specific meaning, which is far removed from the original intent. Abdul Hamid Abu Sulayman counters this Western stereotype by saying that it *(Jihad)* does not preeminently stand for combat or fight and that Islam is not aggressive by nature.[58] However, Jihad, as a form of defensive war, converges with present-day international law as embodied in the United Nations Charter and other international treaties. The latter two recognise the state's traditional right to individual or collective self-defence. Under certain propitious circumstances, *Jihad* may also bring into its focus the connotation implicit in the concept of "Just War". However, political leadership in a given circumstance or a constellation of circumstances retains the task of defining the circumstances leading to "Just War". It is, thus, obvious that *Jihad* opens up itself to a variety of juridical opinion and that there is no such thing as a monolithic definition of the concept disregarding time-space consideration. While it is feasible to talk of "Just War" in the context of *Jihad*, on the other hand, it is quite instructive to recall that the former U.S. President, George Bush, described the American (and by implication, Western) military campaign to liberate Kuwait from Iraqi military occupation also as an instance of a "Just War". To this effect, he also obtained ecclesiastical endorsements from the Church leaders similar to the Muslim leaders' traditional practice of obtaining *Fataawaa* (singular, *Fatwaa*, a religious verdict) from the *Muftees* (singular, *Mufti*, one who issues a *Fatwaa*) on their public policies.

The statements made by Bush during the course of the War, were sprinkled with the invocation, "God Bless America", which smacked of religious overtones. His State of the Union message delivered during January 1991, was reflective of the latter: "Tonight, as our forces fight, they and their families are in our prayers. May God bless each and every one of them and the coalition forces on our side in the Gulf."[59]

The successful campaign of Afghan Mujahideen's against the armed occupation of their country by the erstwhile Soviet

Union is a typical testimony of this defensive connotation of *Jihad*. *Jihad* can, thus, be legitimately employed for throwing off a foreign yoke, which the modern international law recognises as the right of self-defense. Hence, *Jihad* is a potent weapon to secure human freedom when the latter is threatened. Abdul Hamid Abu Sulayman endorses this contention when he says that Jihad as basic Islamic principle does not exclude the possibility of armed conflict.[60] At the same time, he lays an equal emphasis on its other meanings and its application to different situations. This would imply that Muslims need to change their approaches and methods of thought if at all they aim at creating and maintaining a successful Islamic social system including international relations. As the duty to pursue what is true and right, *Jihad* includes protection of the human rights of life, belief, honour, family, education, and the *Khilafah*, common and private properties. Further, Jihad could be a war of words, an effort to make the doctrines of Islam accepted and acceptable. *Jihad* could, therefore, take place by persuasion as the *Holy Quran* enjoins:

> Invite (all) to the way of thy Lord with wisdom and beautiful preaching; and argue with them in ways that are best and most gracious; For thy Lord knoweth best, who have strayed from His path, and who receive guidance.[61]

The Makkah-Taif Declaration (Third Islamic Summit Conference, 25 January 1981) defined *Jihad* in the sense of a legitimate defensive struggle "to liberate the occupied Palestinian and Arab territories and the holy places" and "to defend the independence and sovereignty of a country against an aggression". The Declaration further legitimised *Jihad* in circumstances where Muslims become "victims of innumerable injustices" and are faced with multiple dangers due to the reign of force and aggression and the politics of violence in international behaviour".[62] The Declaration further stated that "Islam enjoins justice and equity both for its followers and others and it also enjoins tolerance and magnanimity towards those who do not combat us, do not force us to leave our homes and do not violate our sacred values and which never takes the side of wrong doing, injustice or oppression". Thus, it became evident that the member-states successfully pursued a detailed explanation of

Jihad (in the context of Muslim states' external behaviour) in order to remove any misconstruction or misinterpretation. In the above context, it would be very instructive to comprehend the poly-dimensional nature of *Jihad* as underlined by Robert L. Canfield, an Anthropologist of repute. As he states at length:

> The *Jihad* is the highest, most honourable quest of the Muslim. It is the struggle for a pure inner life as well as for upright relations in one's social affairs and a just society in the world at large-inner purity, upright relations, and social justice understood, again, in Islamic terms. Because the *Jihad* for purity, uprightness, and social responsibility is the ideal quest of the Muslim, it has normally provided the basis for cooperation in social causes. *Contrary to the supposition of some non-Muslims, Jihad is not a call to mindless bloodshed in the name of God, rather, it is a call to fulfill sublime ideals* (emphasis added). An appeal to *Jihad* is heeded by Muslims as a function of its aptness to particular circumstances; its moral content, in any case, springs from ideals deeply embedded in Islamic notions of virtue and sublimity.[63]

This being the case, it is very surprising to note that the appeal made by Yasser Arafat, the then 'Head' of the Palestinian National Authority, to insert the word Jihad in the Dakar (Senegal) Declaration (Sixth Islamic Summit Conference held during 9-11 December 1991) to describe the struggle against Israel's occupation of Palestine territory (since the mid-1993, Jericho and Gaza Strip became self-governing territories under the authority of PNA) was not accepted by the majority in the Conference. The plausible reason behind this rejection could be that Saudi Arabia, Kuwait, Egypt and other countries were not particularly enthused with the Palestinian leader as he sided with Saddam Hussein in the latter's War against the U.S.- led Coalition in January 1991. This episode makes it clear that when bilateral equations are strained among the members, they tend to affect their common obligations in an adverse way. Islamic solidarity sounds hollow and remains a rhetoric when, in specific circumstances, it is left unpractised. The OIC, in its Third Summit Conference which was held at Makkah-Taif in January, 1981, paid obeisance to the 'ideal of Islamic solidarity' and reiterated the latter's consolidation among member-states as a priority objective.

Nation-State System

Tawhid exemplifies the worldview of Islam. Tawhid governs the mental horizon of a typical Muslim. To him, it is an ultimate reality; to it alone ultimate loyalty is owed, even though there is apparent diversity in the creation of universe by Allah. As the *Holy Quran* says:

And among His signs is the creation of the heavens and the earth and the variations in your languages and your colours; verily in that are signs for those who know.[64]

Further,

O, people, we have created you (all) of a single pair, a male and female (namely, Adam and Eve), and we have constituted you into tribes and nations that you may know one another. Noble among you in the estimate of Allah is more virtuous.[65]

Thus, pluralism as understood from this Quranic perspective is meant to serve the purpose of knowing each other and not to consider it as an ultimate reference point. In the backdrop of the aforesaid, nation-state system confines man's loyalty to a specific group evolved through a historical process involving race, language, territory, economic relations and other factors. Thus, *Tawhid* is an antithesis to particularism, ethnocentrism and racism and that it is an organising principle of universalism which takes into its vortex the political phenomenon too.[66]

The ideology of nation-state has had no equivalent either in the early Islamic thinking or practice. It's introduction in the Muslim world, as elsewhere, was related to Western colonialism. Moreover, the retreating colonial powers put in place a nation-state structure in the notionally free political entities of the Muslim world. Nonetheless, the nation-state system did not acquire an ideological legitimacy from the populace in the Muslim world. Its acceptance or tolerance by the Muslim world on the *Realpolitik* grounds should not be treated as tantamount to ideational or intellectual conformity. In fact, on spiritual and ethical foundations of Islam, it would be a difficult proposition to rationalise/legitimise it in the context of the Muslim World. At best, it enjoys an ambiguous legitimacy as its viable alternative in any concrete form, is found wanting in the present period. Further, the growing band of conformists who view that the nation-state is on the way towards obsolescence attribute it to factors beyond the control of a sovereign nation-state: revolutionary changes in the technology of telecommunications that have rendered the world to the status of a "Global Village" and the growing stranglehold of multinational corporations in global economic relations, to name only the two. On the other hand, in the contemporary world, it is increasingly perceived, particularly by Muslims, that the nation-state order dismembers the *Umma(h)*[67] because territorial delimitation is the hallmark of a nation-state, whereas *Ummah* overrides territoriality and holds its adherents together by a common bond of faith. In fact, it divided the *Umma(h)*, and for the West it became easier to exploit one national Muslim state with another, as the establishment of the Muslim *Umma(h)* poses the greatest threat to their interests.[68] Besides, the rise of nationalism has been a central force in the disintegration of Islamic unity.[69]

Therefore, the arbitrary delimitation of territorial boundaries on the part of the retreating colonial powers is, in the present times, sought to be redrawn, albeit by the use of force, on the plea that the existing boundaries are incompatible with their civilisational legacy, and indigenous traditions,[70] thus attempting to right historical wrongs. One may perhaps attribute this realisation to invasion and eventual occupation of Kuwait by Saddam Hussein. In the context of the convergence that was found between the USA and the erstwhile Soviet Union, the Security Council could, with the consent and consensus among the Five Permanent Members, impose sanctions against Iraq, Libya, and intervene in Somalia and allow the USA to intervene in Haiti.

In the case of Somalia, the UN concern was to create stable conditions so that a semblance of political order might be put in place there. In the Haitian case, the Security Council "empowered" the USA to attack Haiti in order to restore the democratically elected government which was overthrown by the military.

Be that as it may, in the case of Muslim states, a pelthora of transnational Muslim institutions do bring into sharp focus the contradictions latent in the nation-state order, characterising the contemporary Muslim world, when one takes into account the wide gap between the rhetoric of Islamic universalism and the ceaseless pursuit of the so-called "national" interests of the Muslim states pursued by the ruling elites. To enable Muslims to establish *ummatic* institutions in the Muslim world, the ruling elites have not succeeded in overcoming obstacles posed by nationalism, tribalism and ethnicity, in particular. Hence:

> The dilemma of Islam and nation, Islam and tribe and Islam and contemporary ideologies needs to be reduced first by contemporary Muslim political thought before a truly ummatic institution can be conceived and become functional. Islamisation should first be tackled as a conceptual challenge before it can be transposed into institutional forms.[71]

As these dilemmas, on the one hand, severely test the efficacy of the Muslim political thought in resolving them, there lies, on the other, a potential in Islam to play a constructive role in the field of international relations as perceived by Abdul Hamid Abu Sulayman:

> Islam could be used to bring about more emphasis on issues such as human dignity and human rights by taking a stand against racial and nationalist discrimination by emphasising equality and merit, by decentralising political authority and decision-making bodies, and advocating wider cooperation and mutual support in economic, technical, social, cultural, and political matters based on principles of human welfare and progress, equity, merit, and social justice.[72]

In contravention of an international order based on primordialism as outlined above, there lies a potential in the concept of *Umma* to structure international system on the basis of universal brotherhood of mankind. Moreover, for Muslims, the notion of *Umma* does not conflict with the world view of the *Holy Ouran* and the political practice of the early Islam. At subliminal state, the notion of *Umma* stirs the psychology of Muslims and instantly finds an echo of acceptance. This is one of the reasons for being a part of ideologised Islamic groups operating in the Muslim world. Moreover, the concept of *Umma* is intrinsic to the *Holy Qur'an* which the followers of Islam were familiar with and continue to cherish in the modern times too.

End Notes

[1] There are increasing endeavours by scholars to reevaluate the sociological impact of the religion-politics interaction, not only in the Third World but also in the secular Western societies as well, in response to the countries such

as Italy and Germany. The ideology of Liberation Theology (a syncretistic tendency of clubbing Marxian ideas with the ameliorative aspects of the Bible as interpreted by the Christian clergy) in the Latin American states, is a case in point. Typical of such remodeling endeavours are those of Robert Wuthnow, Lamin Sanneh, Edward Mortimer and Richard Falk, to name only four. For details, see:

  a) Robert Wuthnow, 'Understanding Religion and Politics', *Daedalus* (Cambridge: Massachusetts), Vo1.120, No.3, Summer 1991, pp.1-20.

  b) Lamin Sanneh, 'Religion and Politics: Third World Perspectives on a Comparative Religious Theme', *Daedalus* (Cambridge: Massachusetts), Vo1.120, No.3, Summer 1991, pp.203-218.

  c) Edward Mortimer, 'Christianity and Islam', *International Affairs* (London), Vol. 67, No. 1, January 1991, pp. 7-13.

  d) Richard Falk, 'Religion and Politics: Verging on the Post-Modern', *Alternatives* (Boulder: Colorado), Vol. XIII, 1988, pp.379-394.

[2] See James A. Beckford and Thomas Luckmann, 'Introduction', in James A. Beckford and Thomas Luckmann, eds., *The Changing Face of Religion* (New Delhi: Sage Publications, 1989). To Quote them: "..... the tendency towards a Western-led separation of religion from politics began to be reversed in the mid-1970s". p. 3.

[3] The phenomenon is variously designated by analysts as "Renaissance", "Resurgence", "Reaction", "Revitalisation", "Revival", "Reassertion", "Fundamentalism", and the like. "Fundamentalism" in particular, has a specific association with Christian history, especially in its protestant form, during the early decades of the Twentieth century in the United States of America. Most of the expressions, however, betray one's ideological predilections and biases. Such jargon, as the ones used above, are objected to by some scholars, notably among whom is Mona Abul Fadl. See her work, *Islam and the Middle East: The Aesthetics of a Political Enquiry* (Research Monograph, No.2) (Herndon, Virginia: The International Institute of Islamic Thought, 1990), p.38.

For a perceptive insight on the subject, see, John 0. Voll, 'Renewal and Reform in Islamic History', in John L. Esposito, ed., *Voices of Resurgent Islam* (New York: Oxford University Press, 1983), pp.32-47. Esposito, besides buttressing the John Voll viewpoint, also cites other grounds for rejecting "fundamentalism", as the latter is culture-specific (for its association with Protestant Christianity), erroneously implies a monolithic Islamic threat, and draws into its vortex all stereotypes and images being propagated by Western media about Islam and Muslims. In view of these reasons, he settles down for a "less value laden" and "more fitting general terms" such as "Islamic revivalism" and/or "Islamic activism". See John L.Esposito, *Islamic Threat: Myth or Reality?* (New York: Oxford University Press,1992), p. 8; Eric Davis, 'The Concept of Revival and the Study of Islam and Politics', in Barbara Stowasser, ed., *The Islamic Impulse* (London: Croom Helm, 1987), pp. 37-58; and "Political Islam: Pluralism Denied?" *National Institute for Research Advancement (NIRA) Review* (Tokyo: Centre for Policy Research Information, Winter 1995), p.3.

[4] John L. Esposito, *The Islamic Threat: Myth or Reality?* (New York: Oxford University Press, 1992), p. 9.

5 Confining his attention to the Pakistani case in which Islam plays a not-insignificant role in the public policy, Wayne A. Wilcox recognises the urgent need for such a deviation from the accepted wisdom on the subject. See 'The Wellsprings of Pakistan', in Lawrence Ziring, et al., ed., *Pakistan: The Long View*, (Durham, North Carolina: Duke University Press, 1977), pp.25-39.

Tamara also considers that any analysis of Muslim societies need to address itself to the self image without which Muslims' responses to external influences become incomprehensible. See Tamara Sonn, 'The Islamic Alternative: Cause or Effect?' *International Journal* (Toronto), Vol. XLVI, No.2, Spring 1991, p.292.

6 Traditions and Sayings as attributed to Prophet Mohammad. The former are considered as one of the most authentic sources of Islamic Jurisprudence (*Fiqh*).

7 Amir Said Arjomand, 'The Emergence of Islamic Political Ideologies,' in James A. Backford and Thomas Luckmann, eds., *The Changing Face of Religion* (New Delhi: Sage Publications, 1987), p.108; Sami Zubaida, *Islam, the People and the State: Essays in Political Ideas and Movements in the Middle East* (London: Routledge, 1989), p.41; and Khurram Murad, ed., *The Islamic Movement: Dynamics of Values, Power and Change* (Delhi: Markazi Maktaba Islami, 1984), p. 23.

8 WM. Watt, *Islamic Fundamentalism and Modernity* (London: Routledge, 1988), p. 94; Hugh Goddard, 'Spheres United Under God'. *The Times Higher Education Supplement* (London), September 21, 1990.

9 W.M. Watt, *Islamic Fundamentalism and Modernity* (London: Routledge, 1988), p. 92 and Asaf Hussain, *Political Terrorism and the State in the Middle East* (London: Mansell Publishing Ltd., 1988), p. 15.

10 A. Rashid Moten, "Islamisation of Knowledge: Methodology of Research in Political Science", in Mohammad Muqim, ed., *Research Methodology in Islamic Perspective* (New Delhi: Institute of Objective Studies, 1994), p. 42.

11 Bernard Lewis, "Preface", in Gilles Kepel, *Muslim Extremism in Egypt: The Prophet and Pharaoh* (Berkeley: University of California Press, 1986), p. 12.

12 Charles Issawi, *Egypt at Mid-Century: An Economic Survey* (London: Oxford University Press, 1954), p. 15.

13 To speak from the experience of Europe, the religion-politics symbiosis characterised its Medieval and Thirteenth centuries, thereby earning for it the epithet of Christendom. The reality of the bifurcation of these twin processes had got reflected in the epoch-making phenomenon designated as Reformation, a dynamic which was fundamentally shaped and preceded by Renaissance. These twin processes - Renaissance and Reformation - later paved the way for what is called the Enlightenment. The cumulative result of all these processes led the way to the denigration of faith-based organisation of human affairs (including politics) on the principles of Christianity as interpreted by the organised clergy. Moreover, the rise of bourgeoisie in Europe following the overthrow of the feudal order required, for its unfettered development, a socio-political order which recognised no ecclesiastic authority, external to it. It was this bourgeoisie, at the helm of the newly emerged nation-state order, which prescribed the rules of the game so far as politics was concerned.

The oppression inflicted on the believers, as recorded in History, produced its own antidote in the form of nationalised churches and the rise of nation- state system in Europe with secularism as the reigning ideology of European populace. The two-nationalised church and the nation-state system - interacted with each other closely. It is noteworthy in this context, that such a social revolution has not been, till date, reproduced in the case of Muslim societies, even though as an intellectual response to what is currently touted as 'Islamic Fundamentalism', there has developed a corpus of intelligentsia, both among Muslim and non-Muslim scholars on Islam, which has been advocating the emulation of this European experience by the Muslim lands. Notable among the advocates of such a viewpoint is Akeel Bilgrami. See his article, 'Rushdie and Reform of Islam', *Economic and Political Weekly* (Mumbai), Vol. XXV, No. 12, March 24, 1990, pp. 605-608.

[14] Jalal Ali Ahmad, *Occidentosis: A Plague From The West*, trans. R Campbell (Berkeley, California: Mizan Press, 1984).

[15] John O. Voll, 'Islam Fundamentalism and Regional Dynamics', in Harms W. Maull and Otto Pick, eds., *The Gulf War: Regional and International Dimensions* (London: Pinter Publishers, 1989), p. 41.

[16] Ali Shariati, *On the Sociology of Islam* (Berkeley, California: Mizan Press, 1979), p. 23.

[17] Ernest Gellner, *Post-Modernism, Reason and Religion* (London: Routledge, 1992), p. 15.

[18] Ernest Gellner, 'Islam and Marxism: Some Comparisons', *International Affairs* (London), Vol. 67, No. 1, January 1991, p. 2.

[19] John L. Esposito, 'The Study of Islam: Challenges and Prospects', *Middle East Studies Association Bulletin* (Washington, D.C.), Vol.24, No.l, July, 1990, pp. 1-2.

A view similar to the one cited above is also held by Udo Steinbach. See his 'The "Second Islamic Republic" - A Theocracy on the Road to Normality', *Aussen Politik* (Hamburg), Vol. 41, No. 1, 1990, pp. 73-90.

[20] Javaid Saeed, *Islam and Modernisation: A Comparative Analysis of Pakistan, Egypt, and Turkey* (Connecticut: Praeger Publishers, 1994), p.70.

[21] Francis Fukuyama, *The End of History and the Last Man* (London: Penguin Books, 1992), pp. XXII+418.

[22] Suroosh Irfani, 'The Return of History', *Strategic Studies* (Islamabad), Vol. XIV, No.3, Spring 1991, p.45. Compare this essay's title to that of Fukuyama's. The contrast is obvious.

[23] *Ibid*, p.45.

[24] *Ibid.*, pp. 45-46.

[25] They are cited here only for purposes of illustration. They do not, however, exhaust the entirety of the west's ideological/value systems. Some notable Western media persons like John Casey hold the view that the difficulties faced by the West vis-à-vis the Muslim world stem not from Islam itself, but from "Western ideas imported into the Muslim World: nationalism, socialism and secularism". See John Casey, "Why does the West Fear Islam?", *The Pioneer* (New Delhi), August 19, 1994.

[26] A detailed exposition of these resistance movement s falls beyond the purview of this essay. For an historical account of these movements, see G.H. Jansen, *Militant Islam* (London: Pan Books, 1979).

27 Monroe Berger, *Islam in Egypt Today* (Cambridge: Cambridge University Press, 1970), p. 129.

28 Ralph Braibanti, 'Saudi Arabia in the Context of Political Development Theory', in William A. Beling, ed., *King Faisal and the Modernisation of Saudi Arabia* (London: Croom Helm, 1980), p. 37.

29 'Given .... the manifold threats and challenges confronting Islamic societies today, it is not surprising that to some at least within them, the solution to their problems is seen as being essentially religious and as lying in particular in the restoration of the traditionally close relationship between religion and state in Islam. In the near future, it is, therefore, unlikely that this view will lose its appeal for many as possible panacea for those problems in any society where Islam is a significant influence". See Goddard Hugh, 'Spheres United Under God'. *The Times Higher Education Supplement* (London), 21 September 1990.

30 For details on these issues, see Abdul Hamid A. Abu Sulayman, *Crisis in the Muslim Mind*, Second Edition, English trans. Yusuf Talal DeLorenzo (Herndon, Virginia: International Institute of Islamic Thought, 1994), pp.XVIII+160, and also Ismail Raji al-Faruqi, *Islamisation of Knowledge: General Principles and Work Plan*, (Herndon, Virginia: International Institute of Islamic Thought, 1982), p.60.

31 *International Herald Tribune* (Singapore Edition), December 28, 1990. The said bill has the support of Abbasi Madani's Islamic Salvation Front (FIS) which swept the provincial and municipal elections conducted in Algeria in June 1990.

32 *The Economist* (London), 4 August 1990.

33 Bernard Lewis, "Roots of Muslim Rage", *The Atlantic Monthly* (Philadelphia), Vol. 266, No. 3, September 1990, p. 60.

34 *Ibid.*, p.60.

35 Samuel P. Huntington, "The Clash of Civilisations?", *Foreign Affairs* (Washington D.C.), Vol. 72, No. 3, Summer, 1993, pp. 22-48. He later converted this article into a book. For details, see the Indian Edition, *The Clash of Civilisations and the Remarking of World Order* (New Delhi: Viking Penguin India, 1996). After giving descriptive hypotheses of future shape of inter-state relations in civilisational terms, Huntington, at the end of his essay, looks into the implications for the West, and categorises them into "short-term advantage" and "long-term accommodation". The list, covering the twin categories, is exhaustive. After going through the whole essay, one gets an impression that the author feels enveloped by an impending danger emanating from the other side of the barricade. To be fair to the author, he is not alone in this predicament. The Orientalist scholarship as a whole suffers from it. This scholarship, more often than not, comes to the aid of the powers-that-be by way of providing academic inputs to the latter: a process designated by analysts as "epistemological imperialism" of the West, implicit in the scholarly works of Edward Said, in particular, his 1993 study, *Culture & Imperialism* (London: Vintage, 1993). Huntington exactly did this in the closing note of his much-quoted essay.

In this context, it may be noted that Huntington was one of the theoreticians of liberal political development (modernisation): a theoretical paradigm sought to study the Third World societies which attained statehood

Globalisation and Islamism: Rethinking Some Reigning Paradigms 75

in the 60s. This paradigm hardly considered religion and other factors of culture as having any significance in public affairs. From the denial of any role for religion in modernisation theory to its central location in the post-cold war international relations in the 94s, Huntington, in fact, traversed a long way.

[36] Ibid., p.39.
[37] Ibid., p.22.
[38] Ibid., p.22.
[39] This viewpoint is being recognised in most of the scholarly analyses. Representative of them is Maria McKarzel, 'The Middle East since 1945', *World Review: A Journal of Contemporary Relevance* (London), Vol. 30, No. 1, March 1991, p. 22.
[40] Fayez A. Sayegh, *The Zionist Diplomacy* (Beirut, 1966), p. 143.
[41] Quoted in Judith Miller, "Two Faces of Fundamentalism: Hasan al-Turabi and Muhammed Fadlallah", *Foreign Affairs* (Washington, D.C.), Vol.73, No.6, November-December 1994, p.139.
[42] David E. Long, 'King Faisal's Worldview', in Willard A. Beling, ed., *King Faisal and the Modernisation of Saudi Arabia* (London: Croom Helm, 1980), p. 174.
[43] For details on the subject, see C.G. Weeramantry, *Islamic Jurisprudence: An international Perspective* (London: Macmillan Press, 1988), pp. XIX 207. Also, for an excellent treatment on the subject of Islam's contribution to International Law, see Marcel A.Boisard, 'On the Probable Influence of Islam on Western Public and International Law', *International Journal of Middle East Studies* (New York), Vol. II, 1980, pp. 429-450.
[44] Prominent among those who think on these lines is Abdul Hamid Abu Sulayman. See his two works: *The Islamic Theory of International Relations: New Directions for Islamic Methodology* (Herndon, Virginia: International Institute of Islamic Thought, 1987), and *Crisis in the Muslim Mind* (Islamic Methodologies No. 1), Second Editon, trans. Yusuf Talal De Lorenzo (Herndon, Virginia: International Institute of Islamic Thought, 1994).
[45] The *Fatwa* (religious edict) of the spiritual guide of the Islamic Republic of Iran, Ali Khomeini, issued against the presence of Western Armed Forces on the Saudi Arabian soil in the context of Iraqi occupation of Kuwait, constitutes an important part of *Jihad*, as understood in terms of self-defence. On the other hand, Saudi Arabia, to justify its decision to invite the American led Western forces on its territory has, during 120-12 September, 1990, convened a meeting of the world Muslim League *(Rabita Alam-e-Islami)*, an offshoot of the Organisation of Islamic Conference, in which the assembled religious leaders approved of the Saudi decision saying that it is in conformity with *Sharia*. In the statement called the Makkah Document that was issued at the conclusion of this Saudi-sponsored Conference, there was a strident attack of Saddam's "hypocrisy towards Islam" saying that his invasion of Kuwait would "distort the image of Islam and the Muslims before world public opinion, leading most of the international media to make it a point to portray Islam and its adherents in a bloody way, and said that they cannot keep promises, do not respect the rights of neighbours, have no mercy for the young and do not recognise the rights of others." To counter this, Saddam Hussain convened his own "World Muslim Conference" in Baghdad during

September 9-12, 1991, in which the Conference called for *a Jihad* as expected by Saddam Hussein, did not materialise. For details, see, *The Economist* (London), Vol. 316, No. 7673, September 22-28, 1990, p. 55. and also Mushahid Hussain, 'The Persian Gulf Crisis: Impact on the Muslim World', *Strategic Studies* (Islamabad), Vol. XIV, Nos. 1 & 2, Autumn/Winter 1990-1991, p. 38.

46. For details, see Rudolph Peters, *Islam and Colonialism: The Doctrine of Jihad in Modern History* (The Hague: Mouton, 1979).

47. For details on the multi-dimensional aspects of "Cultural Imperialism", see James Petras, "Cultural Imperialism in the Late Twentieth Century", *Economic and Political Weekly* (Mumbai), Vol. XXIX, No. 32, August 6, 1994, pp. 2070-2073.

48. John L. Esposito, ed., *Voices of Resurgent Islam* (New York: Oxford University Press, 1983), pp. 237-38.

49. Asaf Hussain, *Political Terrorism and the State in the Middle East* (London: Mansell Publishing Ltd., 1988), p. 3.

50. WM. Watt, *Islamic Fundamentalism and Modernity* (London: Routledge, 1988), p. 17.

51. *Ibid.*, p. 98.

52. Allan Richards and John Waterbury, *A Political Economy of the Middle East: State, Class and Economic Development* (Boulder, San Francisco: Westview Press. 1990), p, 348.

53. Ralph Braibanti, 'Saudi Arabia in the Context of Political Development Theory,' in Willard A. Beling, ed., *King Faisal and the Modernisation of Saudi Arabia* (London: Croom Helm, 1980), p. 49.

54. Bo Johnson Theutenberg, 'Different Trends of the International Legal System of Today,' in *The Future of International Law in a Multicultural Society* (The Hague: Martinus Nijhoff, 1984), p. 268. "When the European domination and the European bonds now are being lifted from the colonial world, it is natural that these countries revert to their own "values". The interesting thing is, however, that it is not only one single country that takes recourse to its own cultural system, but a big part of the world, the whole Afro-Asian group of countries. Acting in the same direction, those countries can most surely influence the evolution of international law." *Ibid.*, pp. 268-9.

55. *Ibid.* p.268.

56. *Ibid.* p. 270.

57. For particulars on this subject of *Jihad*, see Mohammad Talaat al-Ghunaimi, *The Muslim Conception of International Law and the Western Approach* (The Hague: Martinus Nijhoff, 1968), p. 143.

58. Abdul Hamid Abu Sulayman, *The Islamic Theory of International Relations : New Directions for Islamic Methodology and Thought* (Herndon, Virginia: The International Institute of Islamic Thought, 1987).

59. Fatima Mernissi, *Islam and Democracy: Fear of the Modern World*, trans. Mary Jo Lakeland (London: Virago Press, 1993).

60. *Ibid.*, n. 58, p. 124.

61. *The Holy Our'an*, 16: 125.

62. OIC Document No. 153-83 OGN D. 4/Rev. 5, p. 7 and quoted in Muhammad Shamsul Huq, *International Politics: A Third World Perspective* (New Delhi: Sterling Publishers, 1987), pp. 29-30.

Globalisation and Islamism: Rethinking Some Reigning Paradigms 77

[63] Robert L. Canfield, 'The Collision of Evolutionary Process and Islamic Ideology in Greater Central Asia', in Milan Hauner and Robert L. Canfield, eds., *Afghanistan and the Soviet Union: Collision and Transformation* (Boulder, San Francisco: Westview Press, 1989), p. 23.

[64] The Holy Ouran, 30:22.

[65] The Holy Quran, 49:13.

[66] For an understanding of the *Tawhidi* worldview of Islam in its multifaceted dimensions, see the thought-provoking lectures delivered at the Oxford Centre for Islamic Studies (Oxford University) and compiled in a book form., Masudul Alam Choudhury, *The Unicity Precept and the Socio-Scientific Order* (Lanham, Maryland: University Press of America, 1993).

[67] Kalim Siddiqui, ed., *Issues in the Islamic Movement* (London, The Open Press, March 1983), p. 27 and also *Beyond the Muslim Nation-States* (London: The Open Press, 1980).

[68] Asaf Hussain, *Political Terrorism and the State in the Middle East* (London: Mansell Publishing Ltd., 1988), p. 75.

[69] Ibid., p. 75. Similar view is held by Kalim Siddiqui as epitomised in the following sentence: 'Nationalism is a force which leads to the disintegration of the human personality, and society at all levels.' Quoted in Kalim Siddiqui, 'Nation-States as obstacles to the Total Transformation of the Ummah', in M. Ghayasuddin, ed., *The Impact of Nationalism on the Muslim World* (Selangor: Malaysia, The Open Press, 1986), p. 1.

Kalim Siddiqui further elaborated this theme in his paper titled 'Integration and Disintegration in the Politics of Islam and *Kufr*', Presented at the *World Seminar on State and Politics in Islam*, held in London, 1983.

For further particulars on the subject, see Abd Allah Ahsan, 'The Identity Crisis within the Modern Muslim Nation-States', *Al-Tawhid* (Tehran), Vol. V, No. 2, March-August 1988.

For an argument on the incompatibility of Islam and nationalism, see Murtaza Garia, 'Nationalism in the Light of the Quran and the Sunnah', in M. Ghayasuddin, ed., *The Impact of Nationalism on the Muslim World* (Selangor: Malaysia, The Open Press, 1986), pp. 23-35.

[70] For details on the conformist and non-conformist attitudes towards the system of nation-state in the context of Islam, see James P Piscatori, *Islam in the World of Nation-States* (Cambridge: Cambridge University Press, 1986), pp. 40-116. In this work, the author argues that there is a well-established Islamic tradition endorsing territorial pluralism among Muslim states.

[71] Abdullah Al-Ahsan, *OIC: The Organisation of Islamic Conference: An Introduction to Islamic Political Institution* (Herndon, Virginia: The International Institute of Islamic Thought, 1988), p. 123.

[72] Abdul Hamid Abu Sulayman, *The Islamic Theory of International Relations: New Directions for Islamic Methodology and Thought* (Herndon, Virginia: The International Institute of Islamic Thought, 1987), p. 141.

4

Globalisation: Towards a New Perspective on Political Economy*

NISAR-UL-HAQ

Globalisation with its wide-ranging impact on Political, Economic and Social arenas has led to a culture of 'Thinking Globally and 'Acting Locally'. The paper examines the challenges posed by globalisation to Societies and Economies: State civil society relationship, delimiting the role of the state and reformulating it to create 'new roles' for parliament, executive, civil services, legal system, taxation system and public affairs. The notion of 'Global Governance'/ 'International Governance' has the cost or related effect of limiting the autonomy of national / state level policy making. With the increasing focus and development of trade, investment, Communication and Information Technology and significantly the role of International Financial Organisations, the Sovereignty of individual states have come into question.

The advent of the globalisation processes, especially since the late 1980's has made a tremendous impact upon the entire horizon of international political economy, almost concurrently increasing tension between the Western and the Asian models of

---

* Reprinted from the Indian Journal of Political Science, Vol. LXV No.3, July-Sept. 2004 where this article was first published, with the permission of the current editor of the journal.

capitalism. These political and economic changes have raised uncertainties regarding the openness of the trading system, the adequacy of the rules governing the international economy and prospects for potential economic conflict.[1]

Social scientists around the world have attempted to find out the reasons behind the spectacular economic growth. A school of thought represented by Chalmers Johnson, Alice Amsden and Robert Wade in the United States of America and Fernando Henrique Cardoso of Brazil were some of the earliest pioneers of the concept of the 'Development state'. These scholars questioned some of the basic tenets of the neo-classical theories and instead focused upon the effectiveness of state intervention in the economy through industrial policy, credit control and investment targeting as the primary foundations of a strong and resilient economy.[2] It was also called 'State Capitalism' wherein the state served as the financier, planner, producer and distributor of goods and services. In some countries, the State was also the largest consumer as well as employer.

Three theoretical perspectives of contending theories have been used to understand world politics. The rise of Globalisation offers ideas on its strength and weaknesses as a description of contemporary world politics.

1. For Realists, globalisation does not alter the most significant feature of world politics, the territorial division of the world into nation-states. Whilst the increased inter-connectedness between economies and societies might make them more dependent on one another, the same cannot be hold true about the states-system. Here, states retain sovereignty and globalisation does not render obsolete struggle for political power between states nor does it undermine the importance of the threat of the use of force, or the importance of the balance of power.[3] Globalisation, then, may affect our social, economic and cultural lives, but without transcending the international political system of states.

2. For Liberals, the scenario is very different. They tend to view globalisation as the end product of a long-running transformation of world politics. For them, globalisation fundamentally undermines Realist accounts of world politics since it shows that states are no longer central actors as they

once were understood to be. In their place are a myriad of actors, having differing importance according to the issue-area concerned. Liberals are particularly interested in the revolution in technology and communications represented by globalisation.[4] This economically and technologically led increased inter-connectedness between societies results in a very different pattern of world political relations from that which has existed earlier. States are no longer sealed units, if ever they were, and as a result the world looks more like a cobweb of relations than like the state model of Realism or class model of World-System Theory.

3. For World-System Theorists, globalisation is a bit of a shame. It is nothing particularly new, and is really only the latest stage in the development of international capitalism. It does not mark a qualitative shift in world politics, nor does it render all our existing theories and concepts redundant. Above all it is a Western-led phenomenon, which simply furthers the development of international capitalism. Rather than make the world more alike, it further deepens the existing divide between the core – semi-periphery and the periphery.

It is clear that each of the three focuses on different aspects of world politics; Realism on the power relations between states, Liberalism on a much wider set of interactions between states and non-state actors, and World-System Theory on the patterns of the world economy. Each view claims that it focuses on the most important features of world politics and that it offers a better account than the others. Thus, the three approaches are really in competition with one another; and, whilst one can certainly choose between them it is not so easy to add bits from one to the others. For a World-System Theorist, the state behaviour is ultimately determined by class forces; forces that the Realist does not think will affect state behaviour. In other words these three theories are really offering versions of what world politics is like rather than presenting partial pictures of it.

The pace of economic transformation is so speedy that it has created a new world politics. States are no longer treated as closed units which are unable to control their economies. The world economy is more interdependent than ever, with trade and finances ever expanding. Communications have fundamentally revolutionised the way we deal with the rest of the world. We now live in a world where any event in one part of the globe can be immediately observed on the other end of the world. Electronic communication alters our notions of the social groups we work and live in. There is now, more than ever before, a global culture, resembling most urban areas. The world shares a common culture, much of it emanating from Hollywood. The world is becoming more homogeneous. Differences between peoples are diminishing. Time and space seem to be collapsing. Our old ideas of geographical space and of chronological time are undermined by the speed of modern communications and media. A global polity is emerging with transnational social and political movements and the beginnings of a transfer of allegiance from the state to sub-state, transnational, and international bodies can be witnessed. A cosmopolitan culture is also developing. People are beginning to 'think globally and act locally'. A risk culture is emerging with people realizing both that the main risks, which they face, are global (pollution and AIDS) and that states are unable to deal with the problems unilaterally.

Globalisation is thus an ongoing trend whereby the world has – in many respects and at a generally accelerating rate – become one relatively border-less social sphere. 'Internationalisation' refers to a process of intensifying connections between national domains. As a result of internationalisation, countries may come to have wide-ranging and deep effects mutually, but they retain their distinctiveness and aloofness. In international relations, countries are divided from each other by clearly marked frontiers as well as by the substantial time that is generally required to cover the distance between their respective territories. To put the difference in a nutshell, the international realm is a patchwork of bordered countries, while the global sphere is a web of trans border networks. Whereas international links require people to cross considerable distances in comparatively long time intervals, global connections (for example, satellite newscasts) are effectively distance less and instantaneous. Global phenomena can extend across the world simultaneously and can move between places in no time; they are in this sense supra-territorial. While the patterns of 'international' interdependence are strongly influenced by national-state divisions, the lines of 'global' interconnections often have little correspondence to territorial boundaries. International and global relations can coexist, of course, and indeed the contemporary world is at the same time both internationalised and globalising.[5]

The late twentieth century has been accompanied by numerous and a faster pace of change. Thus, Military dictatorships have been overthrown in Latin America, Communism has collapsed in Eastern Europe and Apartheid has been terminated in South Africa. At the same time despite a growth in liberal democratic regimes, outbreaks of ethnic violence have increased. Even as medical science has reached new heights and the average age of Westerners increase steadily, nearly a third of the global population still lives in hunger, malnutrition retarding the physical mental development of one child out of three in the developing world, and six million children under the age of five die from pneumonia or diarrhoea.[6]

Economically, the picture remains unsettled and inequality between rich and poor increases. Of the US$ 23 trillion global GDP, US$ 18 trillion is in the industrial countries, and US$ 5 trillion in the developing countries, which are home to 80 per cent of the world's population. The assets of the richest 358 people in the world exceed the combined annual incomes of countries with 45 per cent of the world population. In the last 30 years, the ratio of shares of global income between the richest 20 per cent and poorest 20 per cent of people has doubled from 30:1 to 61:1[7]. Developing country debt has multiplied, and even major Western countries now find large proportions of their national debt held by foreign investors.

The global economy has been integrated by a massive increase in international economic activity, particularly in the last 15 years by the concentration of world capital among transnational corporations (TNCs). At the same time the establishment of the World Trade Organisation (WTO) marks unprecedented power in a new global institution while the authority of the United Nations as an agent of global governance remains diminished.

In this context, there is a view that globalisation has not been accompanied by democracy but quite the opposite : globalisation has put democracy at stake. In this view, the crucial role of civil society today is to advocate democracy against the rising anti-democratic tendencies of global capital concentration and a new international economic institution with a singular commitment to 'free trade' as the primary basis for international economic relations. Further, this view holds that it is the role of civil society to democratise global governance by harnessing the advantages that can come from globalisation – such as new communications – while resisting its draw backs, most specifically the centralisation of economic power in the hands of TNCs and the international economic institutions – the WTO, IMF, and the World Bank. There is a deep sense of urgency about 'the fate of democracy in an age of globalisation' and a strong sense that its fate will be decided by the outcome of a new negotiation between representatives of international economic actors and representatives of civil society everywhere.[8] Martin Khor, argues that the World Trade Organisation has:

> Expand (ed) 'the economic and political space' in the world for transnational corporations and for transnationalizing the national systems of production, distribution and trade, and consumption. This transnationalizing process has been sought to be achieved by dismantling the power of nation states to, manage and intervene in their economy, and in particular diminishing the rights and powers of Third World countries in their local communities. ...The raison d'etre for all this. ..is to restrict or dampen the competitive capacity of the enterprises and productive apparatus of the South in a world economy that is being 'globalised' in the interest of the Northern transnational corporations.[9]

In contrast to representatives of the new economic globalisation, who view globalisation, free trade, privatisation and democracy as connected key actors in civil society, many scholars view economic globalisation as an adversary of democracy. Moreover, whereas the seat of democracy was previously considered to be the nation state, many now consider its fate to be determined by civil society.

The State and Civil Society in Global Governance

The basis of modern democracy was the birth of the nation in the eighteenth century. An electoral process decided 'Representation' of the officers of public office, and in most cases a more permanent civil service was also established. The civil service was accountable to parliament, but responsible for the executive functions of the state – its legal system, taxation system and public affairs. It was this concept of democracy that was transferred into the international arena with the establishment of the United Nations, except that the power of the UN as always was subject to the members' need to retain national sovereignty.

In a globalising world, it has become clear that many local problems have global origins and need solutions that are both local and global. The problems of global governance clearly exceed the mandate and possibly the competence of national governments on their own or collectively. There is increasing evidence, for example, of global crises within national and local political processes. Crime, unemployment and environmental depletion are examples of major domestic crises of governance whose origins and solutions lie at transnational or international levels or in other words, they cannot be resolved only at the national political level.[10]

Many forces of globalisation create contradictory trends that are placing enormous strain on the normal institutions of political governance: the nation state and the United Nations. The political authority of the UN is clearly in a period of nemesis. Limping along in the face of crippling financial and moral abuse from the United States, an almost financially bankrupt UN sees its status and role in international governance usurped by the new and ascending nexus of multilateral economic institutions. At the same time, it has never been so urgent, as it is today, that there be a strong, re-invented United Nations within a strong system of global governance.

However, the authority and competence of the state, is also being challenged by globalisation. As national and international government declines in authority and international economic institutions leap into the space of government, civil society not only has to grapple with what a democratic system of global governance may look like, but has to do so in the absence of active players willing and able to take on the executive roles of governance, along with the incompetence of the state to deal with global issues.

With the decline of the authority of the state and increasing national and international levels of social crisis, there are loud calls from civil society for the stronger imposition of global governance (usually meaning the UN and its agencies) to balance the newly empowered economic governance to protect 'free trade' of the WTO and international business. Debate has begun about the shape, form and future authority of institutions of international political governance.[11]

Globalisation and International Governance

There has been much publicity about globalisation, a process or a state of affairs that holds much promise for the future of 'planet earth' and not a little trepidation among the people of many countries, particularly those in sub-Saharan Africa, for whom even nationhood, as analysed in the case of the West African sub-region, has not delivered what that they had expected. These countries are yet hardly nations, and now they are being pressed, especially by the multilateral financial institutions, to forget their nationhood and go for globalisation, something that they cannot yet comprehend but which they know would be too big for them to handle.

There is a widespread perception that globalisation may, at some cost, limit the autonomy of policy making at the national level. The best way to achieve development, in view of the multilateral financial institutions is to enhance the role of the market, while diminishing that of the state. The role of the latter should be confined to creating a suitable environment (including macroeconomic policies) for private enterprise to flourish and competitive markets to function. Scholars like Horsman and Marshall have asserted that the era of the nation state is over, and that national-level governance is ineffective in the face of globalised economic and social pressures.[12]

Trade, investment and technology, especially information technology, are playing key integrative roles in this process of globalisation. Air transport, telecommunications, electronic media and now the Internet have made globalisation a reality that profoundly affects the lives of the people in even the most remote areas of the world. At the same time, these developments have also infringed upon the sovereignty of individual nations.

Great concern exists regarding current trends in globalisation, which some view as selective and designed to serve the interests of rich countries. For example, rich countries promote free trade as long as they can export at will, but when competition from less affluent countries intensifies, the rich nations raises various kinds of new issues, such as labour standards.

'The decline in the willingness on the part of the rich democratic nations to offer substantial help to poorer countries is only one indicator of a potentially problematic relationship between democracies and issues of global governance... this self-centredness of liberal democracies is a troubling aspect.' Selectivity by the richer nations becomes especially noticeable when examining labour flows. Excepting illegal immigration, labour flows are permitted or even encouraged whenever rich countries experience a shortage of highly skilled manpower. However, these same rich countries demand free access to trade and investment opportunities in the rest of the world, and that too on their own terms.

Regarding this framework, Richard Haas in his background paper has listed a set of five or six options for international governance, which includes laissez-faire, unilateralism, regionalism, and institutionalism. His suggestions for institutionalism deserve a more detailed study and examination of options. The present system and institutions of international governance are inadequate, not only because of their limited scope and coverage but also because they do not sufficiently represent the views and interests of the vast majority of the world's population. Even the multilateral financial institutions such as the International Monetary Fund and the World Bank are not good enough, as they are unable to deal adequately with the emerging problems of governance in their fields.[13]

Globalisation, in its broadest sense, refers to a world with increasingly porous borders open to a worldwide flow of money, goods, people ideas and information. Globalisation, particularly of trade and finance, also encourages fragmentation as it enables ever smaller countries to find comfortable niches in which to survive and prosper, as clearly demonstrated by Switzerland and Singapore. It is quite likely that this process of fragmentation, driven by the desire for self-determination, has not yet run its course. But while the number of participants in the international system has increase and may grown yet more, national sovereignty is no longer what it used to be. Globalisation, almost by definition, has deprived nation-states of the power to determine their own affairs simply by maintaining control over physical borders, as in the past. This does not however totally detract from the pleasure, presumed or real, of self-determination, however. Some sovereignty is better than none at all, especially as long as the international system is based on the principle of sovereignty, which treats every country as equal, atleast in theory. But as individual governments lose control of popular support and legitimacy, the need for other, supranational forms of control, such as through global governance, becomes evident.[14]

The UN organisation embodies the central dilemma of a world caught between globalisation and fragmentation. It is asked to do much, but lacks the support to do so, largely because major member countries such as the United States are in arrears paying their dues. 192 member states have made the UN an increasingly complex and bureaucratic organisation. Advances in information and communications technology have accelerated the movement toward a borderless global economy, thereby leading to greater calls for a global system that guarantees the freedom of trade, investment, service, finance and other economic activities. The rules set by the WTO are now widely accepted, and the resolution of trade, frictions has come to depend on the WTO dispute – settlement mechanism rather than on bilateral measures, which were formerly often employed by the United States.

Since the 1980s, many countries around the world have undertaken measures to relax regulations over the economic activities undertaken within and around their national borders. This was political reaction to growing skepticism over consistent failures on the part of the states to simultaneously generate economic growth and social development. The optimism of the earlier development theorists implicitly assuming that states have almost unlimited capacity to intervene in the economy and can run it better than the private sector has been the focus of much scholarly debate and discussion. Several proponents of increased globalisation operate under the assumption that state failure is worse than market failure and, therefore, states should be asked to play a more limited role in the new emphasis on economic globalisation. Withdrawing the obstacles to production, accumulation, and export are advocated as the new priority areas of state action. Some theorists in the pro-globalisation tradition strongly believe that unimpeded competition in the market place will mitigate the counterproductive domestic behaviors encouraged by corrupt state bureaucrats.[15]

But it has been quite frequently argued that an increase in the pace of economic integration with the rest of the world would contribute to a growing sense of insecurity in the face of uncertainties of the market place. If the current state of international economy is fueled by constant demands to increase productivity through technological innovation and other creative ideas, it is bound to create even a bigger pool of people more vulnerable than ever before to changing skill and other demands of the marketplace.[16]

Strong globalisationists, those who argue that the current globalisation is a distinctly new phenomenon, stress the point that previous periods of capitalist expansion lacked the speed, technological sophistication, economic integration and ideological universalism which are the hallmarks of globalisation of the twenty-first century. Strong globalisationists also adhere to the efficacy of the market over the state and take the neo-liberal position that globalisation has universally beneficial economic effects.[17]

Another interesting aspect of the current globalisation is the role of the International Financial Institutions (IFIs), multinational organisations like the United Nations and a host of multilateral and bilateral organisations and international and local NGOs. These are all key players in the formulation and implementation of national policy at various geographic and social scales. Their activities have often forced the state to relinquish some of its sovereignty.

The present wave of globalisation is also characterised by a mixed array of issues – the environment, gender rights, debt relief, AIDS, the rights of children, child soldiers in civilian conflicts, the role of minerals in financing civil unrest, the international transfer of arms and military expertise in the form of mercenaries, nuclear terrorism, immigration etc. Each of these is a priority for one international group or another. Yet, their various agendas do not always converge and actually contribute to the complexity of the globalisation process and what it may portend for the poor.[18]

Proponents of globalisation have transformed market freedom to a type of comparative advantage in the drive towards market liberalisation and privatisation. The definition of market freedom in these neo-liberal terms covers a wide array of issues, including, market and labour de-control, and a catch-all of imperative aimed at removing all forms of government limitations on private sector operations. To put it more vividly but less subtly, market freedom has come to mean that freewheeling, free-dealing and fast-moving capital must have the freedom to control state policies. As the state reacts to these new rules of economic engagement, it has been encouraged, coerced to withdraw from many of its traditional roles in promoting employment and social welfare.

The recent wave of economic policy reform in the developing world has been seen as a necessary consequence of a changed world economic system. The key feature of the changed world economy is the element of heightened economic globalisation, which provides new external challenges as well as opportunities for development. As globalisation accelerates, it has come to loom large in the perceptions of policy-makers and adjustment to it in the form of economic liberalisation and the shrinking of the state has moved to the forefront of their economic agenda, even when not imposed on them. The phenomenon of economic globalisation provides the widest possible context for the examination of economic policy reform. However, as a concept in contemporary social science, it appears in many variants. In one strong version, globalisation refers to the presumed emergence of a 'supra-national', borderless global economy with its own laws of motion, encompassing and subordinating the various local economies in a single worldwide division of labour, rendering national governments into municipalities. A softer version of the concept, treats globalisation less as an end-stage and more as a process in which the 'international' economy becomes more closely integrated, with domestic economic agents increasingly oriented to the global market rather than to particular national markets, even as the state continues to remain central to national economic advancement.[19]

With the end of World War II the intensive or deepening phase of globalisation began. Until then, the economic integration of the world was largely confined to international trade between national economies, with underdeveloped areas in the periphery tied in a colonial economic relationship, serving as sites for the extraction of natural resources, often as tribute and as instant markets for the manufactures of the North Atlantic powers. Industrial production in the world economy was largely organised in national systems, which were largely though not exclusively responsive to their internal markets. In the post-war period after World War II, the United States as the new hegemon reorganised the world's economic institutions, chiefly in the form of GATT and the Bretton Woods system, to establish what has been characterised as a liberal international economic order, but one that was clearly designed to serve the interests of the advanced industrial powers.

Thus, Globalisation poses challenges to societies and economies. Its benefits will not materialise unless countries adjust to increased competition. In the poorer countries, it may accentuate inequality and certain posts of the world could become marginalised. Globalisation of the financial markets can generate new risks of instability, which requires all countries to pursue sound economic policies and structural reform. Better prudential regulation and supervision in the financial markets are essential elements in promoting the stability of the international monetary and financial system. Cooperation among regulatory and supervisory authorities should continue to adapt to financial innovations and to the growth in cross-border capital movements and internationally active financial institutions. It is evident that there are strong arguments favouring of globalisation. However, at the same time it poses formidable challenges too. Evidently the success of globalisation is contingent upon the containment of these challenges.

End Notes

[1] Robert Gilpin, 'Economic Change and the challenge of uncertainty', in Robert, S. Ross (ed.) *East Asia in Transition*, Institute of Southeast Asian studies, Singapore, 1995, p.3.

[2] Minxin Pei, 'Constructing the political foundations of an economic miracle', in Henry, S. Rowen (ed.) *Behind East Asian Growth: The political and social foundations of prosperity*, Routledge, London, 1998, p.39.

[3] M. Featherstone, (ed), *Global Culture : Nationalism, Globalisation and Modernity* London : Sage, 1990 This volume brings together selections from a number of sociologists and anthropologists with interest in globalisation, especially its implications for the way we experience world politics.

4 P, Hirst, and G. Thompson, *Globalisation in Question : The International Economy and the Possibilities of Governance* Cambridge : Polity Press, 1996 This book presents an argument against 'globalist' presumptions that globalisation is now irreversible, and wholly beyond state control.

5 Steve Smith and John Baylis *The Globalisation of World Politics*, Oxford University Press, 1997. p.6.

6 UNRISD, *States of Disarray : The Social effects of Globalisation*, UNRISD, Geneva, 1995.

7 UNDP, *Human Development Report*, Oxford University Press, New York, 1996. p.2

8 Cynthea Hewitt de Alcantara, UNRISD presentation to the World Summit for Social development, Copenhagen, March, 1995.

9 See Third World Network, *The WTO, Trade and Environment* Third World Network, Penang, Malaysia, 1994.

10 UNRISD, *States of Disarray*, op.cit.

11 Commission on Global Governance, *Our Global Neighbourhood* : The Report of the Commission on Global Governance, Oxford University Press, New York, 1995, p.2-3.

12 M. Horsman and A. Marshall, *After the Nation State*, London Harper Collins, 1994, p. 14.

13 V.A. Pai Panandiker, *A Global Agenda for International Governance*, 1998, Japan Centre for IN Exchange p. 107.

14 *Ibid*; p. 109.

15 Satya R. Datnayak, The Economic and Political Impact of Globalisation, *Journal of Peace Studies* Vol. II Issue I, New Delhi January-March 2004, p. 28.

16 *Ibid*, p. 29

17 B.Ikubolajeh Logan – *Globalisation, The Third World State and Poverty Alleviation in the Twenty-First Century*, Ashgate Publishing Ltd., England, 2002, p. 2.

18 *Ibid*, p.3

19 *Ibid*, p.5

5

Globalisation and Good Governance: Redefining the State Precincts

BULBUL DHAR-JAMES

Globalisation by definition is a process of social transformation in the broadest sense of cultural, political and economic spheres. Besides being globalised, the economies of the world are being liberalised simultaneously, which means making the economy more profitable for business by adopting a policy of strategic retreat of the state (in favour of Private business). The policies of economic reform though focusing on a group of 'gainers', simultaneously creates groups of 'losers' within society, which also affects the social base of the state and hence its survival. Alongside the World Bank's 'good governance' terminology with it's technocratic resonance, with clear ideological preferences has very specific notions of what constitute the 'good society'- notably a minimal state and free market. The globalised state is caught in a bind as on one hand, it has to satisfy the requirements of structural adjustment – since its economic and hence political survival depends on the generation of economic growth within the country – and on the other, with its reduced ability to serve the patron-client networks, it has to guard itself against the 'revenge of civil society', which could again threaten its survival. Under these policies the engine of growth have to be private actors and the state obligations to the citizens have to take a back seat. *It would thus be fair to say that globalisation has redefined the precincts of the state and weakened its sovereignty. The paper reviews the irreversible long-term political consequences on the state of the 'unregulated' market driven model of the integrated global economy.*

Globalisation: By Definition and Implication

Globalisation is a process that refers to the movement of capital, goods, human beings and material across trans-national borders. Globalisation remains a malleable, catchall term. Jan Aart (2000) outlines four common usages of the term, Globalisation – internationalisation, liberalisation, universalisation and westernisation. To these he adds – de-territorialisation.[1] It involves the movement of ideas and cultures across the globe, though the nucleus of the phenomenon remains economic processes. The *Blackwell Dictionary of Social Thought*, defines Globalisation as a process of social transformation in the broadest sense of cultural, political and economic (as dismantling of national barriers to the operation of national markets that began in the early 1980's) spheres.

The phenomenon of Globalisation is not new. There was a similar phase of globalisation that began over a century earlier. In many ways the world economy in the late 20th century closely resembled the world economy in the 19th century.[2] The parallels between the two periods are striking – integration of World economy through international trade, investments, Markets for international finance etc. It is in terms of governance that the two phases of globalisation are 'fundamentally different'.[3] According to Karl Marx[4], the logic of globalisation of capitalism was the "need of a constantly expanding market for its products chases the bourgeoisie over the entire surface of the globe. It must nestle everywhere establish connections everywhere" – seems like a perfect match for our world today![5] An account written in 1909, exemplifies the belief that globalisation is not a new phenomena – "The complexity of modern finance makes New York dependent on London, London upon Paris, Paris upon Berlin, to a greater degree than has ever yet been the case in history. This interdependence is the result of the daily use of those contrivances of civilization... the instantaneous dissemination of financial and commercial information... and generally the incredible increase in the rapidity of communication."[6]

Globalisation involves the movement of ideas and cultures across the globe, though the core of the phenomenon remains economic processes. Besides being globalised, the economies of the world are being liberalised simultaneously. This involves making the economy more profitable for business by adopting a policy of strategic retreat of the state (in favour of Private business). Under these policies the engine of growth have to be private actors and the state obligations to the citizens have to take a back seat. Liberalisation, Privatisation & Globalisation are processes of Marketisation. Markets are based on the pure purchasing power of the economic agents. Thus, it is not a democratic institution nor in its pure form it is based on considerations of human values. The Markets though the most efficient are not moderated by human concerns and tend to have fostered inequity and marginalisation of the already weak. Governments (and states), are held responsible to their people, markets are not.

The compelling nature of Globalisation with its directed principles of the over a decade of international trade regime – the WTO and reservations about the spirit of inclusion and exclusion[7] of certain provisions continue. The bringing in of 'non-trade issues' like environment, labour standards, investment, competition policy, etc. are highly debatable – a clear asymmetry of concerns between the rich and poor members of the WTO. Issues of TRIPS, Agriculture, Anti dumping regulations, Textiles, Environment, Opening up of investment & Competition etc, is bound to unevenly affect the innumerable groups and nations participating in the process. The agreements like GATS, TRIPS, TRIMS and AOA are full of controversial provisions. The complexity of issues involved and the centrality that WTO has assumed in the present phase of globalisation needs educated deliberation.

Globalisation impacts the political, economic and cultural dimensions. In a globalised scenario, the entire process of the technically efficient Policy choices – especially related to structural adjustment and liberalisation, have de-linked the masses. In fact we have been cautioned against the concentration of expert knowledge, symbolised by the influence of Public policy specialists over government policy and public opinion.⁸ As policy gradually becomes more and more the domain of the specialists, public control over it inevitably reduces. In contemporary terms, globalisation i.e. the transformation process supported by the full force of capitalism, now unimpeded because of the near absence of other competing economic ideologies, with its breakdown of trade barriers and mobility of capital, technology, know-how and people has its own self-perpetuating momentum. It is a process with a power, dynamism and appeal. Considered the surest route to development and prosperities it is even credited with inculcating democracy.

In the sphere of economics, globalisation has presented alternative choices to the consumers. MNC's have created jobs and opportunities yet the opposite is also true with regard to increased foreign investment and trade benefit reach only a privileged few with the gap between the poor and the rich widening. This is so both within the country and between countries. For instance the GDP of sub-Saharan Africa is less than the combined wealth of 15 richest people in the world.⁹

At a cultural level, information dissemination about other cultures is benefited, with Globalisation. With the breakdown of barriers, inter-dependence tightens the network of interaction that links humanity. This in turn encourages community feeling and partaking in identity Politics that has been segregating on the basis of religion, ethnicity, and language amongst others. A blend of a global product being altered to take a local flavour i.e. "*Glocalization*" (Snarr, 2007), seems to be taking place. For Huntington (1996) the shrinking world will bring 'A clash of civilizations' – especially between the Christian, West against Islam etc. The degree to which cultural values can be exported is the subject of some debates for Huntington who argues, "Drinking Coca Cola does not make Russians think like Americans any more than eating sushi make Americans think like Japanese." Superficial changes are not altering the basic culture of the recipient's society. Moral globalisation is manifest in the human rights question being raised as a universal concern. As a 'cultural bulldozer'¹⁰ critics of globalisation feel that it is furthering dependence rather than inter dependence.

The 'Universality' of globalisation is also questionable, with 'global village' being a restricted urban phenomenon.¹¹ It is felt that the increased flow of information, a characteristic of globalisation, goes primarily in one direction. Problems like poverty, inequity, deprivation have endured and stepped up. One third of the people in the developing world cannot meet their basic human needs and do not even have access to clean water. 840 million people suffer from malnutrition and more than that number of adults are illiterate. Though it is interesting that 100 million illiterate people are in the industrialised world.[12]

Politically, the reduced sovereignty of the state, (from within and without), the epitome of institutional, international system is being slowly challenged by the globalised world. For instance, at the end of the Gulf war in April 1991, UN Security Council endorsed the establishment of interim sanctuary for refugees inside Iraq without Iraq's permission. The logic being that the violent treatment of the Kurds by the government of Iraq threatened international amity and security or the establishment of Tribunals (based on the principle of international law, even before the end of the conflict thus constituting early intervention) to try within their own countries persons responsible for crime against humanity in Rwanda or former Yugoslavia.[13] is clearly militated against the understanding of state sovereignty.

The world of rival political ideologies has given way to a world with a solitary overriding political ideology. The UN and the IFI [14] were created in the context of the great depression, with its need for full-employment, a welfare state and peace. The state in India (as well as in Latin America and Africa), with all its attendant characteristics and in the context of economic crisis, has had to implement the tough policies of structural adjustment at the behest of the IMF and the World Bank. Without such external financial assistance, the state would lose its social base and hence political legitimacy because the impoverishment of the state coffers, due to the economic crisis, sharply reduces the ability of the state to serve the patron-client networks on which it depends for its survival. Alongside, given that the policies of SAP are focusing on a group of 'gainers', it simultaneously creates groups of 'losers' within society, which *also* affects the social base of the state and hence its survival. The state thus is caught in a bind. On the one hand, it has to satisfy the requirements of structural adjustment, since its economic and hence political survival depends on the generation of economic growth within the country and on the other, it has to guard itself against the 'revenge of civil society', which could again threaten survival.

The Economic Reforms Programmes:

Washington Consensus manifests the position of IFI (International Financial Institutions) and the entire Donor community – the US, Canadian, EU and Japanese amongst others with a line of thought that the under development as well as the economic crisis, was due to internal/ domestic structural deterioration that needed a fairly uniform treatment. This involved opening up or liberalisation of the economies to foreign competition, along with a series of market based reforms, including privatisation, de-regulation and an embrace of Globalisation.[15] This formed the Backdrop of economic liberalisation and fiscal austerity in the neo-liberal regimen of the SAPs (also called austerity plans). The conditional ties[16] included market reforms, cuts in spending austerity needs, private economy/selling off the inefficient state owned enterprise, attract foreign investments, *getting the prices right* and finally *getting the politics right* i.e good governance as a criteria for political liberalisation. For the critics of globalisation it was a new colonisation with development along the lines of insuring market for western goods retaining the developing world as a source of cheap labour and raw material and in the process undermining the sovereignty of the state. From the point of view of the recipients of this 'conditional aid', the TINA (there is no alternative) factor predominated.

The Economic Reforms Programmes: The Structural Adjustment Programmes (SAPs) designed as conditionalties for the countries wishing to borrow from the World Bank and IMF (IFI)consisted of two broad types of policies:

- Policies for the stabilisation of the balance of payments, using fiscal and monetary restraint along with exchange rate devaluation, to move to an exchange rate which reflects the relative scarcity of foreign and domestic currency; and
- Policies for structural adjustment within the economy, in the narrower sense of market liberalisation and public sector reform, i.e., an extensive range of sectoral measures designed to improve supply conditions in the economy and to make

domestic prices correspond to shadow prices, including widespread deregulation of product and factor markets, privatisation of state enterprises, public sector resource mobilisation and institutional reform, especially of government.

The economy has been inevitably opened to the inflow of foreign goods, technology & capital. Liberalisation, Privatisation & Globalisation – more commonly referred to as LPG, were thus ushered in.

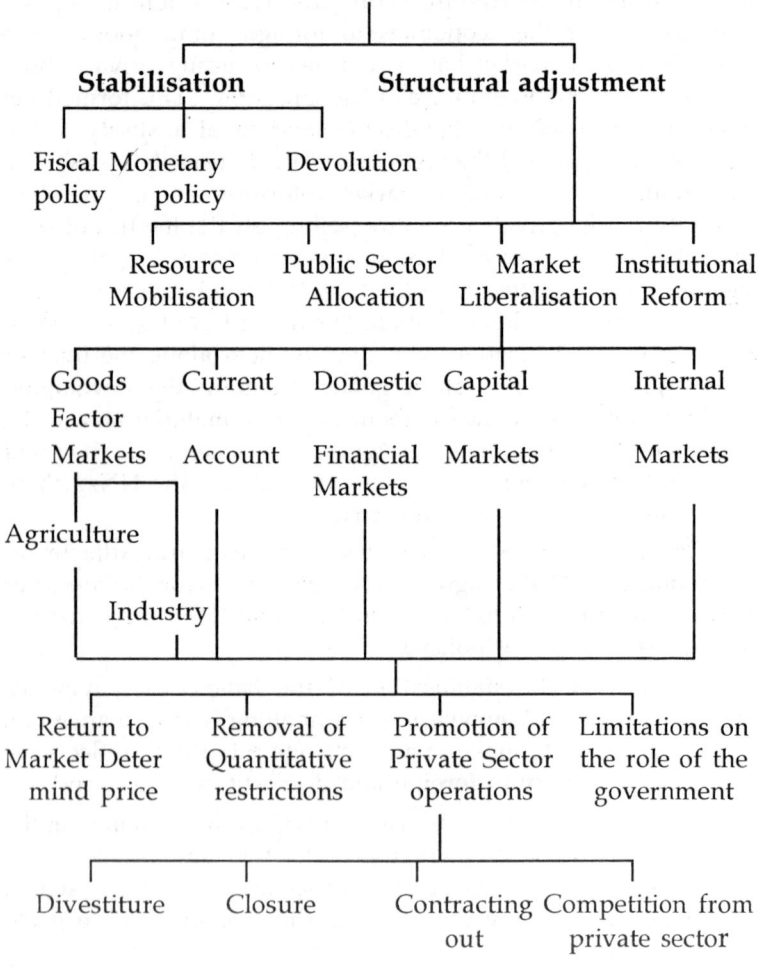

A SCHEMATIC REPRESENTATION OF STRUCTURAL ADJUSTMENT POLICY

Historical Centrality of the State

Historically, notions of the role of the state have shifted dramatically but the discussion has revolved around the mutual rights and obligations of the states and citizens. The State in its wider sense refers to a set of institutions that possess the means of legitimate coercion, exercised over a definite territory and its population referred to as society.[17] The state monopolises rule making through the medium of an organised government.

The Post-colonial state remains the most prominent land mark on an institutional plane. It was constructed on colonial foundation, as opposed to developing 'organically' "from the entrails of Society".[18] The nationalist elite that came to power post colonially was accustomed to a legally strong, hierarchically organised and centralised and economically concentrated governing system. In addition to all the formal attributes of the colonial state, the Post-colonial state was no longer accountable to colonial powers, giving the impression of almost limitless power. But this power was largely deceptive. As much was expected of the new states – thus creating enormous commitment for the new leaders on the one hand, while on the other hand, it had access to much smaller state resources – given that many colonial sources of income had to be abolished in the wake of political independence and given that the new state could not access the extra national resources that the colonial power could furnish to its colony.

In response to these new challenges, the post-colonial state chose the 'statist' mode of development-thus entrusting their bureaucracy with hugely expanded administrative tasks, centralised power and increased the role of the patronage. The state was also seen to be the locus of economic power and access to state resources was a prized accomplishment, whether through the bureaucracy or through political means, direct or indirect, i.e. through patron-client networks. Caught between financial constraints and mushrooming demands on state resources, the state chose to spread itself thin by expanding and accommodating as many interests as possible. The state in other words was 'overdeveloped' and 'predatory'.[19] While 'over-development' carries the connotation of state dominance, the power of the state was illusory to the extent that effective administration was severely hampered by dwindling finances due to the demands of the patrimonial state and the threats to it's political legitimacy implicit in attempts to cut or reduce these patron client relations.

This description clearly militates against the centrality accorded to the state in the 'modernisation' theory that developed in the 1960s which perceives the state to be the central organ to maintain social harmony, political and economic well-being and to foster development and nation building (Almond and Coleman, 1960; Apter, 1965). Huntington, Nettle and others insisted that the place to look for the sources of power to enforce order is in political institutions specifically. International Power relations were the focus of the Dependency[20] and the world system's theory, with the late 70's and 80's returning to Huntington's insight, and that the 'locus of change' was the autonomous state, even the radical notion of the state (see, for instance, Alavi, 1972; Ake, 1981; Skocpol, 1980). The international dependency can be seen as an outgrowth of class structural analysis like Amin (1976), Ake (1981), Saul (1979), Skalr(1979), Shivji, Mamdani(1976) in that it (i) depends on Marxist class theory and (ii) it locates domestic power in the formal apparatus of the state. Pluralists spoke of various groups vying for control over state resources while Neo-Marxists saw the contending parties/groups in terms of class differences and sought to show how the new state apparatus became a vehicle for a new class formation.[21]

The constituent parts and parameters of the modern state- Parliaments, bureaucracies' governmental leadership, courts and law, police and military, remain intact and central. The state has been a sprawling organisation claiming territorial sovereignty, the dominant form of organizing political power, in fact the soul constitutive elements at the exclusion of others in the international system and this is true even today.

In a significant attempt to redefine politics, Leftwich[22] observes the state contributes only one of the many possible foci of socio-economic and political exchange. In other words politics, power and control are not necessarily coterminous with state or public domain and, as Chazan puts it, "power vectors and the search for empowerment take on different meanings in this context". [23]

Civil Society dynamics and its relation to state activity

Thus, the centrality of the state in political analysis is slowly being lost with doubts being cast on the role of fulfilling economic and social aspirations. With the blossoming non-formal socio-economic and political activities – there is much movement between the official and the unofficial, public and private, rural or urban – resulting in a "precarious balance between state and society "and this has ushered in a shift in the "centre of gravity".[24]

When society was brought into the analysis it was merely to explain why the state did not function properly and the reasons for the civil society to come to the stage.[25] Although originally civil society has been used as a generic term for society and the state now it is used to refer to "organisations and institutions in the contemporary social order which are separate from and find expression in their relationship with the state". Whereas the state is identified with a legal and institutional apparatus, the civil society symbolise patterns of relationships and associations like interest groups, professional bodies, membership organisations, which are customary and spontaneous and not necessarily dependant on the law.[26]

The civil society actors – the marginalised and dispossessed social groups, the voluntary associations and institutions, a free press, self help groups, have been coming to the fore, independent of the state according to Chandhoke (1998), with an indisputably participatory arena of civic reflection, debate, and commitment.[27] Thus Chabal (1992) notes: "As the interpretative capacity of state centred conceptual frameworks have decreased over time, it has become quite evident that political scientists have been led astray by the mirage of high politics: constitutions, parties, governments, parliaments, ideology, etc."(p.82).[28]

As opposed to the high politics of the typically Weberian modern bureaucratised sovereign state, Joel S. Migdal,[29] presents the low politics– a state-in-society perspective. This approach demonstrates both the views that states are fragmented and that they face a multitude of social organisations – families, clans, multinational corporations, domestic businesses, tribes, political parties, patron-client dyads that maintain and vie for power to set the rules guiding peoples behaviour. These ongoing and overlapping struggles ally parts of the state with groups in society against other such coalitions. In the process, they determine how societies and states create and maintain distinct ways of structuring day to day life, including the nature of the rules that govern peoples behaviour, whom they benefit and whom they treat as disadvantaged etc. States are shaped by *images and practices* that overlap, contradict reinforce and sometimes are mutually destructive. Images tend to be homogeneous from state to state and practices tend to defy neat categorisation. *Image* implies perception, which assumes the single fairly independent, incorporated and centralised being. It posits two boundaries – the territorial one between states and the social one with public-private divide, separating the state from the non state or the private actors and the social forces. The *practice* serves to recognise, reinforce and indeed validate not just the territorial dimension of state control but also the public-private divide.[30] The idea is to modify the strong structural emphasis in institutional analysis to incorporate cultural variables. Through their practices, the state lays claim to the collective realisation of their population. The Civil society is an indisputably participatory sphere, open to all and has the potential to ensure political accountability. The state, it is believed should play a constructive role in the promotion of civil society by providing the institutional framework within which civil society can thrive and prosper.

A concept that attempts to incorporate this perspective and balance the actors is that of governance (a concept that the Carter Center of the Emory University of Atlanta, and, more specifically, Richard Joseph, Michael Bratton and Goran Hyden, have sought to popularise). The basic idea is that political power is vested outside the government as well and consequently the government is forced to make concessions and bargains with different sections of society in order to maintain its political support and legitimacy. Hyden(1989, 1992) thus, goes beyond the performance of governments to the social roots of authority, pointing out that governance is "characterised by reciprocal behaviour and legitimate relations of power between governors and governed."

A 'Minimalist' State & 'Good' Governance

A central difficulty in redefining the state's role is that the ground beneath government's feet is always changing. In the context of the developing countries, fostering a sustainable blueprint of development in a democratic setting has given salience to the civil society. The end of cold war, the collapse of the command and control economies, the fiscal crisis of the welfare states, the dramatic success of some East Asian countries in accelerating economic growth and reducing poverty and in financial crisis in these very countries in 1997, and the crisis of the failed states in some countries of Africa has also compelled a renewed look at the government from a range of conflicting perspectives. This has challenged the state's place in the world and its potential contribution to human welfare.

It would thus be fair to say that globalisation has undermined the sovereignty of states & governments.[31] For some the increase in global interconnections, has meant a decrease in the policy apparatus accessible to the state to manage activities within and beyond its borders, increase in international forms of association as well as political integration with other states, IMF and GATT provide the basis for global governance.

From the early emphasis on 'rolling back the state' to realising a **'minimalist state'** and a liberalised market with the 'right prices' for private enterprise, especially (the export) trade, to grow unfettered, to a focus on political and institutional factors. IFIs thus perceived that 'a crisis of governance' underlay the problems of the developing countries. Thus, charges of a lack of 'seriousness' or 'political will', of 'bureaucratic corruption', and 'vested interests' led to a focus on **'good governance'** and 'political reform' as a means to support a dynamic economy undergoing structural change (WB, 1989). Good governance was thus intended to improve the effectiveness of adjustment programmes.[32]

If we consider how the global economic and social forces have changed the prevailing notions of the state[33], it is clear that it retains a distinctive role in providing public goods that promote economic and social development. Market failures continue to provide powerful economic arguments for state intervention. But many of the most successful instances of development, recent and historical, entail states working in partnership with markets to correct their failures, not replacing them. The welfare states earlier assigned a strategic role in development is slowly being minimised and has had to retreat from the economy. The market earlier not perceived to be good enough 'to meet the aspirations of the latecomers to industrialisation',[34] was by the early 1990's perceived in an almost diametrically opposite way because of a combination of factors.

Thus Globalisation and its varied manifestations is occurring in a context where governments (whether in India or in other developing countries) are under multiple pressures to undertake different and often contradictory reforms in the established administrative arrangements. The World Bank's and IMF's (IFI) assumption in stabilisation & SAP as applied to the Developing countries economies has been that economic growth would only be resumed by a contraction of the state activity and the development of a liberalised market. In many respects the IFI have provided a framework within which other donor Agencies must also operate.

> The 'shrinking' or the minimalist state is manifest in the growing reliance on marketisation, contracting out major parts of the work to the private sector, networking at best and letting the NGO sector take charge of the developmental responsibilities.[35] In the name of **'effective management'**, the state's user charges for various utilities including health, education, reduced subsidy etc threatens the welfare of the poor and weaker sections of the society. The compulsive character of the phenomenon with its directed tenets of the international trade regime (WTO) is bound to unevenly affect the myriad groups and nations participating in the process.

The economic and social consequences of adopting SAP policies have resulted in unrest and protest[36] both within the government machinery itself and within civil society in general, and these pose real threats to the political credibility and legitimacy of these governments. Threats, which they are not prepared to readily face. This led the IFIs to focus on largely technical economic prescriptions to 'shrink the state' by withdrawing from the functions of production and exchange and to liberalise markets[37]. It was felt that once the correct neo-liberal policies were in place, the process of liberalisation and de-regulation would provide the basis for sustained future economic growth.

Public Administration to perform new tasks

SAP in India and in the other developing countries has ushered in the "new conventional view" that the state should directly supply services only where necessary. State is acting in what could be described as the 'provider' role – ensuring that essential services and goods are delivered but not aiming to be the sole deliverer. Although this needs less direct action by the government sector, the state withdrawal often implies a paradoxical need for public administration to perform new tasks, which are more complex than the old ones. It has now to regulate and support private community, NGO, International Agencies, etc. This is technically difficult, politically sensitive and difficult to accommodate together with established styles of administration.[38]

The imperatives for change in the nature of the public administration include – the attack on the public sector, changes in economic theory (idea that less government would improve aggregate welfare by improving economic efficiency)[39] the impact of changes in the private sector, particularly globalisation as an economic force[40].

The new paradigm poses a direct challenge to what had earlier been regarded as fundamental and almost eternal principles of Public administration[41], viz;

- Governments should organise themselves according to the hierarchical bureaucratic principles (most classically enunciated by Max Weber) – the single best way of operating an organisation.

- The second principle was that once the government involved itself in the area, it became the direct provider of goods and services through the bureaucracy.

- Accountability was sought through separating administrative from the political matters. The administration was to be the instrument to carry out instructions, while any matters of policy of strategy were the preserve of the political leadership.

- Public administration was considered as a special form of administration needing a professional bureaucracy employed for life, having the ability to serve any political master equally.

All these seeming axioms have been challenged. By the early 1990's, a new model of public sector management with several incarnations was emerging in most developed countries – from 'managerialism', new public administration', 'Market based public administration', and 'entrepreneurial government'.[42] 'The new paradigm moves the public sector unavoidably away from administration towards 'management[43]. The government and a public sector are vital to economic success as well as to social cohesion. Thus instead of dismantling of government, we are witnessing a new form of government and governance. The earlier rigidly bureaucratic model is now discredited both theoretically as well as practically. But there are serious questions of *Ethics, accountability, theoretical basis of the new model* as well as the significant question of role and organisation of public services. Despite criticisms and indisputable problems, the change to a managerial model is an irreversible phenomenon.

Globalisation and Governance in India:

The Macro Economic Crisis in India could be traced to the early 1980's[44] with essentially crisis driven reforms, the momentum of which dissipated as soon as the immediate crisis was over. By 1985 – large fiscal deficit (8.4% of GDP) as competition between the Political parties drove subsidies up at every election. In 1985, the reforms were not initiated in the face of any immediate threat, so they could be considered belief-driven. It was by 1991 when Narsimha Rao came to power, that the Current Account deficit and India's foreign exchange reserves were virtually exhausted. The macro economic crisis of 1990-91 was unprecedented in Indian history. Unlike the crises in the past (which were due to war, monsoon failure or oil shock), the crisis of 1990-91 was largely policy induced. The July 1991 reform process had underpinnings of both the factors.

An examination of the fiscal, external and political developments during the decade preceding the crisis highlights the pressures that were leading the economy to a crisis. Mounting fiscal deficits financed through external and internal borrowing had put the Debt/GDP ratio on an unsustainable path. The expansionary policy continued until the situation became so fragile that the country was about to default on its external obligations. In a simple framework of analysis, the fiscal deficit of the government sector as a percentage of GDP far exceeded the annual growth rate of GDP and the debt-service ratio exceeded export growth suggesting an unsustainable macro scenario. Under this backdrop, India embarked upon a stabilisation and structural reform program.

Ongoing since 1991, the reforms in India have opened the national economy to the outside world along with increasing inequalities in the society. With a very sound record of various facets of democracy,[45] - vibrant media, watchful civil society, periodic elections, relatively autonomous judicial and bureaucratic system amongst other attributes these institutions desperately need to be nurtured. Though Linguistic conflicts, regional secessionist movements, communal tensions and riots and political violence had often made its existence rather precarious. On many occasions, it so seemed that the existence of India as a nation was itself in danger. It not only survived all of them but also emerged from them much stronger, reinforcing in the process, its commitment to democratic ideals. Analysing the achievements of Indian democracy attained in a largely hostile environment, vitiated by religious superstitions, caste prejudices and acute economic disparities, for Guha (2007) the genuine triumph of modern India lies not in the domain of economics but in that of politics.[46]

During the first 41 years of Independence, India had six prime ministers. But between 1989 and 2006 there were seven prime ministers, all without backing of a majority party indicating that multi-party coalitions are a regular form of government in which instability was inbuilt. But, as recent analysis substantiates, the fact that such a government could last fcr even three years shows the resilience of Indian democracy and Parliamentary form of government'.[47] Coalitions result from the proliferation of political parties and also work as incentive for such proliferations. With fractured result of an election, even small parties wield enormous bargaining power. Leaders from parties manage to secure few seats into the House and then 'negotiate' for Cabinet posts. The first casualty of such coalition cabinet is the principle of collective responsibility[48]. An accompanying process is that of politicisation of the permanent civil services. Wide-ranging political reforms are imperative to combat the crisis of governance that India faces (and also if coalition governments are to become viable and stable).[49]

In the complex history of India's sixty years experience with democracy, the issue of governance remains debatable and an agreement is almost impossible. In keeping with the spirit of democracy, ultimate sovereignty rests with the people, and their representatives are merely to carry out their will. A mere technical view of democracy and a concentration on the myth of an election system will overlook social and economic disparity that make it difficult for even formal participation to be successful. 'The free exercise of franchise may require freedom from caste superiors, from dominant landlords, or in the case of women, from male heads of household. It may be curtailed when people do not have the power of independent decision making; when they have inadequate access to relevant information, when they are helpless in holding their representatives accountable; and, above all, when their exercise of franchise fails to yield a responsive administration'.[50] National elections in India are dramatic moments that reveal salient themes of contemporary Indian politics. The 2004 elections underline at least three such themes according to Atul Kohli and Amrita Basu (2007)[51]

1. A billion people of diverse cultural backgrounds in India have managed to elect its rulers through regular elections maintaining democratic institutions since its political independence after the Second World War.
2. In contrast with the initial decades following political independence when Congress party 'Dominance' won elections year after year, today the competition is intense with no political party enjoying a position of unchallenged dominance.
3. The national economy has been growing but also becoming more unequal along regional, rural-urban and class lines. Ethnic conflicts and political fragmentation without debilitating inequalities has thus emerged as the most pressing political challenge in contemporary India.

Precarious coalition governments, weakened political institutions and political activism along class and ethnic lines today characterises politics in India. Political crisis are always at hand. Since 1991, the five coalition governments at the union level, have endorsed and served the reform process (Sachs 2005), irrespective of the proclaimed ideology. Successful economic performance is necessary for India. Indian policy makers had initially sought economic self-sufficiency through a policy of state led industrialisation focused on meeting the needs of its large internal market. This protectionist economic strategy has had mixed results with development of some basic industries but generating extensive inefficiencies and increasing poverty.

After Sixty years of Political independence, India is very visible globally manifesting its economic presence. Fourth Largest in terms of purchasing power parity (PPP), India's growing economic buoyancy is becoming manifest on the global arena. Once regarded in diplomatic circles as the chief ideologue of the G-77 group of developing countries, India is taking an assertive self-interest line. As nuclear power, it has snubbed attempts to sign the non-proliferation treaty, entering instead into an as yet fuzzy and contentious civil nuclear deal with the United States. On trade issues, it has moved away from the conventional G-77 position on services, preferring to strike for its rapidly expanding services sector by supporting further liberalisation. On international economic governance, it is a leading voice for reform of the International Monetary Fund's voting system, (since becoming a net and growing contributor to the Fund's reserves). On global affairs, it is working towards a seat on an expanded UN Security Council and enjoys favour with the majority of the P5 (permanent five) members. The other facet of the Globalised scenario is that India is also a country that has not only seen a tripling of its population since Independence, but also a shrinking of its natural resource base and a sharpening of its income divide. But for the huge proportion of the middle class that desires luxury consumables, an equal number (or more) of the population, exists on less than a $1 a day. The paradox of visible India is the high PPP along with dilapidated infrastructure, starvation, illiteracy, poverty and despondency. And both these dimensions survive, and in this sense the Indian state's path to development is still a long way from optimising on Globalisation.[52]

Balancing State and its Institutional Capacity:

Given the liberalising nature of adjustment, the longer-term questions are to do with how the government manages its relationship with the other actors. The inherent contradictions are visible and intense, but the promises of welfare and social justice are kept alive due to the pressure of electoral politics. The long-term sustainability of reforms process requires, atleast, (a) the state to become more decentralised, especially in its decision-making; (b) to develop better ties with the civil society by gathering and processing more information within civil society and (c) most significantly evolving a reciprocal relationship with the market. And this is perhaps best served in a context of true plural politics, characterised by:

- Significant legal reforms to create an atmosphere congenial to potential investors, promoting business confidence, ensuring individual economic rights, a credible means of resolving conflict; and a government bound by institutional checks above authoritarian or personal rule, without control over the Constitution.
- A genuinely free press to promote accountability by creating public awareness of government action (and inaction) with critical and doubtful voices being given their due – and which does not just disseminate government press releases and sycophantic endorsements of government proclamations, reporting little else but government success; and
- Political mobilisation through the promotion of autonomous political associations within civil society that would allow organisations to represent economic actors who may not otherwise be heard.

Winners and losers are rampant in capitalist globalisation's, uneven impacts. It is contestable whether, globalisation is a cause or a cure for the crisis, the point remains that it is inexorable and inevitable. The processes of Globalisation seem to be more successfully adopted and adjusted in those societies where the state has scored wide-ranging success in welfare activities, rather than in the societies where welfare measures are not deeply entrenched.[53] Here the need of the day is a consensus (across different political groupings) on "how" the practice of welfarism can be dovetailed with globalisation to ensure justice and equal opportunity for all.

The historical record suggests the importance of building on the relative strengths of the state, along with the civil society and the market to better the state's institutional capability. The most advantageous market oriented reforms[54], as seen from an economic standpoint, are difficult to implement because of the established political structures. In this lies a clear incentive to combine economic analysis with the political setting analysis - in other words to analyse the political economy of the Reforms in the redefined State Precincts in the globalised era.

End Notes

[1] Jan Aart, *Globalisation: A Critical Introduction*, Macmillan, 2000, "Thought territory still matters in our globalising world, it no longer constitutes the whole of our geography".

[2] Jeffrey, Sachs *'The End of Poverty; How can we make it happen in our Lifetime'* New York, Penguin, 2005; Sachs Jeffrey and Andrew Warner, *Economic Reform and the process of Global Integration*, Brookings paper on Economic Activity, 1, 1995.

[3] For a detailed analysis see Deepak Nayyar, (Eds), *Governing Globalisations; Issues and Institutions*, New Delhi, OUP, 2006; Sachs 2005.ibid

[4] Karl Marx, Friedrich Engels; Communist Manifesto, Martin Malia, Mass Market, 1849

[5] Ellen Wood ('Back to Marx', Monthly review, June 1997) in pointing to the relevance of Marxism says "..just about every economic actor in the world today is operating according to the logic of capitalism, and even those in the outmost periphery . . . are subject to that logic. Capitalism is universal also in the sense that its logic – the logic of accumulation, co modification, profit maximisation, competition has penetrated just about every aspect of human life and nature itself. "

[6] From Angell, 1909, quoted in Micheal T Snarr and D Neil Snarr, *Introducing Global Issues*, Boulder and London, Lynne Rienner Publishers, Viva Books page 3. 2007

[7] Globalisation has created prospects for some countries and people in the developing world but a large proportion of both countries and people have been kept out. As a market-driven process Globalisation has more often than not heightening exclusion or what Amartya Sen calls a lack of entitlements.

[8] Robert Dahl, *Democracy and its critics*, New Delhi, Orient Longman Ltd. Dahl, 1991

[9] Richard Parker, *"From Conquistadors to Corporations,"* Sojourners Magazine, May to June, 2002

[10] Green and Luehrmann, Comparative Politrics of the Third World; Linking Concepts and Cases, Lynne Rienner Publishers Inc, Viva Books page 3. 2004 Pg.10 2004

[11] According to UNDP 1999 statistics only one in ten people worldwide have access to the internet.

[12] The globalisation of communication (Television and Radio etc) in the less developed countries typically is a one-way proposition" the people do not control any of the information; they only receive it. Deepak Nayyar op cit, p. 5.

[13] Examples of technology that have eroded state sovereignty include the Satellite dishes, e-mails and World Wide Web. This besides, 'the state has difficulty controlling the influx of illegal drugs and unwanted immigrants, including terrorists' Snarr op cit, p 6. 2007

[14] Referred to as "lenders of the last resort" implying that the countries go to them when they are unable to pay their bills or have no other choice - the TINA argument.

[15] Privatisation, Liberalisation, and Globalisation have placed new players center stage inducing a strategic withdrawal on part of the nation state in some important spheres. These prescriptions are today subjected to question not from the critics but also the supporters. See for eg. Joseph Stiglitz, *Redefining the Role of the state* March 17, 1998 ; Lance Taylor, *Varieties of Stabilisation Experience: Towards sensible macro economics in the Third World*, Clarendon Press, Oxford, 1988

[16] For the critics of Globalisation, Conditionalities-or the conditions attached to continuation of aid was tantamount to blackmail and getting the prices right may be getting development wrong.

[17] Typically a Weberian sovereign state would be an Organisation/institution that seeks to exercise the preponderance of force within a territory, recognised order and deterring the challengers domestically and externally.

[18] J F, Bayart *The state in Africa: The politics of the Belly*, London, Longman, p.32, 1993

[19] Hamza Alavi, "*Bangladesh and the crisis of Pakistan*", in R Milliband and T. Saville (eds, Socialist Register, London, Merlin Press, 1971; C Leys, *The 'overdeveloped Post Colonial state: A revaluation*, Review of African Political Economy, 5-January-April Leys, 1976, Robert Bates, *Markets and States in Tropical Africa*, Berkley, California University Press.1981

[20] Andre Gunder Frank has moved from his core-periphery thesis to the 'ReOrient' theory suggesting that the West's period of global economic dominance has been limited to a period spanning a few decades after the beginning of the industrial revolution to the present time. Before then the Orient was the center of global economic activity and it may not be long before it regains its dominance with the rapid economic rise of the likes of India and China. A G Frank , *ReOrient, Global Economy in the Asian Age*, Berkeley: University of California Press, 1998

[21] For an analysis of contending views see, Bulbul Dhar, *The Politics of Economic Liberalisation in Urban Tanzania*, PhD thesis, SOAS, University of London, 1995

[22] Adrian Leftwich, *What is Politics*, Blackwell Publishers, 1984

[23] N. Chazan, *Politics and Society in contemporary Africa*, London, Macmillan p.123, 1988

[24] *ibid*

[25] It is since the 1980s that works of the political scientists like Hyden Goran, "*Community Governance and High Politics*", in *Beyond Autocracy in Africa*,

Working Paper for the inaugural seminar of the Governance in Africa Program, the Carter Centre of Emory University, Atlanta, Georgia, Feb 17-18, 1989, M A Klein (eds) Peasants in Africa; Historical and Comparative Perspectives, Beverly Hills, sage, 1980, V. Azarya, and N. Chazan, "*Disengagement from the State in Africa: Reflections on the experience of Ghana and Guinea*", Comparative studies in Society and History, 29 (1), January, 1987. See Bulbul Dhar op cit

[26] J Healey and M Robinson, *Democracy, Governance and Economic Policy; Sub Saharan Africa in Comparative Prespective*, London, Overseas Development Institute, pp 160-161, 1992

[27] Neera Chandhoke, *The State and Civil society; Explorations in Political theory*, New Delhi, Sage, 1998; Naomi Chazan, *Politics and Society in contemporary Africa*, London, Macmillan, 1988.

[28] Patrick Chabal, Power in Africa, An Essay in Political Interpretation, London, Macmillan, 1992.

[29] Migdal Joel S, State in Society; Studying how States and Societies Transform and Constitute one another, C.U.P, 2001.

[30] The Foucault effect: Studies in Governmentality edited by Graham Burchell, Colin Gordon, and Peter Miller, University of Chicago Press, 1991. "the state is no more than a composite reality and a mythicised abstraction ...it is the tactics of government that make possible that continual definition and redefinition of what is within the competence of the state and what is not.... thus the state can only be understood in its survival and its limits on the basis of the general tactics of govern mentality."

[31] Although the sovereignty of states was never absolute, except legally. Limitations on state sovereignty have been recognised by Bodin, Hobbes & Austin, long before Globalisation was on the international agenda.

[32] In one party states of Africa & Latin America, it was translated to political conditionality of multiparty politics, with a two-fold objective: that legitimate and effective opposition would force recalcitrant governments to implement economic reform effectively, and that a democratically-elected government would be better able to gain acceptability for the reform process from civil society.

[33] The Global culture and its impact on Indian society has been widely discussed amongst others by Yogendra Singh (1994), Peggy Mohan (1995), Rajni Kothari (1995), Krishna Kumar (1996)

[34] Deepak Nayyar op cit

[35] Dolly Arora, Mainstream, March 10th, 2001.

[36] SAP cannot function without a well functioning state and retreat of this state is essential as a strategy for liberalising civil society and "empowering the people" World Bank *Sub Saharan Africa: From Crisis to Sustainable Growth, A long term perspective*, Washington D C , World bank 1989.

[37] One characteristic response to economic crisis and insecurity by most of civil society has been to pursue multiple survival strategies, which typically fall into what has been called the 'Second Economy'. Since most of these activities are unrecorded in official statistics, the presence of the Second Economy and the informal sector makes "income and expenditure patterns ... more complex than is normally allowed for in the economic analysis of poor countries.

[38] For instance, transformation of the Planning Commission from its pre-liberalisation role as principal agency devising and justifying the interventions of the command economy, to a surprisingly new role of advocacy for privatisation in particular of the power sector, is a major institutional development. RBI and the Planning Commission are acting as independent agents arguing for liberalisation in terms of specific constituency and arena of responsibility of each.

[39] The most important economic theory applied to bureaucracy is Public Choice Theory- the key assumption of which is a comprehensive view of rationality. And the 'best' outcome will involve a maximum role for the market forces and a minimum role for the government. If the role of government in supplying goods and services will be reduced, the economy as a whole would benefit. Public choice provided alternatives, the most obvious being to allow competition and choice and return as many activities as possible to the private sector. The Principal/Agent theory has also been applied to the public sector. This attempts to find incentives for agents to act in the interests of the principals. These kind of economic theorizing along with an ideological preference among many economists for market solution have provided the intellectual coherence to cutting the Public service, as well as restructuring its management.

[40] In public administration as with other social or scientific theories, the spread of ideas and the impact of technology occurs so rapidly that national barriers become increasingly artificial. In the global economic competition, the role of government Porter (1990) points out can be used as a 'national competitive advantage'. Like the education policy, tax policy, anti-trust policy, regulatory policy, environmental policy, fiscal & monetary policy and many others. All of these provide substantial roles for public administrators and managers.

[41] Owen E Hughes: Public Administration and Management; An Introduction, Hampshire, UK, Macmillan Press LTD, 1994

[42] C. Pollitt, *Managerialism and the Public Services: The Anglo-American Experience.* Oxford: Basil Blackwell, 1990; Jong S. Jun, Deil Spencer Wright, *Globalisation and Decentralisation*, Institutional context, policy Issues..Georgetown University Press 1996; Stephen P. Osborne, *Public Management, Official Perspective*, Routledge, 2001

[43] A positive perspective is reflected in Osborne (ibid) that government needs to be 'reinvented'. They believe in government and that government can do much more than markets. However for that bureaucracy is neither necessary not efficient and that other means should be used. For this they formulated a ten point programme for entrepreneurial governments.

[44] Politically Independent India begun with Planned economy with industrial focus in *Nehru years*, 1947-64, followed by Mrs. Gandhi's (1966-77) focus on agriculture, the *garibi hatao* slogan, bank nationalisation etc. It was the period of spending boom and Fiscal deficits (1977 – 91), that Indian economic policy ushered in a reformist mode.

[45] Barring the few odd emergency years (1977-1979) of authoritarianism.

[46] "The sapling (of democracy)," says Ramchandra, Guha 2007, *India after Gandhi; The history of the World's Largest Democracy'*, Great Britain, Macmillan, New Delhi, Picador, 2007, "was planted by the nation's founders, who lived long enough (and worked hard enough) to nurture it to adulthood. Those who

Globalisation and Good Governance: Redefining the State Precincts 115

came afterwards could disturb and degrade the tree of democracy but, try as they might, could not uproot or destroy it."

[47] Bimal, Jalan *India's Politics; A view from the Backbench*, Penguin, Viking, New Delhi, 2007; Ramchandra Guha ibid et al

[48] The primary concern of each group within the coalition is to protect its own interest. With each cabinet minister becoming an independent master of her/his own ministry, the collective responsibility becomes limited to maintaining majority in the House for survival. If survival is possible in another coalition even this responsibility is shirked off. The procedure and performance of the Parliament also gets affected and even rules are suspended to pass the Budget and the Finance Bill without the Standing Committee considering it.

[49] Laying out an agenda for the future Bimal Jalan, op cit lists a minimum practical agenda that deserves consideration and debate in legislative Bodies, Media and other institution of the civil society viz: Federation of states, the councils of states, state funding of elections, the role of small parties in government, business of the Parliament, reform of the government ministerial responsibility, de-politisation of the civil service, Fiscal empowerment, and legal & Judicial reforms.

[50] In India, where significant minorities - based on religion, language, ethnicity, exist - " majoritarian democracy tends to be unfair as the aspirations of the permanent minorities are either ignored , or else systematically outvoted. Such minorities thus never have a real, let alone equal, opportunity to influence the outcome of the decision making process. Given these constraints, to raise a cheer for Indian democracy purely on the basis of voter participation may be somewhat rash." Neerja Gopal Jayal, (Eds), *Themes in Politics Democracy in India*, New Delhi, OUP, 2001, p. 4

[51] Atul Kohli and Amrita Basu , in Mark Kesselman, Joel Krieger, and William A Joseph, *Introducing Comparative Politics*, Boston, NY, Houghton Mifflin Company 2007

[52] See Ram Chandra Guha op cit , Bimal Jalan op cit, Deepak Nayyar op cit

[53] Elmar Reiger & Steven Liebfried, *'Welfare state limits to Globalisation,'*,Politics & Society, Vol 26, No. 3, Sept 1998

[54] See inter alia John Martinussen, Society, State and the Market: A guide to Competing Theories of Development, Zed Books, 1999, Goddard C. Roe, Patrick Cronin and Kishore C. dash (eds.), International Political Economy: State Market Relations in a Changing Global Order. Boulder, London, Lynne Reinner Publisher, 2003, Robert, Gilpin Global Political Economy: Understanding the International Economic Order, Princeton, Princeton University press, 2001.

GLOBALISATION AND THE NEW WORLD ORDER/AREA STUDIES

6

Globalised Trend Towards Nuclear Proliferation: A Case Study of India and Pakistan as Glocalisation

MOHAMMED BADRUL ALAM

Amidst globalisation and the new world order, the proliferation of nuclear weapons across various regions of the globe has been a matter of paramount concern for the stability of international order and its system. While the United States took the lead in nuclear weaponisation during the final years of World War II, other countries have followed suit since then. My chapter will examine and evaluate the escalatory nature of nuclear proliferation in major countries of the world with its ramifications being felt in terms of sustaining the basic human security to its population. In the South Asian context, with both India and Pakistan having chosen the path of nuclearisation and with neither of them signing Nuclear Non-proliferation Treaty (NPT) and Comprehensive Test Ban Treaty (CTBT), the challenges for arriving at a reasonable arms control regime are too onerous. This chapter will surmise that the ball lies in the court of the United States, the sole super power of the post-Cold War era to take the lead in this regard on a fast-track basis.

The proliferation of nuclear weapons across various countries of the globe has been a major challenge to global security in today's globalised new world order. During the Cold War phase, global proliferation was limited to a few select countries as the world was divided along ideological lines. Of late, many new emerging and developing countries have not only acquired weapons of mass destruction as a matter of deterrence but also with the belief in enhancing a state's status and prestige in the international system.

Varied issues has been dealt in this article, the first among them being the examination and evaluation of the scale and magnitude of nuclear weapons across the globe. Secondly, a comparative analysis of military and defence spending vis-à-vis human security issues in the South Asian regional scene between India and Pakistan will be discussed. Finally, global solutions to nuclear proliferation in the form of Nuclear Non-Proliferation Treaty (NPT), and Comprehensive Test Ban Treaty (CTBT) and the response to these measures by the big powers as well as of India will also be addressed.

India has a defence establishment of over a million troops, while Pakistan has that number close to 600,000. It is believed that some of the defence expenditure of both countries is classified and not open for public domain, specially the expenditure incurred on the development of nuclear weapons and nuclear-tipped ballistic missiles. By a conservative estimate, the cost of nuclear weapons is estimated at $15 billion and $5 billion for India and Pakistan respectively, whereas USA has spent $5821 billion for building, deployment, targeting and defence of the bomb. In terms of human deprivation profile in providing basic infrastructure facilities and amenities to its people, statistics for India and Pakistan paint a dim forecast. (See, Table 1)

Table 1: *Human Deprivation Profile of India and Pakistan*

	India	Pakistan
Population below poverty line 1989-94	53%	12%
Population without access to health services (in millions)	143	63
Population without access to safe water (in millions)	178	56

Population without access to sanitation (in millions)	66.5	98
Illiterate adults as per cent of total adult population	48%	62%
GDP per capita 1996 ($)	370	500
Unemployment rate (2003)	9.50%	7.70%

(*Source*: CIA- The Fact Book, India & Pakistan. Also, Human Development in South Asia 1999, The Mehbubul Haq Development Centre, Oxford University Press, 1999,pp.196-7. See, National Resources Defence Council, New York, 2003, available at http://www.nrdc.org/nuclear/southasia.asp)

Table 2: *Poverty Profile of South Asia*

Country	Earnings $ 1 a day or less
Pakistan	12%
Nepal	53%
Bangladesh	29%
India	53%
Sri Lanka	4%

(*Source*: Human Development in South Asia, 1999, The Crisis of Governance, Mahbubul Haq Human Development Centre, Oxford University Press, Karachi, 1999, p.12.)

A report in *Human Development in South Asia 1997*, has pointed out quite graphically that South Asia (with a population of 1.50 billion people) has emerged as the poorest, the most illiterate and the most malnourished region of the world. It is home to more than half the world's illiterates and more than 40 per cent of the world's poor strive here. (see, Table 1) South Asian economy started flourishing side by side with East Asia in 1960, but East Asia's per capita income is now 27 times higher than South Asia's. In South Asia, 830 million people lack facilities for elementary sanitation, 340 million have no access to safe drinking water, 400 million people are illiterates with two-thirds of them women, and more than 500 million people survive in absolute poverty. But South Asia's poverty has not inhibited its military having a sizeable budget. Military spending is currently running $14 billion a year. This is in spite of the fact that a sizeable section of India and Pakistan's population earns less than a dollar a day. (see, Table 2)

Table 3: *The Defense Budget of India and Pakistan*

Year	Pakistan			India		
	In million $	In million Rs.	% GDP	In million $	In billion Rs.	% GDP
1988	2500	47285	6.2	7941	130	3.1
1989	2499	50961	6	8161	142	2.9
1990	2636	58635	5.8	8051	153	2.7
1991	2823	70187	5.8	7532	163	2.5
1992	2997	81606	6.1	7209	174	2.3
1993	2993	89619	5.7	8137	209	2.4
1994	2917	98144	5.3	8109	230	2.3
1995	2965	112085	5.3	8340	260	2.2
1996	2961	123550	5.1	8565	291	2.1
1998	2833	131803	4.9	9307	339	2.2
1999	2858	146931	4.7	10482	453	2.3
2000	2867	153795	4.5	10900	490	2.3
2001	3071	169950	4.6	11397	531	2.3
2002	3350	188850	4.7	11426	556	2.3
2003	3350	196000		12394	630	

(*Source*: The SIPRI military expenditure database, http://www.first.sipri.org/index.php)

Three disturbing trends in South Asia's military spending

There are three discerning trends in South Asia's military spending. First, military spending in South Asia is largely independent of the human security situation on the ground. India ranks 138 in the world in terms of real per capita income (PPP dollars), but first in total arms imports while Pakistan's rank is lingering at 129 in real per capita income and 10th in arms imports procurement. Second, both India and Pakistan have invested in absolute sums in proportion to their GDP in their defence budget. (See, Table 3) While military spending went down by 37 per cent globally during the 1987-1994 period, military spending in South Asia went up by 12 per cent during the same period. The total number of soldiers were reduced by 16 per cent globally during the same period, but increased by 8 per cent in South Asia. While military holdings of combat aircraft, artillery, ships, and tanks went down by 14 per cent in the world, they went up by 43 per cent in South Asia. Third, there is a major risk involved when two developing nations like India and Pakistan, have nuclear weapon capability and remain locked in historical animosity even after 60 years of independence from the British colonial rule.

Indian official estimates of defence spending covers current and capital expenditure of the three forces (Army, Air Force, Navy) as well as research and development on this front. Reporting of defence expenditure in India has been based on the budget documents of the Government of India. A big chunk of the budget is geared towards defence-related space and atomic energy sectors. It is estimated that 25 per cent of all outlays on space and atomic energy (other than for nuclear power generation) have a defence orientation. India's ongoing nuclear programme is based on work done at the nuclear and space research establishments.

Table 4: *'Official' versus 'Alternate' Defence Estimates for India (Rs crores, At current prices)*

Year	Official	Alternate
1995-96	26879	33940
1996-97	29498	37336
1997-98	36099	46120
1998-99	41200	54255
1999-2000	48504	66232
2000-01	54461	72308
2001-02	57000	75170
2002-03	56000	73777
2003-04	65000	83955

Source: Computed from Government of India Budget documents

In 2003-04 (budget estimates), the budgeted outlay, according to the alternative estimate of defence expenditure was 29 per cent higher than the official figure. The gap between the official and alternate estimate was widened in the late 1990s, exactly when Indian defence expenditure begins to accelerate. The higher outlays, according to the alternative estimate, take the defence spending-GDP ratio to a significant higher level. Thus, while the official figures suggest a defence spending-GDP level of 2.5 per cent in 2001-02, the alternate estimate leads to a ratio of as much as 3.3 per cent. Clearly, when all aspects of defence spending are taken into account, outlays are much more higher than the figures that form the basis for the official data. It is more than a reasonable assessment that a similar exercise conducted for Pakistan will also show even a larger gap between the official and true levels of defence spending.

Global Comparison:

Both India and Pakistan are allocating a considerable amount of resources to the defence sector. Arms imports as a proportion of total imports are higher in Pakistan compared to that of India. According to World Bank data, Pakistan's arms imports constituted 9.7 per cent of total imports in 1999, compared to 1.6 per cent for India in the same year. This ratio varies in both countries from year to year but in general, the ratio for Pakistan is around 6 per cent while that for India it is 2 per cent. Clearly, the imports of arms place a bigger strain on Pakistan's balance of payments than that of India.

Another indicator of the greater role of defence in Pakistan's economy is in the size of the military force. India of course has the larger army, with 1.3 million personnel in uniform, while Pakistan has less than half this number, 590,000 (1999, World Bank data). However, in relative terms, the Pakistani army is proportionately bigger. The Indian defence personnel population constitutes just 0.30 per cent of the labour force, Pakistani military strength, on the other hand, is as much as 1.2 per cent of the labour force – a stagerring four times as large as in India.

With respect to averages of low-income countries and of the world as a whole, India and Pakistan allocate considerably higher resources to defence. Table 5 presents statistics for averages for India, Pakistan, various low-income countries and for the world.

Globalised Trend Towards Nuclear Proliferation: A Case Study... 125

Table 5: *India, Pakistan and the Rest of the World*

Category	year	India	pakistan	Low-income countries	World average
Defence Spending-GDP%	2001	2.5	4.5	2.3	2.3
Defence Spending-Central Govt. Expenditure (%)	2001	14	23	13.1	9.8
Military Personnel-Labour Force (%)	1999	0.3	1.18	0.56	0.7
Arms Imports-Total Imports (%)	1999	1.6	9.7	2.1	0.9

Source: World Development Indicators Database (World Bank, 2003)

It is clear that India and Pakistan are showing higher levels of defence spending than other low-income countries or the world as a whole. On the aspect of the military population, the Indian figure is lower than the global average while for Pakistan it is larger. In arms imports, Pakistan spends relatively much more than what the low-income countries do. On the whole, the message which flows through from these figures is that India and Pakistan attach considerably more importance to defence than other countries which are at roughly the same level of development.

Table 6: *Worldwide Nuclear Stockpiles:*

Country	Total Nuclear Warheads
China	410
France	350
India	50-90
Israel	100
Pakistan	30-50
Russia	17,000
United Kingdom	185
United States	10,000

(Source: Carnegie Endowment for International Peace,
http:www.carnegieendowment.org/images/npp/nuke.jpg)

Table 7: *WMD Terrorism: Countries Suspected to Possess Chemical or Biological Weapons Capabilities*

Chemical Weapons	Biological Weapons
China	China
Egypt	Egypt
India	India
Iran	Israel
Israel	Libya
Libya	North Korea
North Korea	Pakistan
Pakistan	Russia
Sudan	Sudan
Syria	Syria
Taiwan	

(*Source*: Carnegie Endowment for International Peace, http://www.carnegieendowment.org/images/npp/nuke.jpg)

India and Pakistan's Nuclear Forces and Current Missile Capability:

It is difficult to determine the actual size and composition of nuclear arsenals of India and Pakistan, but NRDC (National Defence Resource Council) and Carnegie Endowment for International Peace estimate that both countries have a total of 80 to 140 weapons. India has about 50 to 90 nuclear warheads, higher than Pakistan, which may have as many as 50. (see, Table 6) While India is believed to possess both chemical and biological weapons, Pakistan has chemical weapons capability. (see, Table 7) Both countries have fission weapons, similar to the early designs developed by the United States in the late 1940s and early 1950s. NRDC estimates their explosive yields are 5 to 25 kilotons (1 kiloton is equivalent to 1,000 tons of TNT). By comparison, in 1945, the yield of the weapon the United States exploded over Hiroshima was 15 kilotons, while the bomb exploded over Nagasaki was 21 kilotons.

The United States and Russia maintain by far the largest nuclear arsenals, with Russia possessing 15,000 nuclear weapons and the United States 10,000 weapons. The French, British, and Chinese nuclear bombs number in the low hundreds. North Korea's arsenal is the smallest with fewer than 10 warheads.

Although the Israeli government is ambiguous whether it has nuclear weapons, independent observers estimate that the Israeli arsenal contains between 75-200 nuclear weapons. The sum of all the nuclear arsenals across the globe comes to about 26,000 warheads.

According to *Jane Intelligence Review*, Pakistan has completed development of a solid fuel missile that could strike key Indian cities from deep within Pakistan territory through Ghauri (series of liquid propelled missiles in an offensive operation) and Shaheen (series weapons as defensive measures). On May 24, 2002, (and again on April 6, 2007), Pakistan also tested Intermediate Range Ballistic Missile Hatf V (Ghauri) missiles that have a range of 1,500 kilometers (1,000 miles) and can hit most populous cities of Northern, Central and Western India. Pakistan on July 26, 2007, successfully test-fired the terrain-hugging Babur cruise missile, which is capable of carrying warheads and can hit targets within a range of 700 km, that includes many Indian cities. The Babur or Hatf missile can carry conventional as well as non-conventional nuclear warheads. The father of the Pakistan bomb, Dr. A. Q. Khan, in a declaration has asserted that Ghauri missiles could "wipe out thrice, all the big cities of India." On June 4, 2004, Pakistan also successfully re-tested Hatf-V and Ghauri-1. In addition, Pakistan is now equipped with ballistic missiles like: Abdali-1, Hatf-I, Ghaznavi (SRBM), Shaheen series of MRBM(750-2500 km) and Ghauri series of MRBMs and IRBMs ranging between 1,300 to 3,500 km. India , on the other hand, on June 13, 2004, has successfully test fired Brahmos, the supersonic cruise missiles that can travel at Mach 2.823 and which has been configured to be launched from either land, ship, sub-marine and aircraft using liquid ramjet technology. Furthermore, India has test fired Agni-III longest-range missile successfully on April 12, 2007, which can hit objects from a range of 3000 miles and thus the entire territorial space of Pakistan (in addition to those of China's mega metropolis of Beijing and Shanghai) can be within India's missile range. Agni-III's successful test is likely to put additional pressure on Pakistan's nuclear establishment as the former (India) can claim to have attained minimum credible deterrence and thus form crucial component of India's nuclear doctrine. In coming years, India may opt for nuclear armed submarines, armed with nuclear-tipped ballistic missiles, for assured and effective second-strike capabilities and nuclear-tipped land-attack cruise missiles (LACMs) to provide India a definitive strategic edge. In addition, India's Armed forces have formulated a joint war doctrine to ensure that individual combat capabilities of Army, Navy and Air Force can come together in the event of war. It remains to be seen whether and when Pakistan will match India's cruise missile and related capabilities so as not to provide its rival a strategic edge.[1]

Thinking the Unthinkable:

After India and Pakistan conducted nuclear tests in 1998, experts have debated whether their nuclear weapons contribute to 'ugly stability' in South Asia. Experts who argue that the nuclear standoff promotes stability have pointed to the U.S.-Soviet Union Cold War as an example of how deterrence ensures military restraint.

There are major differences between the Cold War and the current South Asian crisis. Unlike the U.S.-Soviet experience, India-Pakistan have a deep-rooted hatred and have fought three major wars and a limited war over Kargil (in 1999) since both countries became independent in 1947.

A second difference centres round the issue of nuclear arsenals. India and Pakistan's nuclear arsenals are much smaller than those of the United States and Russia. The U.S. and Russian arsenals truly represent the capability to destroy each other's territory beyond recovery. While the two South Asia countries have the potential to produce unimaginable loss of life and destruction, they do not reach the level of "mutual assured destruction" that stood as the ultimate deterrent between the United States and then Soviet Union during the Cold War.

The two South Asian rivals assume nuclear attacks against cities. During the early Cold War period this was the deterrent strategy of the United States and the Soviet Union. But as both countries introduced technological improvements into their arsenals, they pursued other strategies, targeting each other's nuclear forces, conventional military forces, industry and leadership. India and Pakistan may include these type of targets in their current military planning. For example, attacking large river dams with nuclear weapons could result in massive disruption, severe economic consequences and huge casualties. Concentrations of military forces and high profile facilities may provide tempting targets as well.

Global Solution: Status of Nuclear Non-Proliferation Regimes

India and NPT (Nuclear Non-Proliferation Treaty):

India's stand on nuclear proliferation and the decision to stay out of the NPT seemed, in part, to have been motivated by China's entry into the nuclear club in 1964 and the resulting security dilemma to its national interests. However, the official stand taken by India rested on the discriminatory features of the treaty. India considered the Nuclear Non-Proliferation Treaty (announced on 14 May 1968 and sponsored by the USA, the USSR, and the UK) as having serious loopholes. The then Indian ambassador to the United Nations, Azim Husain, made the following points:

a. The Treaty does not ensure the non-proliferation of nuclear weapons but only stopped the dissemination of weapons to non-nuclear weapon states without imposing any curbs on the continued manufacture, stockpiling and sophistication of nuclear weapons.

b. The Treaty does not do away with the special status of superiority conferred on those powers which possessed nuclear weapons.

c. The Treaty does not provide for a balance of obligations and responsibilities between the nuclear weapon states and non-nuclear weapon states. While all the obligations were imposed on non-nuclear weapon states, the nuclear weapon states had not accepted any obligation.

d. The Treaty does not constitute a step by step approach towards nuclear disarmament.

e. The Treaty does not prohibit one nuclear state from assisting another nuclear weapon state in providing technical aid.

f. The long period of a quarter of a century provided in Article X of the Treaty would appear to endorse and legitimise the present state of affairs and legalise, if not encourage, an unrestricted vertical proliferation by the existing nuclear weapon powers.

g. Article VI does not create a judicial obligation in regard to the cessation of the nuclear arms race at an early date.
h. The treaty imparted a false sense of security to the world.
i. It was discriminatory in regard to the peaceful benefits of nuclear explosion.
j. It was discriminatory in regard to the safeguards and controls which were all imposed on the non-nuclear weapon states while none whatsoever were imposed on the nuclear weapon states.
k. The security assurances to the non-nuclear weapon states could not be a quid pro quo for the acceptance of the treaty. This must be binding for the nuclear weapon states.[2]

Broadly speaking, India's opposition to the NPT could be found in four issues: (i) the balance of obligations; (ii) linkage between the Non-Proliferation Treaty and Disarmament; (iii) question of control and safeguards; and (iv) civilian benefits of nuclear technology.

(a) The Balance of Obligations:

India and other nuclear states have differed on the basic meaning of proliferation. To the nuclear weapon states, proliferation is one of horizontal growth that results in the increase of the number of states with nuclear-weapons. India, on the other hand, views proliferation issue as both vertically and horizontally.

According to India, the real problem of proliferation lies in the continuing quantitative and qualitative proliferation of nuclear weapons by the acknowledged and declared nuclear states. India strongly maintains that the root of global tension and insecurity was the possession of nuclear weapons and arsenals by the exclusive nuclear club (USA, Russia, UK, France and PRC). India argued that, in order to have an effective and comprehensive NPT, such weapons and their means of delivery must be eradicated, otherwise, the non-proliferation of these weapons cannot be accomplished.[3]

The discriminatory nature of the Non-Proliferation Treaty is inherent in the structure of the Treaty itself. Article IX (e) of the treaty defines a nuclear weapons state as one which has manufactured and exploded a nuclear weapon or other nuclear device prior to 1 January 1967.[4] India considered this arbitrary watershed of testing of nuclear weapons as an act of legitimisation of a few nations' nuclear monopoly so as to preempt any such move or intention by other states. India also objected to the first draft of the treaty because it excluded any mention of mutual obligations of nuclear weapons and non-nuclear weapon states. There was absolutely no provision in the treaty to dissuade the nuclear weapon states from acts of further proliferation. The control applied to the non-nuclear weapon states could very well be applied to the nuclear weapon states. That would have given a semblance of balance of obligations between these two categories of states. India was also critical of the treaty because of the possibility of technical assistance between nuclear weapon states. It is quite possible that the Indian policy makers were apprehensive of a likely Sino-American rapprochement or Sino-Soviet reconciliation.

(b) *Linkage between the Non-Proliferation Treaty and Disarmament:*

India voiced serious objections to the treaty because there was no linkage between the Non-Proliferation Treaty and disarmament. Article VI of the NPT did not provide any credible commitment by the nuclear weapon states. In addition to that, Article X of the treaty appeared to endorse and fully legalise the vertical proliferation by the nuclear weapon states. From India's standpoint, a real and credible security guarantee could only be provided through nuclear disarmament. New Delhi refused to sign the NPT as it perceived the security assurances of the NPT to be inadequate and insufficient.

(c) *Question of Control and Safeguards:*

The issue of control and safeguards are dealt within Article III of the draft treaty. The obligations to accept control and inspection or "safeguards" apply to non-nuclear weapon states. The nuclear weapon states are free from any sorts of obligations whatsoever.

India considered the NPT safeguard system as another symbol of discrimination between nuclear and non-nuclear weapon states. India insisted that the control and safeguard systems should be universal in nature and applicable to all states with respect to their earlier nuclear programmes (military and peaceful).

(d) Civilian Benefits of Nuclear Technology:

India also criticises the draft treaty because of its failure to provide the non-nuclear weapon states with the civilian benefits of nuclear technology on a non-discriminatory basis. Article V of the NPT says that the nuclear weapon countries should provide the non-nuclear weapon countries with access to nuclear explosive devices for peaceful applications. The same article also calls for the creation of an international body with adequate representation of non-nuclear weapon states for facilitating a special international regime. So far, the nuclear weapon states have not taken any positive steps to create such an international regime nor have they agreed to share the spin-off benefits of Peaceful Nuclear Explosions (PNEs). The NPT and IAEA have institutionalised PNEs and both the Soviet Union and the United States have been conducting PNE studies since the mid-fifties.[5] The United States initiated "Project Plowshare" in 1957 and conducted 41 nuclear explosions reportedly for peaceful purposes between 1961 and 1974.[6] India had clearly opposed the provisions regarding PNEs in the draft treaty. In a speech before the ENDC, India's representative, V.C.Trivedi, observed: "There is full justification for preventing the proliferation in weapons, but this is the first time it is suggested that there should be non-proliferation in science and technology."[7]

India proposed that the PNEs should be institutionalised under an international regime. It further stated that PNEs should be linked directly to the conclusion of a Comprehensive Test Ban Treaty.[8]

To summarise the main objections raised by India against the Non-Proliferation Treaty, the following points may be noted.

a. India considers the Non-Proliferation Treaty as discriminatory, making a clear distinction between the nuclear 'haves' and nuclear 'have-nots'. The treaty fails to provide the proportional obligations to the parties involved.

b. The Treaty prohibited Peaceful Nuclear Explosions (PNEs) which non-nuclear weapon states and in particular the developing nations require urgently for their economic and technological advancement.
c. The Treaty does not address the security problems of non-nuclear weapon states facing security threats from nuclear weapon states.
d. India strongly objects to the Treaty's inability to discourage vertical proliferation and the ongoing proliferation of weapons.
e. India, in particular, takes a serious view of Chinese non-participation in the treaty. The experience of the bitter border war of 1962 and the subsequent nuclear explosions by China in 1964 have compelled Indian policy makers to become more cautious. Since Beijing remained a non-signatory to the treaty, New Delhi used that as a sufficient rationale not to be a signatory to the treaty either.

Since India did not participated in the NPT Review and Extension Conference, the spotlight shifted to Comprehensive Test Ban Treaty (CTBT) negotiations that continued in earnest since 1994 when the Conference on Disarmament (CD) met in Geneva to spell out the various provisions and nuances.

The five declared nuclear weapon states along with the then three nuclear threshold states (Israel, India and Pakistan) participated in these deliberations. A number of other countries outside these groups also participated in the delibeartions. This meeting concluded in August 1996.

Rationale for India's opposition to CTBT

From India's point of view, it does not see any serious and sincere approaches being made by the nuclear weapon states toward genuine nuclear disarmament. On the other hand, there has been proliferation of nuclear weapons at various levels in an emasculated form and only some cosmetic efforts such as START (Strategic Arms Reduction Treaty) talks have been made to hide the huge arsenal of nuclear weapons which the nuclear weapon states are possessing. For Indian policy makers, asking her to sign CTBT and not making any real effort to eliminate the nuclear weapons will be construed as an act of double standards of the arms control negotiations. The Indian Minister for External Affairs made a major policy statement at the 50th session of the U.N. General Assembly in October 1995.

> "It can not be argued that the security of few countries depends on their having nuclear weapons, and that of the rest depends on their not—we note that Nuclear Weapon States have agreed to a CTBT only after acquiring the know-how to develop and refine their arsenals without the need for further tests. In our view, the CTBT must be an integral step in the process of nuclear disarmament. Developing new warheads or refining, exhibiting ones after a CTBT is in place, using innovative technologies, would be as contrary to the spirit of the CTBT as the NPT is to the spirit of non-proliferation. The CTBT must contain a binding commitment on the international community, especially the Nuclear Weapon States, to take further measures within an agreed time frame towards the creation of a nuclear weapon free world."[9]

India has also argued that CTBT only forbids atmospheric explosive testing, though it is silent on sub-critical (non-nuclear) experiments or computer simulations.. Moreover, the nuclear weapon states are not interested in sharing this technology with other nuclear threshold states. It is interesting to note the comments made in 1958 by the then French President Charles DeGaulle, representing a former non-Nuclear Weapon State , about the futility of a viable nuclear disarmament in the absence of reduction of stockpiles. DeGaulle said,

"We will continue to press the Russians, the Americans and the British to agree to halt production and to eliminate their stocks of nuclear weapons and to agree to effective international control. If this goal were attained, the famous question of nuclear tests would immediately disappear. If this were not to be, to those who continue to accumulate bombs, how would a halt of testing make any difference? Their power would not be diminished. It would be, on the contrary, a hoax on the poor world if these three states make the world believe that by suspending tests, we would be enhancing world security. It would, on the other hand, give them an alibi for not disarming."[10]

India would be placed at a disadvantage had it signed the CTBT in its original form. In a speech made before the U.N. First Committee on Disarmament, ex-Prime Minister Atal Behari Vajpayee called for a treaty to ban all types of nuclear weapon tests. Vajpayee added,

"As the PTBT (Partial Test Ban Treaty) drove testing underground, we do not wish the CTBT to drive testing into laboratories by those who have the resources to do so. We must ensure that the CTBT leaves no loophole for activity, either explosive-based or non-explosive based, aimed at the continued development and refinement of nuclear weapons—The situation would be untenable, where, even with a CTBT in place, development, refinement and production of new nuclear weapons continue."[11]

India has also objected to the CTBT's provisions regarding Entry Into Force (EIF). The EIF clause states that the sixty-one-nation CD had to come to a unanimous decision for the treaty to take effect. As stated by Inder K.Gujral on June 20, 1996, for the nuclear powers who proposed the EIF, the treaty would be meaningless without the participation of all the nuclear threshold states, one of which is India. The EIF clause envisioned a preliminary signing with an international conference coming in the year 2000 to ratify the treaty. India demurred, refusing to be held solely accountable for the treaty's failure, and fearing the possibility of international sanctions if it did not ratify. But the EIF debacle suggested that many nuclear powers, coerced into supporting the treaty by the United States, were trying to use India's rejection as an excuse to dismantle the treaty. "The sincerity of those who are pretending to be high priests of the test ban is questionable," stated Gujral. As the saying went at the CD, these countries were "hiding behind India's sari."[12]

India also asserted that, as a sovereign nation, it had every right to maintain its strategic flexibility. During the CTBT debate, Ambassador Prakash Shah, India's permanent representative to the United Nations stated that India "cannot permit our option to be constrained as long as countries around us continue their weapons programmes either openly or in a clandestine manner" and as long as "Nuclear Weapon States remain unwilling to accept the obligation to eliminate their nuclear arsenals."[13]

Since the time India gained independence in 1947, it has faced four major wars, three with Pakistan and one with China. Apart from that, India has had low intensity wars with the insurgent forces in Punjab, Kashmir and in the North-East who are directly being aided by its arch enemies, including its neighbors. From the Indian standpoint, Pakistan has embarked upon an active effort to acquire nuclear technology for their

Kahuta plant ever since India detonated a peaceful nuclear explosion in 1974. China has provided military aid to Pakistan on a regular basis and since the period of the Zia ul Haq regime in Pakistan in the 1980s, this has grown substantially. India views the ongoing military cooperation between China and Pakistan at the highest level to have only exacerbated the security environment in the Indian sub-continent. China, on its own, does have very sophisticated nuclear weapons with long range ICBM capabilities and with nuclear test explosions taking place on a regular basis. Only after making sure of its existing huge arsenals of nuclear weapons did China sign the CTBT and it is not under any pressure to curtail or dismantle its nuclear programme. CTBT has also not been ratified by the US Congress and the prospects of the Treaty going the way of the League of Nations Charter can not be ruled out.

There is also a political component as to why India opposed signing CTBT. In its election manifesto in 1998 and 1999, the BJP had made clear its stand on the nuclear bomb issue. For the BJP, in order for India's foreign policy agenda to be credible, it was not willing to project India as a nuclear apartheid nation and was actively opposed to imposition of a hegemonic nuclear regime. The pro-bomb lobby of the Sangh Parivar also felt that the Hindu majority of the country would be inclined to side with BJP's position as Pakistan, its arch enemy, was believed to have covert nuclear activities. That suspicion was later validated with the explosion of nuclear devices by Pakistan in May 1998. BJP also feels very strongly that it is not India's fault that there has been a slow progress on nuclear disarmament negotiations. In fact, Jaswant Singh, a BJP stalwart and ex-External affairs minister, said in a press statement that India had been a staunch advocate of global nuclear disarmament. It has participated actively in all such efforts, convinced that a world without nuclear weapons will enhance both national and global security. India was the first country to call for a ban on nuclear testing in 1954, for a non-discriminatory treaty on non-proliferation in 1965, for a treaty on non-use of nuclear weapons in 1978, for a nuclear freeze in 1982 and for a phased programme of complete elimination in 1988.[14] The Congress Party, particularly during the premiership of Rajiv Gandhi and P.V.Narasimbha Rao, on the other hand, had not spelled its nuclear policy clearly. The leaders of Congress Party had asserted the right to have the nuclear options open without advocating for a full fledged nuclear tests and nuclear weapons programme. It was only after India demonstrated its technological skill in detonating nuclear capabilities in the May 1998 blasts that the Indian National Congress Party, under its new president, Sonia Gandhi, reversed and argued for a tougher line on CTBT; it insisted on opposing it. With India's nuclear tests having earned popular mass appeal and with Congress and BJP in support of it, it is very unlikely that the CTBT in its present form and without sufficient carrots will be accepted by the present regime.

In the United States itself, there has been a growing support in favour of ratification of CTBT after the US Senate voted against it in October 1999.[15] However, the basic rationale for India not signing the CTBT is due to its discriminatory and parochial nature in its overt tilt towards those countries who were members of the nuclear club before NPT went into effect. It is noteworthy that Russia supports India's nuclear weapons as those are "based on its dire necessity to ensure national security and such weapons playing a positive role in ensuring peace and stability in South Asia."[16] Unless the situation at the international and regional level changes drastically, this may very well be India's position for the foreseeable future.

It will be counter-productive if the international community resorts to unilateralism such as the plans made by the current US president George W. Bush with the National Missile Defence program and selective morality on the part of the Big Five nuclear weapon states in maintaining the existing status quo of nuclear powers prior to India and Pakistan's explosion and not work towards a genuine nuclear arms control agreement. Although US and Russian leaders have shown willingness to drastically cut their nuclear arsenals to a historic 2,000 warheads, START-III is yet to pick up the right momentum. According to Ashley J. Tellis, a Rand corporation analyst, "Several critical impediments are still there in the arena of global nuclear reform, despite all the other beneficial developments that have occurred on the aftermath of the Cold War. For example, neither Russia nor the small nuclear powers, the United Kingdom and France, appear willing to contemplate reductions in nuclear capabilities as part of some larger process that will eventually culminate in nuclear abolition. Even US has demurred about carrying nuclear arms reduction to its logical terminus, preferring instead to pursue a "lead and hedge" policy well into the future."[17]

In this context, India's stand favouring a genuine nuclear reduction sounds credible and plausible. "Indian government called all nuclear weapon states to join with it in opening early negotiations for a nuclear weapons convention so that these weapons can be dealt with in a global, non-discriminatory framework as other weapons of mass destruction have been — dealt with in the past. While it appears self serving, coming as it did on the heels of the 1998 nuclear tests, it is certainly consistent with India's past proposals and represented a continuation of traditional Indian policy which has always held out the threat of overt nuclearisation so long as the global nuclear order remained unreformed."[18] Perhaps that day is not far off when all the nuclear weapon states can work together and make proactive effort for a genuine new world order based on a reasonable nuclear arms reduction package in commensurate with the defined national interests of individual nation states of the globe.

End Notes

[1] See, www.rediff.com, October 5, 2001, and July 26, 2007, also, see, *The Times of India*, New Delhi, November 10, 2003, also, See, *The Times of India*, New Delhi, April 13, 2007; also, see, http://www.thebulletin.org/minutes-to-midnight/nuclear.html)

[2] K. Subrahmanyam. *Nuclear Proliferation and International Security*, Lancer International, New Delhi, 1985, pp.1-3

[3] Mohammed B. Alam. *India's Nuclear Policy*, Mittal Publications ,New Delhi, 1988 ,pp.52-53; also, see, Alam, Mohammed B.(ed.), *Constructing Nuclear Strategic Discourse: The South Asian Scene*, New Delhi: India Research Press, 2007

[4] SIPRI, *The NPT: The Main Political Barrier in Nuclear Weapon Proliferation*, Tahler and Francis, London, 1980, pp 42-46

[5] T.T. Poulose. " The Third World Response to Anti-Nuclear Proliferation Strategy", *India Quarterly*, April-June 1978 , pp.145-67

[6] Mohammed B. Alam (ed.). *Essays on Nuclear Proliferation*, Vikas Publishing House, New Delhi, 1995

[7] Statement by V.C. Trivedi, in the first committee of the UN, 31 October 1966, UN Document, A/C, a/PV.1436, pp.22-27

[8] *Ibid*, pp.23-37

Globalised Trend Towards Nuclear Proliferation: A Case Study... 139

9. Statement by Mr.Pranab Mukherjee, Minister for External Affairs, U.N.General Assembly, 50th Session, New York, October 1995. See, *The Times of India*, New Delhi, 16 October 1995
10. Press Conference by Charles de Gaulle, Paris, 23 October 1958. See, *The Hindu*, Madras, 25 Ocotber 1958
11. Statement by Mr.Atal Behari Vajpayee, Member of Parliament and Leader of Opposition, and Chief Delegate to U.N. First Committee on Disarmament, New York, October 1995. See, *The Times of India*, New Delhi, 16 October 1995
12. Vikas, Kapur. "Nuclear Empowerment", *Harvard-Radcliffe Liberal Monthly*, Vol.1, Summer 1996.
13. Statement by Mr.Prakash Shah, 50th session of the U.N. General Assembly, *UN Chronicle*, New York, 9 September 1996, p.5. Also see, *The Hindustan Times*, New Delhi, 11 September 1996
14. Press Statement by Mr.Jaswant Singh, Deputy Chairman, Planning Commission, *The Times of India*, New Delhi, 18 May 1998)
15. *Indian Express*, New Delhi, March 26, 2001, p.4, available at http://www.expressindia.co
16. Samina Ahmed and David Cortright; *South Asia at the Nuclear Crossroads*, Working Paper, Joan B. Kroc Institute for International Peace Studies, University of Notre Dame, March 2001, p.6, also, see, David Baldwin; "The Power of Positive Sanctions", *World Politics*, Vol.24, October 1971, p.25
17. See, Ashley Tellis; Ibid, p.240, Also, see, Stuart Croft and Phil Williams, "The United Kingdom," and Klaus Schubert, "France," in Regina Cowen Karp (ed.) *Security with Nuclear Weapons?*, Oxford: UK, Oxford University Press, 1991, pp.145-188
18. John F. Burns; "India calls for talks on New Treaty limiting nuclear arms," *The New York Times*, June 1, 1998)

7

Conflict and Development in the Age of Globalisation: A Case of Rwanda

M. MUSLIM KHAN

The period of globalisation has been marked by inter and intra-state conflicts in various regions of the world. Among the examples of ethnic conflicts leading to failed states, Rwanda is a prime example. In developing countries, the major concerns are still nation-building and development – both of which are still problematic in Rwanda. This article speaks about international intervention, in intra-state conflicts and how even 'genocide' was clumsily handled by the UN in Rwanda. Further, suggestions have been given as to how the role of regional and international bodies, can be made more effective in handling conflict and developmental issues in the Third World.

The small African country of Rwanda was considered to be the Switzerland of Africa in the past till the 1980s due to adequate greenery, mild climate, average temperature and fast rate of economic development with millions of dollars of development aid coming to the country. This also provided a great boost to its agriculture. During its colonial period, Rwandan economy reflected a healthy state as can be referred in the writings of Aldolphus Frederick (1910) that 'milk and honey' flowed in Rwanda.[1] But Rwanda started facing economic crisis since the start of the 1990s when development aid stopped flowing into the country.

The Rwandan economy had become very weak due to ethnic conflict between Hutus and Tutsis and prolonged civil war. The reduction of international aid immediately allowed the conflict to worsen. Poverty, land scarcity, unemployment and population explosion in Rwanda surfaced in an explosive manner; partisan approach by rulers further intensified the process of ethnic conflict in Rwanda. The civil war turned into genocide of Tutsis in 1994 by the Hutu regime of Col. Bagosora and Hutu militia. This genocide regime was over thrown by RPF (Rwandan Patriotic Front) which was dominated by Tutsis. In the whole conflict there has been great loss of human lives and development. The conflict in Rwanda between Hutus and Tutsis has a long history and politics. The ethnification of Rwandan politics has resulted in ethnification of development. In such a scenario the ethnic group controlling political power controlled development process and most of the benefits were directed to the same ethnic group.

A. *Genesis of Ethnification of Politics and Development*

At the beginning of the colonial rule by Germans in 1890 the Tutsis formed just fifteen per cent of the population but they had established a centralised monarchy and an aristocratic feudal regime over the Hutu majority. The Tutsis belonged to the Nilotic-Hamitic race. They were tall, slim, with high forehead, narrow nose, long fingers and pale (fair) skin. They traced their tribal origin to civilisations of Abyssinia and Egypt, who migrated to Rwanda during the 14th or 15th century and gradually established their rule. The majority population was of Hutu who roughly constituted 85 per cent of the population. The Hutus were short, stockier, negroid in appearance with sturdy bones and broad structures.

Both Hutus and Tutsis spoke the same language, lived on the same hillsides and intermarried to such an extent that the ethnic distinctions between the two groups are often blurred and the specialists on the region consider these ethnic distinctions as artificial[2]. Most of the ethnic distinctions between Hutus and

Tutsis are inventions of German and Belgian colonial administration and the missionary churches. During the German colonial rule between 1890 and 1916, the racial and tribal differences between Tutsis and Hutus were fully exploited. German administrator Richard Kandt preferred Tutsis and regarded them more racially developed than Hutus to rule.[3] Rwanda was transferred to Belgium under the League of Nations mandate after the German defeat in the First World War. The colonial administration of Belgium also made full use of the traditional power structure and highlighted the racial and tribal differences of Hutus and Tutsis. As the colonial masters ruled from a distance, they established indirect rule. The Tutsi king and nobility were retained with a reduction of their formal power, but they were able to enhance their economic and social influence. More and more Tutsis were employed in local administration. In the fields of education, administration, trade, agriculture, land and livestock, Tutsis were preferred. Pierre Ryckmans Belgian Governor General of Congo and Rwanda-Urundi openly adopted the policy that Tutsis were a highly developed race and born to rule.[4]

The Christian missionaries' role in augmenting racial and tribal consciousness and antagonism in Rwanda is irreparable. The Belgian Catholic missionaries and the Catholic church under bishop Leon Classe was primarily interested in converting the Tutsi aristocracy and their king,[5] during the colonial rule. Their approach was that once the local king and nobles accept Christianity then it could easily spread to the rest of the people. They even removed Tutsi king Musinga who refused to accept Christianity and his baptised son Rudahingwa was enthroned in 1931 as king Murata III. The policy of giving importance and favour to Tutsis by colonial rulers and missionaries generated a strong class – culture (tribe) identity among Tutsis and a feeling that they were bound to rule over the majority Hutus. A sense of elitism developed among Tutsis and an inferiority complex developed among the Hutus in the beginning. The French missionaries were next sent to Rwanda. They had a relatively more charitable approach. They spread Christianity mostly among Hutu majority who were seen as poor and marginalised. This was a horizontal approach. But in their zeal to spread Christianity, the French missionaries held Tutsis responsible for the poverty and marginalisation of Hutus. Such a policy brought more antagonism between Hutus and Tutsis. The Belgian colonial administration's benefits to Tutsis at the same time, surcharged Hutu majority thinking against Tutsis and their feeling of being marginalised. After Second World War, the Hutus began to question Tutsi rule.[6]

B. *The Hutu Revolution of 1959*

The inferiority complex of Hutus turned into aggressive resentfulness after finding support of French missionaries and even French government. With this the antagonism was bound to be generated on at least two grounds one of which was class – culture ethnic identification. The poor Hutus against rich powerful ruling Tutsis was a powerful imagery. Another identification was that of Tutsis being exploiters and rulers who came from outside while Hutus being local but exploited and marginalised by Tutsis. Even the Hutu-Tutsi sharing a common history and territory forming a single nation speaking Bantu language and nearly 85 per cent Christians by religion (68 per cent catholics), and having numerous mixed marriages could not minimise their antagonism.

In 1959 the Hutus revolted against the Tutsi king and captured power. A large number of Tutsis were killed and nearly five lakh Tutsis fled from Rwanda to the neighbouring countries.[7] Out of this, 250000 Tutsis fled to neighbouring Uganda alone, while rest of them fled to Burundi, Tanzania and Zaire (Congo). Land and properties of Tutsis were occupied by Hutus. The Belgian colonial administration also accepted the wave of Hutus and subsequently gave approval to Hutu revolutionaries as new rulers. Under this changed situation Rwanda became independent and Rwanda – Urundi were separated as separate countries of Rwanda and Burundi. In the new situation elections were held under the supervision of United Nations in September 1961. Rwanda fell under the rule of Hutu dominated Hutu Emancipation Party which became victorious in election, while in Burundi, Tutsis gained majority and formed the government. But the irony of the fact was that despite the installation of a new government and adoption of an electoral system, the problem of half a million Tutsi population which had fled from the country remained unsolved. Even the United Nations which monitored the first general elections, did not pressurise the Hutu ruling elite at that time to work out plans for the return of exiled Tutsi refugees. Had this refugee problem been solved at that time the subsequent civil war and genocide of 1994 would not have occurred. The exiled Tutsis had to live as refugees and later on a civil war was started by them against the Hutu led ruling Rwandan regime.

C. Civil War and Killing by Govt. Forces

After Hutu revolution the Hutu elite which occupied power became dictatorial. Even the coming to power in 1962 as a result of democratic elections, the Hutu President Kayibanda (1962 – 1973) continued the previous Tutsi like centralised rule. The post independent Republican rule was hardly different than earlier Tutsi Monarchy except it was mainly Hutu rule. Moreover, next President Habyarimana (1973 – 1994) was also Hutu. Under his rule a system of worst form of personal power system developed.[8] Nepotism and corruption became very high. Though some Tutsis were included in the administration at this time, it was a kind of military dictatorship heavily depending on foreign financial aid and mostly Tutsis were marginalised. From 1985 onwards the economic growth had halted and the country became economically very weak.

In such a situation the Tutsi dominated rebel force of RPF from Rwandan refugees in Uganda had intensified civil war since October 1990. As over the years animosity between Hutus and Tutsis had been kept alive, the civil war further generated mutual fear and hate. The Hutu led Habyarimana regime and after his assassination on 6th April 1994, Col. Bagosora regime used Tutsi RPF fear by telling Hutus that if RPF captured political power in Rwanda, the Hutus would be massacred. The Hutu militia leaders widely used the fear of RPF to mobilise and incite the Hutus to kill Tutsis. President Habyarimana and his Hutu group widened divisions between Hutu and Tutsi by the end of 1992 through attacks, virulent propaganda and persistent political maneuvering. Habyarimana's supporters also killed Hutu opponents who were the principal political challengers. The Radio Television Libre des Mille Collines (RTLM) and the movement called Hutu Power were widely used by Habyarimana regime for propaganda and to counter RPF leaders. When the Rwandan government began massacring Tutsis in 1990, crimes were solidly documented by local and international human rights groups and by a special rapporteur for the United Nations Commission on Human Rights. Some donors protested this massacre. Belgian government even recalled its Ambassador briefly but none of the donors openly challenged Habyarimana's regime. The Hutu group in power in Rwanda along with President Habyarimana directed massacre of hundreds of Tutsis in mid October 1990 and in five other episodes before the 1994 genocide.[9] By early 1992, Habyarimana had begun providing military training to the youth of his party, who were transformed into militia known as INTERAHAMWE. After President Habyarimana's assassination the Presidential Guards and other troops commanded by Colonel Bagosora, backed by militia, murdered Hutu government officials and leaders of the political opposition, creating a vacuum in which Bagosora and his supporters could take control. The soldiers and militia began systematically slaughtering Tutsis[10].

On the other hand Rwandan army, the RPF rebel attack kept on increasing day by day. The RPF had established a strong military force of over 19000 soldiers. The RPF had strengthened its position by secretly bringing arms and several hundred troops into Rwanda. The movement which began throughout Rwanda had also grown politically in the capital Kigali. The peace agreement (Arusha Accords) had assured power sharing to RPF in the Rwandan government. The Human Rights Watch Report in 1993 pointed out that supporters previously reluctant to declare their loyalties now acknowledged that they were RPF members.

The RPF had some 600 cells throughout the country by early April 1994.[11] Out of them 147 were in the capital Kigali alone. According to an estimate of Human Rights Watch Report, a total between 3600 to 7200 persons had openly or privately declared their support for RPF.[12] It also made efforts to form joint militia with Rwandan MDR and PSD to counter possible attack. The killing of Rwandan President Habyarimana by shooting down his plane on 6th April 1994 was blamed on this RPF militia men. Even the Hutu politicians opposed to Habyarimana and the circle of his own Hutu supporters and military might have wanted Habyarimana dead and could have found means to bring down his plane. The reason behind this stand was that the President was coming back after attending a meeting of heads of state where he had supposedly finally consented to put in place the broad-based transitional government by accommodating a sizeable number of RPF men in it. While the RPF might have launched the missile either because they believed that Habyarimana would never permit the accord to be implemented or, conversely, because they thought he was about to do so and they preferred a clear military victory to sharing of power as part of coalition.

Inside Rwanda, the killing of President Habyarimana was made the pretext to attack the Tutsis by Hutu Military and militia, which turned into a genocide (1994). On the other hand, the RPF troops began their attack from north side of the border and marched towards south. The RPF ultimately captured political power in Rwanda by emerging victorious on 18th July 1994. Though RPF was Tutsi dominated, it had tried to have Tutsi – Hutu cohesion within its organisation, as in 1994 Paul Kagame the chief general was a Tutsi while Kanyarengwe, a Hutu was its President. The Tutsi – Hutu cohesion gave added advantage to RPF in extending its influence inside Rwanda during the civil war. The Hutus with RPF could move and carry out their mission easily within Rwanda without attracting much suspicion of the Hutu regime. The strategy proved beneficial for the RPF. The victory of RPF stopped Tutsi's genocide by Hutus, but the war brought great destruction.

D. *Genocide of 1994*

During the genocide from 6th April to 18th July 1994 which was nearly three and a half months, eight lakh people were killed in Rwanda as per the United Nations report. Out of this the number of children who were killed was 3,00,000. This genocide was mainly directed against minority Tutsis. But the Hutu extremist militia and the Hutu government agencies as well as their mobilised and motivated supporters who were involved in killing Tutsis also targeted and killed moderate Hutus who either opposed the policies of the killer government or sympathised with the Tutsis. According to Prof. Gerard Prunier, an United Nations expert who evaluated population loss in Rwanda, about 5,07,000 Tutsis were killed out of 6,57,000 and rest of them mostly fled from the country.[13] Demographer Willam Seltzer estimated the annihilation of about 77 per cent of the population registered as Tutsi.[14] However, now it is a widely accepted fact that 75 per cent of the Tutsi population was killed in 1994.

The civil war and genocide had a great impact on development. Apart from the huge loss of human lives there was a total collapse of the country's economy. Innumerable houses, agricultural fields and markets were destroyed or burnt. Rwanda depended heavily on foreign financial support in 1994 and also in preceding several years. The donor nations and the World Bank had withheld aid or threatened to do so to pressurise the Rwandan government at several critical moments, including when it balked at signing the Arusha Peace Treaty (1993) during pre-genocide President Habyarimana's rule. However, during the April - July 1994 genocide, the world community failed to react on time to condemn and issue explicit warnings that they would never fund a genocide interim government led by Col. Bogosora after the assassination of President Habyarimana. Perhaps such an act by the world community and especially by the World Bank would have proved effective in making genocide less sanguine. The interim genocidal government of Bagosora survived for a brief period of three and half months and it was overthrown by the Rwandan Patriotic Front (RPF) militia in a war later.

By that time severe damage to the economy had already been done by groups engaged in genocide. Large number of Tutsis fled to neighbouring countries and had become refugees. The RPF waged a war from outside and halted the genocide but in the process the RPF itself killed large numbers of people. Seth Sendashonga, former minister of interior and early member of RPF, estimated that the RPF killed some 60,000 people between April 1994 and August 1995 . The troops of RPF, dominated by Tutsis, committed grave violations of international humanitarian law by attacking and killing unarmed civilians. The soldiers of RPF killed political and military leaders of past government and persons close to Habyarimana. Even their women and children were not spared.

E. Refugee Problem

Fearing persecution by RPF in 1994 after the genocide, the three million Hutus fled to neighbouring countries, mostly in Zaire. This included large number of perpetrators of the genocide, who turned themselves into a rebel force. They are frequently attacking Rwanda from outside and menacing its borders. Civil war is still continuing. The ruling RPF government which is projecting an image of Tutsi – Hutu cohesion within RPF, has been asking the Hutu refugees to return back to Rwanda, but only a few have come back. The Rwandan president Paul Kagame has reiterated his comeback offer to the Hutu refugees in 2006 also, however, their response is not encouraging. If the vast number of Hutu refugees do not return back to Rwanda to get rehabilitated, another genocide is not far away.

F. Problems of Development

Rwanda has a predominantly agricultural economy. As it has been said earlier, in the post-colonial years till the 1980s the rate of development was fast with millions of dollars of development aid coming to Rwanda, among which the French aid was of a very large size. This foreign development aid provided a boost to its agriculture. Contrary to this, the population of the country was increasing very fast which ultimately lead to population explosion. The three million population in 1960 became 7.5 million in 1993. According to Hartmut Diessenbacher Rwanda had an average of ten pregnancies and 8.3 live births per woman of child–bearing age. Even President Habyarimana, who ruled from 1973 to 1994, was himself a father of eight children. Diessenbacher used this population explosion to explain genocide in Rwanda– that how the population growth and a shortage of land helped to bring about the massacre and civil war.[15] On the other hand the economy and agricultural land were largely dominated by Hutus after the 1959 revolution, as there was exodus of 5 million Tutsis in to neighbouring countries whose sufferings were innumerable. Those Tutsis who remained in Rwanda were marginalised from economic and political power. The population explosion in Rwanda, led to scarcity of land resources, food and jobs. Such scarcity was witnessed among

Conflict and Development in the Age of Globalisation: A Case... 149

both Hutus and Tutsis. Kapuscinski described in 1994 that 'the farmers are fighting a bitter battle for land against each other and this results in hate, envy, animosity'.[16] The land and job scarcity in a condition of socio-economic and political inequality on ethnic lines gave a boost to ethnic conflict.

On the one hand, the corrupt ruling class and administrators of Rwanda were more bothered about their personal gain. They were habituated of making calculated use of Ethnic divisions between Hutus and Tutsis. On the other hand, efforts to make agriculture more productive were not able to increase production to the level to cope with rising population. There was heavy soil erosion due to volcanic base and rain. Due to rain nearly 40 kilograms of Nitrogen are leached out per hectre every year in Rwanda.[17] The earth erosion is 26 tones per hectre every year. This resulted in reduction of land available for cultivation in already over-populated Rwanda. The country having surplus food production earlier started importing food by 1994. The production of export oriented cash crops like Coffee, Tea and Tobacco fell sharply. The export revenues from mineral resources like Tin and some other items were not sufficient to make up and supplement the foreign reserve required for import including food import. The potential tourism sector could hardly be boosted because of conflict. Rwanda has the lowest urbanisation rate in Africa.[18] Thus a small labour class could be employed or engaged in urban areas. Hundreds of thousands were seeking work and bread, a future, a better life, in their own country, but unable to find it.[19] This dissatisfied unemployed youth were lured by ethnic militia.

In 1990s, when foreign development aid reduced drastically the conflict in Rwanda grew enormously. A fanatic and militant approach was adopted to control what ever gain, benefits or resources were available. Hutu militia and promoters of genocide (April 1994 to July 1994) adopted this approach and targeted Tutsis. Tutsis were killed and their houses and properties were occupied by Hutu organisers of genocide. After the victory of RPF over Hutu Military and militia in July 1994 the returning Tutsi exiles captured the deserted Hutu houses and properties. Many Hutu perpetrators were killed and other Hutus mostly fled to the neighbouring country of Zaire (Congo) and Tanzania fearing persecution.

This reflects a unique development phenomena based on class–culture–power linkage. The ethnic group controlling power controls resources and becomes a class. In armed conflict the young men, unemployed and poor members of ethnic group find opportunities to gain money, properties, position and political and military career. The rich and powerful members of the ethnic group exploit and use them for the gain of power and property. This reflects a worst kind of blending between anarchy and tyranny in Rwanda; tyranny surviving in anarchy and anarchy created by tyranny. There is also the lack of legal accountability for any ruler or militia leader for the crimes they commit.

G. Regional Impact and Role of Neighbours

There has been frequent Hutu–Tutsi killing in the region which has its contagious effect on Rwanda due to the presence of same ethnic groups in several countries. In Burundi nearly ten thousand Burundian Hutus were killed by a Tutsi dominated army in 1965. The Tutsis are in majority in Burundi while the Hutus form minority in contrast to Rwanda where Hutus were in majority till 15 July 1994 and Tutsis formed small minority. In 1972 more than 1,00,000 Burundian Hutus were killed in Burundi. The year 1988 saw the killing of 20,000 Burundian Hutus by the Tutsi dominated army of Burundi. In 1991 three thousand Hutus were killed in Burundi again by the army. The year 1993 witnessed the killing of 50,000 Burundian Hutus and Tutsis after a failed Tutsi led coup. Thereafter, 150000 Hutus and Tutsis have died in Burundi's continuing bloodshed.[20] Such incidents kept the animosity among the Hutus and Tutsis intact in the region. Its worst impact was visible in Rwanda, the immediate neighbour. The Tutsis led civil war against the Hutu rule in Rwanda since 1990 with the help of Uganda. The Hutu dominated army of Rwanda resorted to killing Tutsi minority many a times. Its worst impact was seen in the 1994 genocide in Rwanda in which 8,00,000 Tutsis and moderate Hutus were killed by Hutu militia and government agencies after the assassination of Hutu President Habyarimana. Uganda was an active participant in civil war from the side of Tutsi rebels (RPF) by all means including arms and shelters. In addition to the huge loss of human lives and properties, the conflict at regional level developed animosity among countries and worstly affected inter–country trade and economic cooperation. The inter–country borders became war zones, affected by rebels and marauding gangs unsafe for trade, transport and tourism.

H. French Neo-colonialism and Development Aid

After the 1959 Hutu revolution and capturing of power by Hutu majority, France supported the Hutu ruling regime and provided millions of dollars as development aid. But Rwandan military regime used most part of the development aid for buying arms, military training and supporting government expenditure. France had military agreement since 1975 with President Habyarimana's regime. The French neo-colonialism was directed at maintaining *status-quo* in Rwanda under the Hutu rule. More than this, France became an active participant in the civil war between Hutu government and Tutsi rebels from 1990 to July 1994. France was providing arms, ammunition, and training to armed forces of Hutu regime against Tutsi rebels of Rwanda Patriotic Front (RPF) operating from Uganda . During the killing of Tutsis by Habyarimana regime and genocide by Hutu regime of Col. Bagosora and militia, France continued its support to the killer regime by weapons, training and financial aid. Bill Berkeley has mentioned that the Rwanda's Hutu elite had established a clear example of the ' state as a racketeering enterprise'.[21] President Habyarimana who governed Rwanda for twenty three years on the model of his mentor Mobutu Sese Seko of Zaire, was amply funded and armed by the French. President Habyarimana ran lucrative rackets in everything from development aid to marijuana smuggling, poaching of gorillas, selling skulls and feet of primates.[22] Even the French peace keeping force was reported to be engaged more in training the Hutu military than doing peace keeping work. France did nothing to prevent the civil war and genocide. An adviser to the French President Francois Mitterrand gave a confused picture by saying that brutal slaughter was an usual practice among Africans and could not be easily eradicated.[23]

When Tutsi dominated RPF captured Rwanda in July 1994 after a war from outside and its Tutsi leader Paul Kagame formed the government, France changed the 'horse' and started supporting Paul Kagame's government. The French support still continues. This shows that France has been more bothered of its neo–colonial interest than the lives of human beings. It could even go to the extent of actively helping a genocide regime for its neo–colonial interests. Neo–colonialism is not better than colonialism for Rwanda.

I. Role of United Nations, Belgium, UK and USA

The United Nations and the United States of America played ambiguous roles with regard to the conflict and development in Rwanda. The United Nations deployed its Peace Keeping Force in Rwanda in 1992 when conflict had become vigorous between the Hutu military of Habyarimana and Tutsi dominated RPF. The peace keeping troops had been contributed by France, Canada and Belgium. But the UN staff in Rwanda failed to prevent frequent killings and genocide of 1994. They even failed to mobilise Security Council to intervene at appropriate time during 1994 genocide when 8 lakh people were killed in Rwanda by Hutu regime's army and militia. The Government of Belgium withdrew its troops when its ten soldiers were killed during the genocide. Before this, the Government of Belgium refused to contribute the requested 800 soldiers and agreed to send only half that number saying that it was a poor country and could not afford the cost. Human Rights Watch Report has pointed out that the troops from other countries that were less well trained and less well-armed filled the remaining places, producing a force that was weaker than it would have been with a full Belgian batallion.[24]

In January-February 1994, when preparations were intensified for further conflict which led to genocide, General Romeo Dallaire the Commander of UN Peacekeeping Force as well as the Government of Belgium asked for a stronger mandate from the Security Council to control the deteriorating situation in Rwanda . But they were rebuffed by the United States of America and the United Kingdom, which refused to support any measure that might add to the cost of the operation.[25] When the genocide began in Rwanda, the U.S. government took seven weeks to lease armoured personnel carriers for Rwanda required by the

Peace Keeping Force. The United States was more bothered about who will pay for it and what would be the colour of the vehicles.

When in 1994 the killing began in Rwanda, the UN Secretary General's special representative, Roger Booh – Booh minimised both the extent and the organised nature of the slayings. Even when the genocide was in full swing, the UN Security Council instead of providing full mandate came out with small changes in the role of troop deployment The United Kingdom provided only fifty trucks. The United Nations took the conflict and killings in Rwanda a little seriously only when in late April 1994 the representatives of the Czech Republic, Spain, New Zealand and Argentina sought more information beyond what was provided by the Secretariat of the UN. The UN Security Council, however, avoided to use the term Genocide for the Rwandan killing . It preferred the term civil war and refused to intervene vigorously,[26] as after accepting genocide the UN would be obliged to intervene according to the Genocide Convention of 1948 . The civil war fell under a domestic issue where the UN should refrain from intervening. Ironically, the United States of America had specially instructed its Ambassador to the UN to make sure that the word Genocide was not included in the Security Council resolution.[27]

J. Hope for the future

Had there been timely and proper intervention by the United Nations, the huge loss of human lives and destruction of properties could have been saved in 1994. Thus there is a need of proper and timely UN initiatives in such cases of conflicts. Fearing persecution by Tutsi dominated RPF, three million Hutus who fled into neighbouring countries are still remaining there as refugees. This has generated a huge refugee problem in the region. The present ruling government of Paul Kagame, which is Tutsi dominated but presenting a cohesive approach, has asked Hutu refugees to return back to Rwanda. But only a few Hutu refugees have dared to come back. The huge refugee problem is one of the biggest hindrances to development in the region. Many Hutu refugees are now engaged in civil war against the present Tutsi dominated regime of Rwanda. Unless the vast number of Hutu refugees return to Rwanda and get rehabilitated, the conflict will never be over. The neo-colonial power in France is more bothered in safeguarding its interests rather than looking forward for the real development of Rwanda or resolution of conflict. The ambiguous approach of some big powers like the United States of America will also not bring conflict resolution. The international community and the United Nations continue to remain insensitive. As the cases of conflicts and civil wars are frequent and numerous in Africa – for example the Sudan, Zaire, Burundi, Somalia, Ivory Coast, Liberia etc., and outside Africa in Iraq, Israel, Chechnya etc. the United Nations must arrange a standby well equipped Peace Keeping Force with quick response capabilities. The United Nations should feel responsible. As the Security Council is dominated by few, the UN actions will keep on reflecting their interest.

The reforms in the United Nations and democratisation of the Security Council are the need of the hour to make the organisation responsive and responsible. On the other hand, the international community has to think whether it should respect and tolerate a responsible government and responsible sovereignty or an irresponsible government and irresponsible sovereignty and refrain from intervening in cases of state organised killings. In Rwanda, as well as in many other countries of Africa, the lack of proper democratic institutionalisation is one of the reasons for ethnic dissatisfaction and conflicts. The UN should exert pressure on such states for proper democratic institutionalisation. The development issues and food scarcity issues must be handled immediately and properly, both by the United Nations and the African Union. The African Union needs to adopt a regional and a local approach to handle such mass conflicts and civil wars as well as the development issues. On the pattern of the United Nations, if the African Union arranges a local (African) Peace Keeping Force, it can be very 'effective and responsive in such conflicts.

References

1. Adolphus Frederick (Duke of Mecklenburg), *In the Heart of Africa*, Cassel/ London, 1990.
2. Hildegard Schurings, ' Ethnien haben ihre Geschichte', in Schurings (ed.), *Ein Volk verlasst sein Land – Krieg und Volkermord in Ruandu Cologne*, 1994.

Conflict and Development in the Age of Globalisation: A Case... 155

3. Pierre Ryckmans, *La Politique Coloniale*, Rex, Louvain, 1934.
4. Pierre Ryckmans, *Dominer pour Servir*, Brussels, 1948.
5. Ian Linden and Jane Linden, *Church and Revolution in Rwanda*, Manchester Univ. Press, New York, 1977.
6. Rene Lemarchand, *Rwanda and Burundi*, Pall Mall Press, London, 1970.
7. David Van Biema, 'Exodus from Rwanda', *Time*, July 25, 16,1994.
8. Peter Molt, 'Ein Product der Kolonialherrschaft', *Frankfurter Rundschau*, vom 20, Juni 1994.
9. *HRW Report – Leave None to Tell the Story: Genocide in Rwanda*, March 1999, 'Genocide',p.1of 8.
10. *Ibid*, p.3 of 8
11. *HRW Report* ... 'April 1994: Month that would not end', p. 1 of 20.
12. *Ibid*.
13. *Human Rights Watch Report – Leave None to Tell the Story: Genocide in Rwanda*, March 1999, 'Numbers', p.1 of 2.
14. *Ibid*.
15. Hartmut Diessenbacher, 'Explaining the Genocide in Rwanda', *Law and State*, Vol. 52, 1955, pp. 58-88. (Institute for Scientific Co-operation, Tubingen, Federal Republic of Germany).
16. Ryszard Kapuscinski, 'Massaker im Paradies. Aus einem Gesprach zum Fall Ruanda: Diktatur gegen Demokratie, Kein Stammeskrieg' in *Lettre Internationale*, Heft 26, III Vj, 1994 a.
17. E. Smaling, 'Two Scenarios for the Sub-Sahara', in *Ceres*, 126, Nov. 1990.
18. Hartmut Diessenbacher, *op.cit.*, p.81.
19. *Ibid*.
20. M. Muslim Khan, 'Politics of Genocide in Rwanda 1994', in *Indian Journal of Politics*, Vol. XXXIX, No.3, July-September 2005, p.134.
21. Bill Berkeley, 'Road to a Genocide', *Dissent*, Winter 2002, p.72.
22. *Ibid*. p.73.
23. *HRW Report – Leave None* ... 'International Responsibility', p. 3 of 8.
24. *Ibid*. p. 2 of 8.
25. *Ibid*.
26. 'United Nations Peacekeeping', *The Economist*, 25 June 1994.
27. Hartmut Dissenbacher, *op.cit*, p.68.

8

Impact of Globalisation on the GCC States: Cultural Dimension

FARAH NAAZ

The all pervasive phenomenon of globalisation has generated a lot of debate regarding its impact. The various dimensions of globlisation; economic, political, ideological and cultural, has affected the third world countries in varied proportions. The Middle East and North Africa region is one of the least globalised regions of the world but in the GCC states, globalisation is taking place at a rapid speed. However, despite being an active participant in the process of globalisation they have strong reservations to some of its aspects because of its cultural implications. The main reason behind this is, the ideas, institutions and attitudes which are spread by globalisation originated in one part of the world and are mostly western in origin. The major problem faced by these countries is how to protect their national identity and culture in the face of globalisation. While on the one hand they have adjusted to globalisation, they have also become very cautious to protect their cultural identity. Under the circumstances, harmonisation of economic and cultural diversities seems to be the best alternative for the GCC states. Society's traditional ways can be blended with foreign ideas without affecting the traditional roots.

The phenomenon of globalisation has been all pervasive and is felt even in the remotest corner of the world. The term globalisation has been used to describe a process, a condition, a system, a force and an age. It has generated a lot of debate and has resulted in controversies regarding its impact. There have already been varied groups of scholars defending or rejecting globalisation. Globalisation has been understood as "a multidimensional set of social processes that create, multiply, stretch and intensify worldwide social interdependencies and exchanges while at the same time fostering in people a growing awareness of deepening connections between the local and the distant."[1] This definition reflects at some of its characteristics. It involves the multiplication of existing social networks and activities that overcome traditional, economic, political, cultural boundaries. It intensifies worldwide social relations, interdependence and links distant localities. Financial markets extend around the globe, offering the consumers commodities from various parts of the world. The use of internet and satellites make possible distant information for the consumers with real time pictures of remote events. All this has resulted in the global affecting the local and the local affecting the global. People are developing a keen sense of becoming a part of the whole, which gradually change people's individual and collective identities and impact the way they act in the world.[2]

As it operates simultaneously and unevenly on several levels it is able to create several dimensions, the major dimensions being economic, political, ideological and cultural.

Economic dimension of globalisation refers to the intensification and expansion of economic interrelations across the globe. As a result, trade has been stimulated and markets have expanded thus, creating new linkages among national economies. Transnational corporations, powerful international economic institutions and large regional trading systems are shaping the global economic order. Political globalisation refers to the intensification and expansion of political interrelations across the globe. Contemporary manifestations of globalisation have led to the partial penetration of old territorial borders and softening cultural lines of demarcation. It is most visible in the rise of supra-territorial institutions and associations held together by common norms and interests. It (political globalisation) is also indicated by the considerable uniformity amongst the states in terms of their goals, structures, and programs. Almost all states assume responsibilities for a wide range of activities, including education, healthcare, economy etc. Globalisation contains an ideological dimension also as shown by the range of norms, claims, beliefs and narratives about the phenomenon. The debate whether globalisation represents good or the bad occurs in the arena of ideology.[3]

Cultural dimension of globalisation refers to intensification and expansion of cultural flows across the globe. It involves the movement of ideas, information, images and people. According to Berger, in cultural dimension of the phenomenon, culture is understood in "conventional, social, scientific sense as the beliefs, values and lifestyles of ordinary people, in their everyday existence."[4] From anthropological context, culture is more indigenous. The main ingredients are probably language, history, religion, customs, artifacts, cooking, values, traditions and also dependent upon man's capacity for learning and transmitting knowledge to succeeding generations.[5]

An emergence of global culture is evident, which is heavily American in origin. Language is a crucial factor in this cultural diffusion. English language in its American form rather than British is the koine of this culture. Millions of people all over the world use English language for practical reasons. "Each language carries with it a cultural freight of cognitive, normative and even emotional connotations. So does the American language, even apart from the beliefs and values propagated through the American mass communication media."[6] The emerging global culture is diffused through both elite and popular vehicle. The most important elite vehicle is the international culture of business and political leaders. Its basic engine is international business which also drives economic and technical globalisation. Another elite sector of the emerging global culture is the globalisation of the western intelligentsia carried by academic networks and governmental and non-governmental agencies. By far the most important manifestation of the emerging global culture is the vehicle of popular culture. It is propagated by business enterprises of all sorts such as, Adidas, McDonalds, Disney, MTV, and so on. Popular culture penetrates broad masses of people all over the world.[7] With the help of technology and communication this culture is transcending borders easily and reaching all countries without any distinction. "It is a fact that the United States dominates the global traffic in information and ideas and as statistics show: 75 per cent of the prepackaged software; 60 per cent of pre recorded music; 32 per cent of books come from America not to say how American way of life is becoming the mode."[8]

Most scholars hold that a sort of homogenised popular culture is developing in the world, which is dominated by the western culture. There have been serious attempts by some countries to resist these forces of globlisation, as they feel that it is affecting their cultures in a negative way. Other scholars argue that despite all this, cultural diversity is going to remain and would not be affected by the homogenising tendencies. For example, according to sociologist Roland Roberson, global cultural flows often reinvigorate local cultural niches. He also speaks of glocalisation – a complex interaction of the global and the local characterised by cultural borrowing, which would result in the process of hybridisation and are most visible in fashion, music, dance, film, food and language.[9]

Impact on the Gulf Cooperation Council states (Saudi Arabia, Kuwait, UAE, Oman, Bahrain and Qatar)

Globalisation is largely viewed in economic terms in West. It is seen as an integration of markets, the free movement of goods, services and labour across borders. However, in the third world countries, particularly in the Middle East and North Africa (MENA) region, globalisation has often been discussed in largely ideological terms. It has been promoted by a few, but more often attacked as a new version of imperialism. Critics regard it as a threat to their political, economic and cultural independence.[10] However, the case in the Gulf particularly the GCC (Gulf Cooperation Council) states is different. "The MENA region as a whole remains one of the least globalised regions in the world. The exception is the Gulf states, where globalisation is proceeding at a break neck speed. No part of the world has come into the global market more rapidly and with more change in material abundance than the oil states along the Arabian Gulf. Within two generations, the peoples of Saudi Arabia, Kuwait, Bahrain,

Qatar, the United Arab Emirates, and Oman have turned small desert towns and seaports into urbanised states. The now overwhelmingly ultramodern Gulf societies have grown expotentially."[11]

Because of globalisation, modernisation is also taking place at a rapid speed in the GCC states that have benefited greatly in communications, transport, information technology and health care. They have adopted modern economic and financial norms and have been able to built most modern social and economic infrastructure.

The social life has been greatly affected by globalisation. There is tremendous growth in population owing to the advent of modern medicines and healthcare facilities. "By way of comparison, the rate of population growth (excluding expatriates) in all six GCC states was estimated to be collectively about 4.5 per cent between 1985 and 1995 for a total of 17.5 m people."[12] There is tremendous growth in population in metropolitan areas and increasing urbanisation and distinct improvement in literacy rate, food, water supplies and health of the people. Nomadic communities have become settled and have access to all the amenities of urbanities. Many members of the younger generation are getting educated outside their native countries, like UK or US and bring back to the Gulf their technical skills, knowledge of business practices and exposure to foreign cultures. Transportation has become modern and efficient. Advanced technology is imported and applied in industry and households. Technology has also increased entertainment and exposure to the world. The trend towards nuclear families is also increasing. Access to information has increased. The younger generation understands the future business trends of the Gulf and they are also becoming a part of the decision making.[13]

In the GCC states as else where the family businesses are also being affected. In this a family monopolises a business and obviously the income. The main concern of these families is that the coming generation grow up to be responsible and become good managers. The GCC states have a highly traditional culture where the patriarchs of the family regulated the life and the younger generation is discouraged from taking a different stand. Business elders are aging without turning over the reins to the younger next generation diminishing initiative and

Impact of Globalisation on the GCC States: Cultural Dimension 161

entrepreneurship. Now with increasing liberalisation of Gulf economies, there are some fundamental changes in their economies. The governments of this region are encouraging privatisation in their economies. As a result, family companies have to face competition from other companies and require better performance. In order to encourage the younger generation they very often send them abroad to gain technical and managerial skills.[14]

Another aspect related to the above is that a huge expatriate workforce manages family companies. In this the family controls all leadership positions as well as decision making while give management positions to talented people even if they are outsiders. In the coming years, the non-family managers are expected to play a greater role and have to be made an important part in the decision making process. They also have to encourage entrepreneurship in the coming generation in order to adapt to their environment.[15]

The Gulf Cooperation Council members have made big strides in the field of education since the eighties of the last century. There has been an increase of 28.8 per cent in the number of pupils at various levels of education. All states give priority to the development of educational curricula because of the role of education in developing the human resources which constitute the cornerstone of state advancement. However, there has also been a call for maintaining the independence of educational institutions while preserving the Arab and Islamic identity.[16]

All countries of the Gulf are interested in reforming their educational system. The options before the governments have been, to follow the inherited colonial model or opt for the nearest cultural influence or built an indigenous framework. However, there is constant tension between acceptance and resistance of the imperial models as well as between higher education and sense of national identity. The need has increased for more pragmatic approaches to higher education- training provision. Although there is the presence of a large number of federal institutions that cater to a vast majority of the nation's students, there are also many private and semi-private institutions in areas that qualify them for work in the global economy. Some of them are Ajman college of Science and Technology, American university of Sharjah, Dubai Politechnic etc. Some higher colleges are developing affiliation with overseas institutions like universities in UK, Canada, France, North America. For example, the American University of Sharjah has affiliation with the American university of Washington.[17]

The GCC states have strong reservations to some aspects of globalisation because of its cultural implications. The basic elements of globalisation are seen as hostile. The main reason for this is that, the ideas, customs, institutions and attitudes which are spread by globalisation have originated in one part of the world and are mostly western in origin. Regions which are open to globalisation and westernisation, already have considerable western components in them, like North and South America, Europe and Africa and even Asia. This is not the case with the GCC states.[18] Much of globalisation is related to modernisation that challenge traditional society. As Gulf society is very traditional, they see globalisation as a major threat to their traditions.

Globalisation has different impact on different religions. In the case of GCC states, religion constitutes an important part of their culture. And as they do not want to compromise on this front, they are all the more cautious about globalisation. Globalisation affects two major trends of religions – number of followers and intensity in belief. A religion does not loose its relevance due to temporal changes. The major religions in the world have existed for more than 1000 years and have displayed great capacity to adapt to new circumstances. It is argued that globalisation should not affect religion. All religions have their own momentum depending upon the circumstances. The followers of some religions declined, whereas two world religions are expanding either in number or in intensity of belief. Christianity faces serious problems in coping with the problems of secularisation. Same is the case with Buddhism and Confucianism. Concerning, Judaism, the Jewish population is mainly concentrated in Israel and New York. So far as Islam and Hinduism are concerned, matters are different. Hinduism is a religion that is increasing in intensity but is restricted to India. Islam has been considered as the fastest growing religion in the world as its number of followers continues to increase. Also, the intensity of belief has also increased within Islam. Thus fundamentalist groups stand strong in almost all Muslim countries. It also involves the spread of western lifestyle (besides other elements), which affects Christian values in one way and Islam in the other.[19] This has resulted in a lot of opposition within Islam against globalisation and westernisation.

Other reason for criticising the traits of globalisation is the lack of previous cultural penetration of GCC states by the Western ideas and culture. Most of the regions of the world (North America, South America, Europe, Australia, New Zealand and even former Soviet bloc, Sub Saharan Africa, and even Asia) are adapted to the Western culture. Some like South and South East Asia, opted for a cultural synthesis and accepted English language as a lingua franca. In the Middle East, particularly the GCC states, the cohesion of the Islamic community builds a religious as well as a cultural wall against many aspects of globalisation.[20] As most of the values of Islam contradict the western values, which are promoted by globalisation, globalisation itself is seen as a threat. There is also a limited use of European languages, English too being restricted. The powerful Arabic community also builds a linguistic wall (of Arabic language) against the penetration of the western languages which are an important aspect of globalisation.[21]

The major problem faced by these countries is how to protect their national identity and culture in the face of globalisation. The US is seekng to project American culture as a model for a global culture. It must be remembered that there is a lot of difference in the evolution of the cultural identity of the US and the Arabs. In the Arab world, culture evolved around dominant ethnic centers where common values, legends and cultural symbols facilitated the formation of Arab identity, on the other side, US culture was built by immigrants who later acquired American nationality. Cultural affiliation began afterwards. US is not threatened by any kind of cultural globlisation, whereas the GCC states see a threat in the forces of globalisation and even fear the transfer of decision making process regarding many aspects of life to foreign governments.[22]

Globalisation is more problematic among nations, who maintain fragile and easily penetrable economies. This is the reason why Arabs have succumbed to the cheap commercialisation of the global market. McDonalds and Burger Kings are all over Arab countries. They are often involved in uncensored music. The unfiltered global market culture is forging a collective identity crises among the Arabs. They have also not been able to utilise their invaluable human assets. There is a great problem of brain drain as many Arab scholars, scientists, physicians emigrate to the West solely because they feel that they have not been able to get their due and are not treated on the basis of their merit. They got preference on the basis of their race, family affiliation and citizenship. For example, for high jobs, Americans and Europeans are preferred, for cheap laboureres, Filipinos are best and are quite well paid. Even Arabs come after Americans and Europeans.[23]

The cultural dimension of globlisation has its positive and negative values. Globalisation promotes integration of the world and calls for the removal of all cultural barriers. Conservative Arab nationalists and fundamentalists argue that it has a negative affect on their culture and their cultures cannot adhere to many globalised nations as this would lead to disintegration of identity. UN Deputy Secretary General Louise Frechette while supporting the opportunities from globalisation argued, that it can also be very threatening... "rapid, economic, technological, social and political intrusion of foreign culture into the Arab world may put their cultural magnitude in jeopardy and will force people to fear for the loss of their religious and societal characteristics".[24] Its advocates however rationalise that with the support of technological devices, such as computers, satellites, Arab culture can be acclimatised to retain most globalised concepts regardless of the distinctions between their historical and religious roots.[25]

At the same time, the GCC states are found to be most responsive to globalisation. People from about 120 countries and diverse culture now work in the GCC countries. The number of foreign schools found in the Gulf is more than any other Arab country. There are goods coming from all corners of the world. GCC countries are also one of the largest users of the internet and e-mail.[26]

While on the one hand the GCC states have adjusted to globalisation, they have also become very cautious to protect their cultural identity. This is reflected in the viewpoints of various scholars and leaders. As cited in the Arab News, Prince

Turki Ibn Mohammad Al Kabeer, assistant undersecretary for political affairs and head of the department of Indian Ocean at the Ministry of Foreign Affairs, "People in the Gulf should take up the challenge and play their role in globalisation, while retaining their identity."[27] One of the regional leaders associated with the international leadership summit, in Dubai said, "leaders need to keep pace with the changing world. We are in an era of alliances and merging boundaries and borders. However we must take care to prevent a loss of cultural identity. In many countries the traditional way of life is getting lost and the public feel that their way of life has to be protected against foreign influences."[28]

In a symposium held jointly by American Univesity in Sharjah (AUS) and the Cultural Office of the Egyptian Embassy at Juma Al Majid Centre for culture and Heritage, Dr. Asfour said, "Globalisation contains a lot of aspects that are related to the phenomenon of Americanisation. So in order to fight this phenomenon and protect our national identity and revive our Arabic and Islamic culture, we need to protect our culture by understanding what globalisation is and know how to fight it...we need to stand more and depend on our cultural heritage and origin."[29] At the same symposium, Dr. Muhsin Jassim Al Mousawi from the AUS said, "Educated Arabs and Muslims ought to play an important role in reviving their culture and facing up to globalisation. All Arabic and Muslim leaders need to back up their cultures and educated people if they want to help revive the Islamic and Arabic culture in its war against globalistion."[30]

Conclusion

Globalisation is accepted when it provides opportunities as well as security to the people. It must be remembered that if globalisation makes life better, raises living standards, people would prefer to accept globalisation. Tradition and change do not have to be opposite. Society's traditional ways can be blended with foreign ideas to make a stronger hybrid and a synthesis can be constructed. Moreover, the society can be selective in choosing what values it wants to accept and reject. Globalisation should be introduced with significant educational, social and economic support that could make the Arab countries flourish alongside foreign cultures. Harmonisation of economic and cultural diversities should be pursued. This seems to be the best alternative.

The tension between the 'local versus global' and 'tradition versus modern' definitely exists. But it is also true that because of globalisation, the features of modernisation like - MNCs, jobs, expatriate presence, exist side by side along with traditional features including quasi-traditional political institutions, majlis, council of hereditary sheikhs, appointment through family ties, institutionalisation of religion. By and large these two influences operate side by side and the Gulf youth are found to be equally at ease at both. Even the most modernised western educated Arab from that region have evinced little or no desire to forsake their Islamic cultural heritage for what is widely seen as the secular values of the West.

It seems a drive has already been going on to protect the identity of the Arabs. Their identity is deep rooted and is not likely to be affected so easily. Even though the GCC population is an active participant of the process of globalisation, it is keen to protect its traditions and language. In the culture of the GCC states, religion plays a very important part in their lives. There is no likelihood of religion loosing its importance for a long time to come. In no case do they want the Arabic language to be replaced by English. Some aspects of culture like lifestyle is being changed but it does not alter their culture. Use of information and communication is being utilised for better purposes. The best they can do is to blend their culture and sythesise it without affecting the traditional roots.

The third world countries bear the brunt of the negative impact of globalisation. Trade agreements have removed all the barriers to corporate invasion and control of the third world. With the liberalisation of telecommunications, corporate culture is set to rule. Today, large part of the world is addicted to the TV programmes, movies news, music, lifestyles and entertainment of the North. Satellite cables, VCDs, DVDs and retail giants are creating mass marketing of culture. More than 75 per cent of the world's population have access to daily TV reception. In Asia, US films and TV programmes have a great impact. Through these channels and networks, corporations homogenise the consumer culture of the North. There is something positive about globalisation. It definitely widens ones horizons and makes one familiar with the larger world and can further lead to a more mature cross cultural understanding.

End Notes

[1] Manfed B. Steger, Globalisation: *A Very Short Introduction*, (New York, Oxford University Press, 2003) p. 13.

[2] *Ibid.*, pp 9-12.

[3] *Ibid.*, pp. 37, 56-57, 64, 93.

[4] Peter L. Berger, and Samuel P. Huntington ed., *Many Globalisations: Cultural Diversity in the Contemporary World*, (New York, Oxford University, 2002), p.2.

[5] Louis de Lamare, http://www.users.bigpond.com/I_arom/archives/cultural%20Globalisation.htm.

[6] Berger and Huntington, op. cit., p. 3.

[7] *Ibid.*, pp. 3-6.

[8] Lamare, op. cit.

[9] Manfred, op.cit., p 70-75.

[10] Robert Looney, The Arab World's Uncomfortable Experience with Globalisation, *Middle East Journal*, vol. 61, no. 2, Spring 2007.p. 341-342.

[11] *Ibid.*, p 342.

[12] David E. Long, *Culture and Customs of Saudi Arabia*, (Westport, Greenwood Press, 2005), p. 27.

[13] John Davis, The Gulf: It is a Family Affair, http://hbswk.hbs.edu/item/2191.html. See also, David Long, op.cit., pp 27-28.

[14] *Ibid.*

[15] *Ibid.*

[16] Muhammad Saleh al Musfir The Concluding statements of the Gulf Cooperation Council (GCC) Sessions 1981-2001: An analytical study of the Content, *Journal of South Asian and Middle Eastern Studies* vol. 30, no. 1, Fall 2006, pp 67-69).

[17] Sally Findlow, Global and Local Tensions in an Arab Gulf State: Conflicting Values in UAE Higher Education, (Paper presented to the International Conference, "Travelling Policy/Local Spaces: Globalisation, Identities and Education Policy in Europe", Keele University), *http://www.keele.ac.uk/depts/ed/events/conf-pdf/cPaperFindlow2.pdf*.

[18] Barry Rubin, Globalisation and the Middle East, Part I, www.http//yaleglobal.yale.edu/display.article?id=744.

[19] Jane Erik Lane, *Globalisation and Politics: Promises and Dangers*, (England, Ashgate Publishing House, 2006, pp. 88-89)

[20] Rubin, op. cit.

[21] *Ibid.*

[22] Houda Gamal Abdul Nasser, Arabs, Arab Americans and Globalisation, http://www.alhewar.com/HGANasser.htm
[23] Ramzy Baroud, Arabs and Globalisation, http://weekly.ahram.org.eg/print/2004/722/op12.htm
[24] Mohammad Moussalli, Impact of Globalisation, http://www.globalpolicy.org/globaliz/cultural/2003/0826islam.htm.
[25] *Ibid.*
[26] Abdul Rahman Al Rashid, Arabs should take pride in Openness, *Arab News*, January 3, 2004.
[27] Cited in, Ghazanfar Ali Khan, Gulf Arabs Urged to Take up Globalisation Challenge, *Arab News*, May 27, 2007. http://www.arabnews.com/?page=1&section=0&article=96718&d=27&m=5&y=2.
[28] Al Zamil, Cultural identity must be Protected in the wake of *Globalisation*, http://www. Ameinfo.com/66762.html.
[29] Bassam Za'za, Arab Speakers See Threat to Culture by Globalisation, *Gulf News*, March 21, 2002. (http://www.globalpolicy.org/globaliz/cultural/2002/0321arab.*htm*)
[30] *Ibid.*

GLOBALISATION AND HUMAN RIGHTS

9

Implementing International Human Rights Standards in a Globalising World

K. SAVITRI

This article attempts to argue that globalisation in the human rights field is older than its present economic avatar. The effects of globalisation on human rights are most evident in the way member states have been compelled to accede to international human rights instruments and harmonise their domestic laws in line with them. In doing so, member states are experiencing unprecedented pressures, both externally and internally. The second part of this article looks at the impact of international obligations under Convention on the Elimination of All Forms of Discrimination against Women (CEDAW) and the Convention on the Rights of the Child (CRC) on India as reflected in India's first periodic report submitted to the respective monitoring bodies under the respective conventions. The article in ultimate analysis concludes that although a lot still needs to be done to secure a better protection of women's and children's rights, significant strides thus far have been taken because of the pressures on the Indian state from external and internal actors.

Globalisation and Human Rights Interface

Globalisation is a process as well as a complex phenomenon which includes among others, economic deregulation by the states, privatisation, trade liberalisation and, free movement of people and ideas across the borders. International human rights law is a network of treaties, documents and norms adopted by the international community that set the standards for adherence by states. The international human rights regime endeavours to rein in states and its agencies from abusing rights of individuals and groups by creating binding obligations and monitoring mechanisms for them.

It can be argued here that globalisation in the human rights field is older than its present economic 'avatar'. The effects of economic globalisation on human rights has been both positive and negative, beneficial and challenging, but its benefits are most evident in the way member states have been compelled to accede to international human rights instruments and harmonise their domestic laws in line with them. In doing so, member states are experiencing unprecedented external pressure from the international institutions to implement the human rights standards. Added to this, internally, civil society and non-governmental organisations are exerting never-before influence on states, both directly and via the international bodies, to demand adherence to the international norms and standards.

For the purpose of this article, globalisation is understood as a set of complex and dynamic processes that create interrelationships, cutting across geographical and cultural borders.[1] Evaluating in this sense, it is not a recent phenomenon. Globalisation, leading to a network of interdependencies and common goals, aspiring to synchronise one's domestic system of laws and norms in line with universally accepted standards, occurred in the field of human rights long before it made its appearance in the economic field. Human rights as a universal objective and collective goal have come to occupy the centre-stage of international relations discourse and decision-making process since the Universal Declaration of Human Rights (1948). The significant progress made by the United Nations in the field of human rights is an indicator of the fact that irrespective of the cultural specificity and ideological orientation, most countries across the globe have pledged their commitment to the international human rights principles and sealed that commitment further by acceding to various UN Conventions. Each ideological orientation has made contribution to the evolution of different kinds of rights. More often than not, the commitment displayed by the member states to accept international obligations requires harmonisation of one's domestic laws with the established principles and proclaimed norms of international human rights law. That countries were willing to initiate and accomplish such a change in one's domestic law is a testimony to the importance attached by a country to being seen as a promoter of human rights at home. However, all countries do not willingly ratify the UN Conventions; nor do all of them voluntarily adopt changes in their domestic laws. Many a time, moral force and political pressure is brought on the states to be part of the international human rights obligations. That human rights can be and has been an arena of harmonising interests and a common ground for growing interconnectedness proves their centrality and inviolability in initiating the global concern towards them. It will suffice here to reiterate that globalisation in the form of evolving interrelated processes in human rights field *predates* similar developments witnessed in international economic, financial and trade relations much later.

Globalisation presents newer challenges to the states striving to establish and maintain a human rights regime. Here, the challenges are two-fold. One set of challenges flows from the fact that the arena of state control and regulation is constantly shrinking under the impact of globalisation. As a result, state activity and expenditure in the social sector has receded considerably in recent years in most of the countries, notably the developing ones. Structural Adjustment Policies (SAP) delimits the capacity of states to independently determine their development priorities. Moreover, economic and social policies driven by the directives from international institutions like the World Bank and International Monetary Fund (IMF) erode the avenues of participation of local communities in decision making on socio-economic policies and thus create a democratic deficit which has negative implications for human rights. In countries where SAP has been initiated, there is an element of disenchantment with the lack of state's involvement in social sectors, be it the sphere of education, health, housing or social security.

The second set of challenges hovers round the role of the states. The state has increasingly come under scrutiny for its role in the protection and promotion of human rights. The agents of such scrutiny are both the international and intra-national actors. International donor and lending agencies impose on the recipient countries, mostly developing countries reeling under debt burden, such non-economic conditionalities as good governance and respect for human rights even as the states are pursuing severely restricted policy choices. Within the state, civil society organisations, political and social groups and NGOs are raising uncomfortable questions and issues related to survival and dignity of those marginalised by the shift in policy choices initiated by the state. As a spin off of the international and intra-state pressures on the state, human rights issues have re-emerged and have come to occupy the centre-stage of the discourse on individual's relationship with the state.

The ambivalent relationship between globalisation and human rights is further reflected in the divergent and opposite views held by scholars on the utility of the complex phenomenon of globalisation to the promotion and protection of human rights. Some[2] view globalisation as having had a positive impact on improving the human rights regime within the state and thereby reinforcing state's commitment to universal human rights standards. There has been a phenomenal increase in the number of NGOs active in the human rights field and in the level of their participation, during the last decade-and-a-half. The new-found vigour and resurgence of NGO participation is positive fallout of the free flow of information and ideas, avenues of communication, and cooperation across the borders made possible by globalisation. Many of these NGOs have a consultative status with the Economic and Social Council (ECOSOC) of the United Nations and are therefore able to voice their concerns and record their protests before the various international monitoring bodies. They also submit alternative reports to the treaty bodies to counter a state party's laudatory reports and grand representation of the human rights situation at home. In fact, NGOs have been instrumental in internationalising human rights violations concerns and demanding their redress. NGOs are an important component of

Implementing International Human Rights Standards in a... 175

global civil society and they share a commitment to values and universal human rights norms. They have brought pressure on the state to accept responsibility for the poor and dispossessed and on the "corporations to accept social responsibility in their global dealings."[3]

There are others who believe that globalisation has presented newer challenges and threats[4] that are yet to be convincingly addressed by the international community. The challenges are due to the anxiety caused by the extent and scale of violation of basic human rights standards, paucity of the means of survival and of group-specific nature of marginalisation. At the grassroots level, it has raised individual's concern for survival and security and has created a large section of dispossessed population that harbours a seething anger towards the state for its inability to check the two quintessential impacts of globalisation; poverty and inequality. Globalisation of 1990s has resulted in unparalleled income disparities. On the one hand, there is an increase in the number of billionaires in the world while on the other it has rendered many more millions impoverished. World's richest 1% received as much income as the poorest 57%.[5] According to the UNDP's *Human Development Report 1999*, the assets of three wealthiest individuals in the world are more than the combined gross national product of all least developed countries.

When globalisation becomes pervasive, social and economic rights are the first victims.[6] The implementation of socio-economic rights depends on the availability of resources and the involvement of the state in social sector planning and implementation. Three groups bear the brunt and ill-effects of globalisation the most; women, children and minorities. These groups bear the brunt disproportionately because some or the other areas of the social sector are central to their lives. Women are also uniquely disadvantaged in the sense that they have to bear a greater burden of poverty and falling standard of living, which often result in disintegration of the family set up. Some of this burden is reflected in the migratory trends of work force worldwide. A major segment of migrant workers consists of women, both internally and internationally. Moreover, majority of women migrant workers are employed in unskilled or semi-skilled jobs in the unorganised sector which means that they are excluded from the purview of employment benefits and protection. A part of the ill-effects of poverty and lack of health are passed on by women to children in the form of a high incidence of infant and child mortality rates. The Committee on the Elimination of All Forms of Discrimination against Women has contended that these facts are indicators of the evidence of the feminisation of poverty and the impact of economic policies on the rights of women.[7] UNDP's *Human Development Report 1995* on gender famously stated that 'human development, if not engendered, is endangered'.

Notwithstanding the challenges and its shrinking role in the era of globalisation, the state, however, remains an indispensable agent whose position must be secured in implementing human rights. In the institutional system at the international level, member states remain important interlocutors in the implementation system, which means that it is ultimately the state which has to ensure that the rights are available to its citizens. There is a need to repeatedly access the state for implementing the human rights standards because "state sovereignty remains the international frame of reference, even if the exact contours of sovereignty change overtime."[8] Equally important to bear in mind is the fact that state's preponderance must be checked if human rights are *not* to be grossly violated and infringed upon, because, very often, agents of the state are the primary violators of individual's rights.

International Monitoring Mechanism

The UN human rights system has evolved a committee system for monitoring the implementation of human rights norms contained in the six principal treaties. The promotion and protection of women's rights is an integral part of all human rights instruments evolved under the aegis of the United Nations. Both Charter-based and treaty-based bodies monitor the women's rights. The Charter-based system has established the Commission on the Status of Women in 1947 as a subsidiary body of the Economic and Social Council (ECOSOC). The Commission is an inter-governmental and political body responsible for preparing recommendations and reports to promote women's rights in civil, political, social, economic and cultural fields. The Commission also makes recommendations to ECOSOC on urgent problems requiring immediate attention in the field of women's rights with the object of implementing the principle of equal treatment and non-discrimination on the basis of sex. The Convention on the Elimination of All Forms of Discrimination against Women (1979) [hereafter, the Women's Convention] is the culmination of all the earlier instruments on the subject in that it subsumes the principles enunciated in them. This is the first instrument on women's rights that provides for a monitoring mechanism through a committee of independent experts (Committee on the Elimination of Discrimination against Women, hereafter CEDAW). The Commission on the Status of Women and CEDAW are the two gender-specific bodies dealing with women's rights.

Committee on the Elimination of Discrimination against Women

Ever since its inception, CEDAW has monitored the compliance of the obligations of the states parties to implement the Convention through consideration of their initial and periodic reports. Originally, the mechanism of implementation in the Convention provided for only one procedure, i.e., the mandatory reporting procedure in which the state parties were to indicate the factors and difficulties affecting the degree of fulfilment of the obligations under the Convention. According to Article 18 of the Convention, the states parties undertake to submit a report on the legislative, judicial, administrative or other measures that they have adopted to give effect to the provisions of the Convention and progress made in this regard.[9]

At the risk of being descriptive, an account of structural mechanism will begin and recur suitably in this section. CEDAW consists of twenty-three expert members in the field and they work in their individual capacities. CEDAW has the largest number of members in comparison to any other treaty body. The Convention under Article 20, requires the Committee, to meet annually for single two-week session to consider state reports.

Reporting Procedure: CEDAW had adopted guidelines on the nature, content and structure of the reports to be submitted to it. However, many state reports are incomplete, inadequate and do not follow the reporting guidelines. Most states tend to report only on legislative measures they have taken without adequately reflecting the situation on the ground. One of the objectives of reporting was to enable the states to benefit from each other's experiences in implementing the provisions of the covenant. This objective has not been realised completely because the reports are often glossy and provide only a grand laudatory summary and from which it is impossible to deduce the extent of implementation of women's rights in that particular country.

Reservations: Large number of reservations filed by the states parties has greatly hampered the implementation of rights protected in the Women's Convention. Most reservations pertain to Article 16 concerning marriage and family relations by many states including India.[10] The ratifying states have often justified reservations in general and to Article 16 in particular in the name of cultural relativism since religious minorities tend to have their personal laws relating to marriage and family relations. The large number of reservations to the Convention has become regrettably 'a notorious feature of the Convention',[11] in that the Women's Convention is the first human rights treaty to have such a high number of reservations upon ratification. The problem of reservations is serious because many of them are regarding the fundamental provisions of the Convention although, under Article 28, the Women's Convention specifically prohibits reservations that are incompatible with its *object* and *purpose* (emphasis added). Reservations are made, as Rebecca Cook comments, because,

> *most states are apprehensive about the possible consequences of accepting a human rights treaty, not least because such treaties may have a dynamic force and interpretation of their scope and impact is less certain than that of commercial treaties.... Reservations are seen to offer an assurance that the state can protect its interests to the fullest extent possible.*[12]

Traditionally, treaty texts have allowed reservations to facilitate wider ratification, as they are useful in accommodating cultural and religious preferences of the member states. It is typically believed that seeking to monitor member states and gradually bringing pressure on them to drop the reservations is easier when they are within the treaty fold than they are out of it. Universalists have deployed the argument that reservation is an effective mechanism to rein in states with differing perspectives on human rights and that it provides an objective yardstick against which state behaviour may be assessed.[13]

India's Initial Report to CEDAW

India ratified the Women's Convention on 9th July 1993. India's initial report was submitted on 10th March 1999, late by four years.[14] The Indian Government deposited two Declaratory Statements and one Reservation while ratifying the Convention. The assessment of the implementation of women's rights in India, and their monitoring by CEDAW, must be seen in the light of these Declaratory Statements and Reservation. The two Declaratory Statements pertain to Article 16(1) and (2) of the Convention which calls for the elimination of discrimination against women in all matters relating to marriage and family relations, the elimination of child marriages and the introduction of compulsory registration of marriages respectively. The Declaratory Statements restricting the application of these provisions have been made as a result of India's policy of non-interference in personal laws of any community without its (community's) own initiative and consent. The Indian Government also made reservation in Article 29 (1) of the Convention establishing compulsory arbitration and adjudication of disputes between one or more states parties by the International Court of Justice concerning interpretation and application of the Convention.

The Indian Government held consultations with the domestic NGOs working in the area of women's rights while preparing the initial report. It held one meeting specifically on the preparation of the report and subsequently 20 other meetings were held over a period of three years. In these meetings, the NGOs highlighted the need for withdrawal of Declaratory Statements and Reservation entered by India to the Convention. The NGOs also made a suggestion that while ascertaining the views of the minority communities in reforming their personals laws, the views of women belonging to such communities must also be taken into account.

Contents of the Report

It is a very comprehensive report dealing with various constitutional, legal, economic, democratic and social aspects. Some of the issues raised in the report relate to life expectancy, literacy rate, income, legal remedies etc. The report diligently follows the Committee's guidelines: in the first part, general information regarding the status of women and institutional developments are included; in the second part, article-wise information is detailed.

The report informs that the various provisions on gender equality and non-discrimination are firmly established in Part-III (dealing with Fundamental Rights) and Part IV (the Directive Principles of State Policy) of the Constitution and that these provisions are in line with the principles enunciated in the Universal Declaration of Human Rights. The most important provision concerning gender equality in the Constitution is Article 15(3), which provides for affirmative action. It enables the state to set aside a quota of seats in local and urban Governments for women representatives. Constitutional amendments to incorporate the quota provision were put in place after ratification of the Women's Convention (The 73rd and 74th Constitutional Amendments Act, 1993). Through these amendments, a 'quiet revolution' is in its making in terms of women's participation in decision making. Considering India's population and vast size, even a conservative estimate suggests that when all elections to local bodies in rural areas are held, at least eight hundred thousand women will have entered public office.[15] For a country with a largely rural population and a traditional social outlook on the role of women in public life, this is a remarkable change.

Institutionally speaking, the Indian Government established a statutory body – The National Commission for Women – in 1992 to oversee the working of constitutional safeguards for women on gender equality, for reviewing laws and regulations where necessary, and for looking into specific complaints of violation of women's rights. Several states in India have also set up State Commissions for Women after country's ratification to the Convention. A separate Department of Women and Child Development under the independent charge of a cabinet minister at the Union level has also been created to focus on women's advancements in various facets of life.

In accordance with Article 9 of the Convention (equal right to nationality), the Citizenship Act of 1955, which provided for the acquisition and termination of citizenship, has been amended to bring the national law in conformity with the Convention provision. Prior to the amendment, a child born outside India was considered an Indian national only if the child's father was an Indian at the time of its (child's) birth. This provision discriminated against Indian women marrying non-Indian males, living outside India and, wishing to retain Indian citizenship for their child. This anomaly has been corrected through an amendment effected in 1992. Now, a child born outside India is eligible to acquire Indian citizenship if either of its parents is an Indian citizen at the time of its birth. Thus, the law now takes into account a child's descent from either of parents' side.

Discussion in the Committee on India's Report

The Indian report was examined by CEDAW on 21st January 2000. Opening the discussion, the expert members noted certain lacunae in the report: the report had limited itself to the trafficking in Indian women, without mentioning the fate of "mail-order brides" (Indian women being sold in marriage to Indian or non-Indian males living outside the country – mainly in the Middle East. The phenomenon is more common among the poorer sections of certain minority communities); women had limited access to legal redress in areas of armed conflict, where the armed forces could forcibly enter the houses without warrant and use lethal force under the Armed Forces (Special Powers) Act, 1958; the report did not highlight the plight of untouchable women who were doubly disadvantaged due to their gender and caste; no data had been provided regarding women bonded labour and as to what percentage of women had benefited from the affirmative action programme; and finally one could not gather what protection women had against custodial violence. An expert member also suggested that India should withdraw its provision of reservation provided in article 16(2) and ensure both birth and marriage registration compulsorily. Merely conducting door-to-door survey would not solve the problem.[16]

The Indian representative responded to the Committee that police, customs and the Ministry of External Affairs 'coordinated action against newer forms of sexual exploitation' (subsuming the mail-order-brides phenomenon); that serious efforts were being made to implement the Prevention of Atrocities Act, 1989 against the untouchable women and that members of that community had risen to the highest echelons of public service, but old attitudes and mindsets could not disappear overnight. The Representative admitted that there were still many areas of concern and it was a fact that women bore the brunt of caste-based atrocities. Regarding the Armed Forces (Special Powers) Act, she responded by revealing that the Act was applied only in areas which were declared as 'disturbed areas' by the government of a state. The Act did not grant the security forces immunity from prosecution or other legal proceedings. It only provided that prosecution could not be taken up without the prior consent of the central government.[17]

One may note here that the Indian representative did not explained few of the questions raised, such as how many cases had come up as complaints against the arbitrary behaviour of the armed forces? In how many cases the permission was granted to initiate the legal proceedings against the erring personnel? and what percentage of them were punished?. She also failed to see the inherent logic in the expert member's comment that women, in the first place, did not have adequate information regarding the legal options and access to seek government's permission to initiate legal action, adequate wherewithal to collect *prima facie* evidence and endure the sheer burden of a long-drawn legal process. The Indian representative did not appreciate the mental state of women coming from areas of armed conflict. In fact, no data is available to indicate how many policemen have been prosecuted for their misconduct in states affected by terrorism and insurgency like Punjab, Kashmir and the north-eastern states.

A very good suggestion regarding the dissemination of information put forth by the Committee was that the Convention text had only been translated into Hindi, the official language of the Republic, and that it must be translated in all the national languages of the states.[18] Furthermore, the National Commission for Women should monitor this primary effort in disseminating information on the Convention. The Committee also suggested that India should consider ratifying the Optional Protocol (which until now it has not done) to the Convention granting individual petition procedure.

Domestic Application of CEDAW by Courts

Unlike the USA and Germany, treaties are not self-executing in India, and their provisions do not automatically form part of the domestic law. India is following the Anglo-Saxon tradition in this regard, according to which, customary international law is considered as part of the law of the land only so long as it is not inconsistent with national statutes. Or else, necessary changes will have to be made in the national laws to incorporate the international treaties. The compliance of provisions of CEDAW in India must be seen within this legal framework. In a landmark case of *Visakha v State of Rajasthan*[19], the Supreme Court of India dealt for the first time with a woman's right to work and her working environment. This case was brought as a Public Interest Litigation (PIL) on behalf of a woman social worker employed by the State of Rajasthan to tour the rural areas to educate the people against child marriage and dowry. Some village elders, who were annoyed by the educational activities of the concerned woman, raped her. In passing the judgment against the village elders, the Supreme Court based its' reasoning, besides the Indian Constitution, on Articles 11 and 24 of CEDAW (Right to Work and application of the Convention at the national level respectively). This is the first time that the Indian Supreme Court expressly quoted from the Convention and the CEDAW's general recommendations. Two years later, this reasoning was reiterated and confirmed in another case *Apparel Export Promotion Council v A.K. Chopra*[20] relating to sexual harassment at the work place.[21]

Omissions in the Report

The India Report is as much important for being the initial report submitted to CEDAW as for its significant omissions. Three glaring omissions includes issues like female foeticide, dowry deaths and bride burning. Laws exist prohibiting all the three heinous practices but their implementation leaves much to be desired. The Report does not make any mention of these although the first two are widely practiced in many parts of India. It has often been suggested that promoting education among girls and spreading information regarding the international instruments available to them can best promote women's rights. This can also bring about additional changes and an ability to resist stereotypical practices by women. Unfortunately, CEDAW members did not raise questions or elicit any information concerning these three practices from the Indian representative. Had these questions been raised, they would have formed part of CEDAW's annual report to the General Assembly and sensitised the world community towards these heinous practices. The CEDAW's comments on Indian Report were very general and brief. Had CEDAW members taken care to procure information from women NGOs in India, they would have seen the report in a more critical, searching perspective.

Committee on the Rights of the Child

The Committee on the Rights of the Child (Article 43 of the CRC) consists of eighteen independent members elected by the states parties for a period of four years who are usually recognised experts of high moral standing and work in their independent capacity. Originally the Committee met annually but in view of its increased, and still expanding volume of workload, it has met three times a year since 1995. It has basically one (mandatory) procedure - to consider reports by the member states. The states parties are under an obligation (article 44(3)) to submit an initial report within two years of entry into force of the Convention for them and subsequently periodic reports every five years. The initial report is usually a statement and of the policies and laws concerning children whereas the periodic reports review the progress made in their implementation. Unlike the Women's Convention, the CRC does not provide for either inter-state complaints or individual communication procedure.

Three articles of the Convention on the Rights of the Child are important to analyse the general measures of implementation, namely, Article 4 on the duty to take all possible measures to ensure implementation of the Convention – including the incorporation of the Convention in domestic law; Article 42 on the duty to make the principles of the Convention widely known to children and adults; and Article 44(6) regarding the duty to make countries' reports widely available domestically to generate public debate and domestic scrutiny. India has attached reservations to Articles 4 and 32 regarding the progressive implementation of social and economic rights to the maximum extent of available resources and the protection from recruitment/ employment in general and in hazardous industries in particular. It has thereby partially absolved itself from the present scrutiny.

Reporting Procedure: The purpose of this procedure is to aid the Committee in understanding the level of adherence to the Convention achieved by a state party so that possible options can be suggested for overcoming the difficulties in implementation. The Committee has repeatedly emphasised that reporting procedure itself should not be seen as a mere administrative exercise; rather, it is intended to give a state party an opportunity to review the existing legislation, harmonise it with the Convention provisions, evaluate their implementation, interact with NGOs and to appreciate the attendant problems.[22] The objective of the entire process is to make the domestic environment more child-friendly and thereby enhance the understanding of and the capacity to implement, the Convention. The states parties are obliged to provide sufficient information on the measures adopted and the progress made in the actual enjoyment of those rights to let the Committee have a comprehensive understanding.

Since the states parties have to assess their own compliance, it is not surprising that they do so favourably, highlighting the positive achievements and downplaying the negative aspects. In order to gain a realistic picture, the Committee has a pre-sessional working group that liaises with non-governmental organisations (NGOs)[23] and other competent bodies to gather independent, non-official information about the state policies. This is particularly essential if the expert members of the Committee are not well conversant with the cultural and religious ethos of a society where policy formulations are guided by those considerations. It further comes handy in sorting out the inconsistencies in states reports and lends further credibility to the discussions. This has been effective and particularly evident in the questions raised by Ms Judith Karp[24] on measures of implementation. She had been briefed sufficiently by the Indian NGOs about certain pressing issues of caste-based discrimination against children in rural areas.[25] Expectedly, the official report had glossed over this controversial and emotive issue. It exposed the inadequacy of the Report that discussed at length about the constitutional provisions of equality but did not inform about the practical steps taken, if any, to promote it. Such permeating role accorded to the NGOs at various levels of reporting procedure is in recognition of their vibrant contribution during the drafting of the Convention. In addition to the NGOs, the Committee may invite to its sessions (article 45(a)&(b)) representatives from UNHCR, UNICEF - the latter treasures cumulative knowledge, database and experience in the area - and specialised agencies like ILO and WHO to seek advice on suggesting effective ways of implementing the Convention or in providing technical assistance to the countries in need.[26] The Committee may also request the UN to undertake special study on issues of concern.[27]

The Convention has paid attention to the democratic process of preparation of report. The states parties are under an obligation to consult a wide section of domestic opinion in the formulation of the report. Sometimes, neither such consultation is carried out nor is any information forthcoming from government departments charged with the responsibility of producing reports. In short, the democratic process of acquiring domestic input is lacking.[28] In India too, there was little domestic consultation or constructive dialogue during the preparation of the report. This is a reflection on the opaque nature of democratic procedures existing in some member states.

India's Initial Report to CRC

The question under scrutiny here seeks to critically assess and evaluate the effectiveness of the CRC in monitoring the implementation of the Convention in the context of the first report submitted by India.[29] In order to delimit the discussion on this vast area, the present focus is only on the Committees' capacity to monitor and advance substantive rights and their impact on the domestic laws of the ratifying states.

In the context of India's reservations to articles 4 and 32 regarding non-availability of resources, the Committee requested additional information on the allocation of technical, human and financial resources to the Department of Women and Child Development as it was dissatisfied with mere information that a separate Department of Women and Child Development had been set up for the coordination, monitoring and implementation of the Convention. It sought to query the level of resources allocated for the effective functioning of the said department.[30] India was bluntly reminded of its whopping defence expenditure when insufficiency of resources was pleaded as a reason by India for not implementing articles 4 and 32. Realistically speaking, at least some of the shortcomings in India's implementation are actually attributable to lack of resources. Comparing resource allocation for children with the defence expenditure of a country would be to engage in unlikely comparisons as the two areas represent altogether different sectors of planning, rooted in divergent national and policy priorities.

The process of questioning, seeking additional information and finally, making recommendations has worked effectively to raise issues concerning children in India. As part of its constructive and accommodative approach, the Committee has usually refrained from criticising in harsh terminology and has couched its 'recommendations' and 'concerns' in an agreeable language. This has been a common strategy followed by the Committee. Its concluding observations usually devote first few paragraphs to thank and appreciate the achievements of the states parties. After this palliative, an extensive list of 'regrets' and 'concerns' follows. But none are entitled as 'criticisms' or 'gross inadequacies' even where they are so.

The method adopted by the UN bodies to seek compliance is by putting repeated pressure and appealing to the perception of public image by a government. Recently, the Indian parliament has adopted a constitutional amendment that makes universal, free and compulsory primary education a fundamental right. No modalities have been drawn up for its implementation yet. But the noble intent has certainly helped in boosting India's image when this was highlighted in India's second report.

The Committee has often emphasised in its concluding observations to the state parties on the need for establishing independent monitoring structures to implement the Convention.[31] Due to repeated pressures from the CRC to establish an independent national institution for children, India has recently established the National Commission for the Protection of

Children's Rights (NCPCR) that has started functioning under the guidance of Dr. Shantha Sinha. In view of these successes, it would be difficult to hold the view that rigorous enforcement powers are inevitable for a successful implementing mechanism.

It may seem that the Committee lacks enforcement measures but it is unlikely that the member states will be willing to let the Committee have such overriding powers. In any case, the Convention's mechanism is still preferable because it is the only exclusive international instrument available to the world for the promotion and protection of children's rights. The fact that the member states and the NGOs seek to influence its discussion demonstrates its ability to serve as the focal point for advancing the rights of the child. The NGOs particularly have found a receptive body to articulate their views where their participation and contribution has been institutionalised.[32] It is argued that international law is a highly gendered system as in these women and children are accorded a passive and dependent status. Since children are excluded from the political and law making process at the national and international level, their concerns are likely to be marginalised.[33] This is where one would appreciate the Committee's efforts to overcome the limitation of international law by adopting innovative methods of co-opting the NGOs.

Conclusion

The implementation of women's rights through CEDAW and children's rights through CRC has been an uneven process. The problems arise due to both structural and resource inadequacies. Shortage of time, busy professional commitments of the expert members during the inter-sessional period, lack of coordination with NGOs, reservations to the Conventions, non-adherance to the Committee's recommendations, all these have seriously affected the committees' capacity to effectively implement their mandate.

Despite these shortcomings, some positive developments have taken place at the Committees' level. The duration of sessions of CEDAW has been doubled, an Optional Protocol has been adopted and an effort is being made to initiate confidential investigations. It has been suggested that the question-answer procedure be made crisp, advisory opinion be sought on reservations and, better dissemination of information regarding the international instruments be attempted to make the system more effective. The monitoring mechanism of the CRC has been, in comparison, reasonably successful so far. Its significant achievements have been in enhancing the level of participation and dialogue between the Committee, the reporting states, the NGOs and other UN organs and bodies through dispassionate, constructive engagement of all. It has regularly contributed towards standardisation of procedural and substantive norms through the adoption of various guidelines, general recommendations and enunciating principles through general comments.

The CEDAW and CRC's principal tool in promoting compliance has been to repeatedly bring pressure on the states parties to implement the general recommendations and to make the latter more sensitive towards the rights enunciated in the Conventions in general. They have largely succeeded in this endeavour. The monitoring mechanism has had a positive impact on all those involved in it including the Committees.

The impact of the mechanism on India has been noteworthy and has made India sensitive to the concerns raised by the Committees. Several encouraging changes have been initiated in the policy and institutional mechanism by way of establishing new national human rights institutions, adopting legislative or constitutional measures to incorporate the international norms and recommendations, initiating studies on issues concerning women and children and finally, initiate dialogue with other partners in civil society concerned with these two groups. The establishment of the National Commission for the Protection of Children's Rights (NCPCR) in 2006 and the constitutional amendment making right to free and compulsory education a fundamental right are a case in point. India has also motivated the NGOs to get involved in the process of consultation and implementation. The National Commission for Women was established in 1992 and India ratified CEDAW in 1993 in the run up to the Fourth World Conference on Women in Beijing in order to present itself in a more agreeable light at the global level. The claim here is not that all of this is successful or exhaustive. In fact, some of the institutional mechanisms have proved to be just that: national trophies to be presented before the international community without substantial powers to initiate radical changes in their field. But the international monitoring mechanism has made a difference to the way these rights have been perceived now than when the committees did not exist.

Some principal areas of concern remain. The problem of huge backlog of reports to be submitted (India has also been behind its schedule in this regard) and those waiting to be considered needs to be tackled with a sense of urgency. Also the Committees will have to spell out their parameters for judging performance of states in implementing the Conventions. Lastly, the Committees' ability to evolve innovative methods, as in the past, to face possible challenges to the effectiveness of the mechanism in a globalised world (with international lending agencies tightening their control over national human rights policy choices) holds the key for their continued success and a promise for the future. There are difficulties in the implementation of the rights of the concerned two groups but international human rights instruments cannot be seen as an all or nothing proposition.

End Notes

[1] This rather simplified meaning of globalisation does not subsume everything that the term stands for. It is used in a limited sense here to situate the development of human rights regime at the international level.

[2] Anthony Giddens, Thomas Friedman and M D Pendleton support the view that globalisation is inevitable but is also beneficial to all and a sign of progress.

M.D. Pendleton, "A New Human Right—The Right to Globalisation", *Fordham International Law Journal*, vol. 22, 1999. Giddens maintains that economic benefits bring in their wake political freedom and human rights.

[3] Dinah Shelton, 'Protecting Human Rights in a Globalizing World', *Boston College International and Comparative Law Review*, vol. 25, no.2, 2002, pp.273-322, at p. 299.

[4] Joseph Stiglitz is a staunch opponent of globalisation due to its adverse consequences on the poor. See, Joseph E. Stiglitz, *Making Globalisation Work*, London: Allen Lane, 2006. Anne Orford argues that globalisation privileges property interests of transnational corporations over the human rights of local communities. See Anne Orford, "Contesting Globalisation: A Feminist Perspective on the Future of Globalisation" in Burns H. Weston and Stephen P. Marks, ed., *The Future of International Human Rights*, 1999.

[5] See generally, Adamantia Pollis, "Human Rights and Globalisation", *Journal of Human Rights*, vol.3, no.3, September 2004, pp. 343-358.

Implementing International Human Rights Standards in a... 191

6. The UN Committee on Economic, Social and Cultural Rights issued a statement in this regard in May 1998. See http://www.unhchr.ch/tbs/doc.nsf/ The UN Sub-Commission on the Promotion and Protection of Human Rights asked a member to prepare a working article on the impact of the activities of TNCs on the realisation of economic, social and cultural rights. The report unequivocally condemns economic globalisation. See, El Hadji Guisse's report, UN Doc. E/CN.4/Sub.2/1998/6 (1998).

7. *Report of the Committee on the Elimination of Discrimination against Women*, UN GAOR, 52nd Session, Supp. No. 38, UN Doc. A/52/38/Rev.1 (1997). Similar concerns have been expressed by Committee on Economic, Social and Cultural Rights and the Committee on the Rights of the Child.

8. Dinah Shelton, n.3, p.277.

9. The initial report is due from a state party within one year of the entry into force of the Convention for the state concerned. Thereafter, every four years or whenever the Committee so requests, the states parties have to submit a periodic report.

10. For a summary of reservations see, Annex II, *Discrimination Against Women: The Convention and the Committee*, Human Rights Fact Sheet no. 22, pp. 63-72.

11. Henry Steiner and Philip Alston, *Human Rights in Context: Law, Politics and Morals*, 2nd edn., Oxford University Press, 2000, p. 439.

12. Rebecca Cook, 'Reservations to the Convention on the Elimination of All Forms of Discrimination against Women', *Virginia Journal of International Law*, vol. 30, 1990, pp. 643 and 650.

13. The provision of reservation as a way of reconciling respect for culture within the universal human rights standards is made by e.g., Rosalyn Higgins, *Problems and Process: International Law and How We Use It*, Clarendon Press, 1993, at p. 98; also see, Hilary Charlesworth and Christine Chinkin, *The Boundaries of International Law: A Feminist Perspective*, Manchester University Press, 2000, at 223.

14. CEDAW/C/IND/1 of 10th March, 1999.

15. *Ibid.*, at 26.

16. CEDAW, *Consideration of India Report*, 22nd Session 453 meeting, 21st January 2000.

17. *Ibid.*

18. The Constitution of India recognises 21 national languages in Schedule VIII.

19. *Supreme Court cases* (1997) 6 at 241. This judgment by Justice J S Verma has been one of the most widely referred judgments world over for innovatively applying the international norms in adjudicating a case. Inspired by this, the highest federal court of Canada and many courts in other countries have similarly applied international norms in their rulings. No discussion on women's rights and CEDAW is ever complete without a referring to this.

20. *Supreme Court cases* (1999) 8 at 759.

21. The two cases discussed above have been cited in Sujata Manohar, 'Application of International Human Rights Law in India' in United Nations Department of Economic and Social Affairs, *Bringing International Human Rights Law Home* (United Nations, 2000), at 170-171.

[22] Gerison Lansdown, 'The Reporting Process under the Convention on the Rights of the Child' in P. Alston and J. Crawford, ed., The Future of UN Human Rights Treaty Monitoring, Cambridge University Press, 2000, p. 114.

[23] *A Guide for NGOs Reporting to the Committee on the Rights of the Child*, NGO Group for the Convention on the Rights of the Child, 1994.

[24] Committee's member and rapporteur on India Report. The novel practice of appointing individual rapporteur was suspended for a while due to undue pressure sought to be brought on them to influence the content of the debates and concluding observations. See Lansdown, n.22 at 123. Although she refers to 'pressure from governments', one may presume that the NGOs too seek to influence the questioning by the rapporteur to highlight the lacunae in the official report and perhaps attract greater funding (particularly if they are dependent on external funding). However, Madam Karp's questions were arguably thoroughly justified and reflected the concerns of the Indian NGOs.

[25] Summary Record, 589th meeting: *India*, CRC/C/SR.589, 14/01/2000.

[26] Kilkelly, Ursula, 'The UN Committee on the Rights of the Child - an evaluation in the light of recent UK experience' *Child and Family Law Quarterly*, vol. 8, no. 2, 1996, p. 106.

[27] There was a special rapporteur on children involved in armed conflict and on sale and illegal trafficking that later led to the First and Second Optional Protocol on the subject.

[28] It does appear that the Indian government is ready to make amends for its past follies. A circular by the Department of Women and Child Development responsible for preparing the report has requested the concerned bodies and NGOs to send their comments for the second periodic report. See URL <http://wcd.nic.in/child1.htm.>

[29] India submitted its Initial Report in 1997, two years behind the due date. *Initial Reports of States Parties due in 1995: India*, UN Doc. CRC/C/28/Add.10, 7 July 1997. India has also submitted the second report in 2001.

[30] *List of Issues: India*, CRC/C/Q/IND/1, 30/06/99.

[31] "To encourage the states parties to establish", and recognising the importance of, such institutions, the Committee has recently issued a General Comment No 2, *The Role of Independent National Human Rights Institutions in the Protection and Promotion of the Rights of the Child*, CRC/GC/2002/2,of 15/11/2002; The Committee emphasised to India that an independent structure be established for the purpose. Concluding Observations, CRC/C/15/Add.115, 23/02/2000. As a result, a law establishing a National Commission for Children was passed in India. It has recently started functioning as the National Comission for the Protection of Children's Rights. It may be noted that these recommendations by the Committee predate the General Comment No 2.

[32] Indian NGOs have been very active in laiasoning with the CRC. Several alternative reports have been submitted by the Indian NGOs, notably by Butterflies and the Asian Centre for Human Rights, to counter the claims of the India Report.

[33] As an illustration, van Bueren makes a valid point that the body representing children's interest (UNICEF) has not been accorded the status of a specialised agency. See, G. van Bueren, *The International Law on the Rights of the Child*, Martinus Nijhoff, 1995, p. 52. The Committee in its General Comment No 2, para 5 acknowledges this vulnerability of children.

10

Human Rights Discourse in a Globalised World: Mumbai Metropolis*

NAVED JAMAL

This article seeks to posit the global discourse of human rights in terms of Liberal, Marxist, Islamic and other assorted perspectives. The UN discourse of human rights is predominantly informed by the ethos of Enlightenment in which Liberalism constitutes an important segment. States which have become members of the UN after successfully undergoing the process of decolonisation have embarked upon the task of nation-state building in which the promotion and protection of human rights and fundamental freedoms have been made obligatory. These obligations have received urgency in the context of the ongoing phenomena of globalisation and neo-liberalism. The latter have started impacting on the nature of state and society in the Third world developing countries. Besides, most of the States of the Third World are also compelled to take account of the presence of the civil society in their midst. In the backdrop of this framework cited above, the present

---

* Reprinted from Naved Jamal's published article in the Indian Journal of Human Rights Vol.-2, No.182, 1998 titled 'Human Rights Discourse : A Derivative' used by permission of the publisher of the said journal, the University of Hyderabad.

article seeks to establish and explain its viability towards one of India's most diverse Metropolises: Mumbai. There does seem to be evidence to suggest that status of human rights in relation of domestic social, economic and political forces may vary depending on the level of economic development and nature of political elite in power.

Human Rights are generally understood in terms of freedoms which are essential for the existence, survival and personality of human beings. The crystallisation of human rights in the 20th century is clear in the Universal Declaration of Human Rights (UDHR). It proclaimed human rights as a common standard of achievement for all the people's and nations of this globe. The important role of the state with regard to human rights is signified by the fact that only in an organised society does the notion of human rights make sense. Notion of human rights as norms concerning relationship between individual and state intimately links it with the notion of state. The idea that states must respect basic human rights of individuals is one which extends to the social and economic field. A point to be kept in mind in this regard is that in trying to provide a rational pattern for need satisfaction the role of the state varies with variations in the economic structure. In heterogeneous societies where there are unequal structures of authority dominant social groups have the potential to manipulate and influence state machinery to their advantage. These forms of authority have built in system of norms that are against general principles of civil rights. Understanding rights in a society specific context becomes necessary because of the peculiar problems we face in third world societies like India.

This article is broadly about relations between human rights and socio-political structures in the new emerging globalised world. Most specifically it concentrates on the contradictions between the two, which in turn is conceived to give rise to rights violations at multiple levels. The main question in this article concerns round the question that what are the underlined traditions in society, which greatly limit prospects for implementing human rights? The question explicitly places the issue of human rights within the state-society framework. If it is the case, for example that human rights are becoming increasingly controversial, then the question becomes one of examining the consequences of that controversy for the state and society. Or as the governing process becomes authoritarian in nature, how are the prospects for implementing human rights limited? Answering the question helps us to understand the changing role of the state and the growing and declining importance of human rights.

At the outset, there are complexities and differences involved in trying to answer this question satisfactorily. Second, there are competing theories, each one tending to produce a different answer to the question about nature of state and society. The third section discusses the notion of human rights. The fourth section moves from these considerations to an examination of a contradiction within the socio-political structure and their consequences in relation to human rights. The final section returns briefly to the main question.

STATE, SOCIETY AND HUMAN RIGHTS— COMPLEXITIES INVOLVED

Problems arise in the domain of state and society and the state of human rights within it, if it is not clear as to what is the nature of the social order. There is a basic relationship between state-society and human rights, and at first glance the relationship may look fairly straight forward. There is an organic connection between the two. Then the Interventionist State began with the mandate of bringing about socio-economic change so as to better the living standards and to achieve distributive justice, popular participation and poverty alleviation. The state is vested with the responsibility of protecting rights and liberty of the people. The State which protects the human rights of an individual is better able to integrate the individual within itself and thereby maintain its legitimacy. Politics is the process by which the state is able to steer society, a process involving the transformative capacity of the state including state's power to intervene in social events. It is not difficult to see that these two are inter-related. Thus, (i) societies are affected by the political actions of the state; (ii) political actions of the state are affected by what is happening in society. The difficulty however lies in specifying the nature of these connections and how they work and give rise to rights violations. Exploration of such problems tends to end up as detailed descriptions or case studies of real events and there is no satisfactory theory that considers these contradictions.

Secondly, the difficulty of coping with the questions about state-society and human rights is compounded by the growing importance and complexity of such relations. Thirdly, there is a difficulty of cultural variety. There is a certain moral arrogance about the very idea of trying to conceptualise in this context. The exercise tends to presume a moral imperative of some universal conception of a good life towards which everyone is striving and towards which social development and sensible state politics will bring us all in due course. Operating on such universal assumptions guides to description and analysis can lead one astray. The global existence of cultural heterogeneity thus adds further to the difficulties involved in trying to cope with human rights questions within the state-society framework.

A simple and clear answer to the question is not immediately available. The sole purpose of the article is to lay out ideas and illustrations relevant to a reasonable answer. One thing that emerged from the exercise is that the question needs careful exploration and willingness to accept tentative formulations. To some extent the question can be seen as rhetorical: much can be learned from exploring its complexities.

II. COMPETING THEORIES

Since one needs a theory to cope with the question and as there are several competing theories of schools of thought, there can't be a single correct answer to bring home the point. A tentative answer to the human rights question is going to be shaped by the particular theory or 'rights' being used. The purpose of this section is to identify briefly the positions the theories tend to take.

Liberal View

According to the liberal school, state is a 'conscious creation of man'. It is a contract device to protect rights. The liberal tradition starts from the premise that all human beings possess a state of perfect freedom to decide on the choice of action and the manner of dealing with their possessions.¹ Liberals proclaim pluralism in regard to values which they assume that human being may have quite different performance and conceptions about values being pursued and the only thing they have in common is the freedom to make choices. The freedom of rights according to this thinking is liberty, including freedom of religion, speech, assembly, association and movement. In traditional liberalism there is no place for economic, social and cultural rights.

Marxist View

Viewed from the Marxist angle, state is an instrument of the ruling class. It advances interests of the class in domination. It conceives of the state in a very different way. In this view, state had different historical functions in different historical stages. Marxism sees state under liberalism as a committee of the bourgeoisie, which in a transitional stage has a useful function but generally becomes more oppressive in order to maintain the class structure. Hence according to the Marx, the bourgeois state has to be overthrown by revolution in a new state which is built by the dictatorship of the proletariat. The role of the proletariat state is to accomplish two tasks: (i) to eliminate class differences and increase material abundance through technological progress and rational organisation; and (ii) elimination of scarcity and class difference will together eliminate the rationale for the state which will then wither away and make room for a communist society.

Islamic View

The Shari'at at once religion and law, invests the state with religious sanctity. There is recognition of rights and justice in Islam, but only in so far as it is compatible with God's will as expressed in the Koran and the Hadith. The Islamic Declaration of Human Rights of 1981, thus proclaimed in its preamble that –'Islam gave to mankind an ideal code of Human Rights fourteen centuries ago.'²

Eastern religions with Islam in the lead are increasingly questioning the western perception of human rights and challenging the human rights ideology as devised and understood in the West. It treats human rights as an 'external law of nature which serves to maintain' moral equilibrium of social existence.[3] As such it brings about order out of chaos. Like all major religions, Islam proudly lays claim to furthering human rights.[4] Proceeding in principle from the prescribed reason in Shari-at the member states of the Organisation of the Islamic Conference, emphasised upon the role played by fundamental rights and universal freedoms in Islamic religion. Article 1 (a) of the Cairo Declaration (August 5, 1990) held that 'all human beings form one family...all men are equal in terms of basic human dignity and basic obligations and responsibilities without any discrimination on the grounds of race, colour, language, sex, religious belief, political affiliations, social status or other considerations...'[5].

CULTURAL DIVERSITY AND HUMAN RIGHTS

It is sometimes stated that human rights are a western invention and therefore their adoption throughout the world is cultural imperialism. This argument cannot be dismissed out of hand. There are features in the human rights system that reflects western individualism, a product of both cultural and economic evolution. There is a case for cultural diversity and respect for functioning local traditions and communities. The right of local communities to maintain a degree of autonomy in regard to outside transference is important.

The argument of cultural relativism however is often used for the wrong purposes and by the wrong people. In many cases dominant groups happily accept the penetration of external interests whether it be the form of multinational corporation or other forms of external economic penetration or in the form of the utilisation of modern military and police technologies in order to maintain control over peoples who are otherwise not persuaded that the government promotes their interests. The argument of cultural relativism directed against the human rights systems is therefore sometimes used by those dominant groups in order to prevent the dominated or suppressed groups from absorbing the human rights principles and utilising them in confrontations with those powerful groups which have already abandoned for their own benefit traditional cultures.

In this process there is a tendency in male-dominated societies to emphasise the cultural traditions in respect of women but not of men. The argument of cultural relativism may then become a trap designed by the strong for the weak. This is an issue which human rights movement should take seriously; they should find the right balance between respect for genuine and functioning cultural traditions on the one hand and on the other equal rights of all members of society to absorb those parts of external cultures including human rights concerns diversify and respect for functioning local traditions and communities. The rights of local communities to maintain a degree of autonomy in regard to outside interference is important.

Summing up, the different schools appear to take diverse stands, dwelling on state and society vis-à-vis human rights, as follows:

Liberalism—a product of western individualism wherein lexical priority of liberty applies to societies that have undergone cultural and economic revolution.

Marxist—a communist society brought about following universal proletarian revolution, protects human rights.

Islamic—human rights are an eternal law of nature, and are maintained in a state sanctified by Islam.

Cultural Diversity—definition of human rights varies according to cultural diversities amongst human societies.

The cultural diversity approach will be examined more fully in later sections. There are two lessons to be drawn from this summary of different views. The first concerns about the state and society. The question which arises here is what is the nature of the state and society within it? The initial answer to this question is that it depends on the theory you are using; some allocate a greater importance to the state and society and some to the individual. Recognition of such theoretical differences is an essential first step in coping with such questions.

The other thing amounts to a note of caution. It is essential to appreciate that the brief summaries of the different schools are highly simplified versions. These theories are far more complex and sophisticated than the summaries reveal. Also there are many different and even conflicting theories within these schools. This is especially true of the liberal school.

Libertarianism is a conservative political philosophy centred around 'individual rights' and liberties which argues strenuously against re-distributive state policies. Its egalitarianism is justified precisely thorough its emphasis on property rights and the argument of self-ownership of the individual. Nozick's entitlement theory rules out collective right, group rights and community rights. His defence of rights including the theory of property expressed in his account of distributive justice is a defence of the rights of inviolable individual persons.[6] The justification of minimal state is also grounded in such an argument. The minimal state which is described as classical liberalism is not liberalism because in its very essence it is a violator of human rights. Beyond minimalisms 'obvious incompatibility with international human rights standards its commitment to protecting private property while denying all other economic and social rights borders on logical contradictions'.[7]

The notion of egoistic autonomous individuals figure prominently in the writings of Locke. According to Locke, individuals inherent right to life, liberty and property could not be removed or abrogated by the state. MacPherson argued that Locke's views on property make him a 'bourgeoisie apologist'.[8]

Mill supports the individualistic notion of rights.[9] He observes that the only purpose for which power can rightly be exercised over any member of a civilised community is to prevent harm to others. Mill excludes the backward nations, women and children from rights to liberty.

Bentham criticised natural rights as 'nonsense upon stilts'. According to him rights are conferred by law, they can be made intelligible by reducing them to positive laws utilitarian underpinnings.[10] If natural rights and positive rights are viewed within the integrated perspective it could lead to a plausible definition of human rights. This however has been difficult to achieve as positive laws are not always predicated to socio-economic rights. Democracy is associated with realisation and toleration of man's rights and political equality. But it must be stressed that political equality cannot be realised without socio-economic equality. With reference to positive law Marshall believed that it had contributed to democratisation and guaranteeing of political rights in the West. However socio-economic inequalities in the West pose a serious threat to the realisation of man's democratic ideals.

Although civil, political, social, economic and cultural rights as envisaged in the UDHR are universally accepted by all states of the UN, a full realisation of them remains to be seen. The laws devised tend to justify inequalities on the grounds of preserving the social order.

CHANGING CHARACTER OF STATE AND SOCIETY

Before concentrating on human rights, a brief comment is in order regarding the rapidly changing character of state and society. There is a tremendous heterogeneity from country to country. One should be aware of accepting uncritically any general proposition about the state-society system. Any answer to the question about human rights cannot assume that society is some static formation. State relations within society are going to change through time because social processes are dynamic in character.

The rights discourse within the third world emphasises the need to redefine rights. The traditional oppressive structures in the post-colonial democracies hinder comprehensive growth of human beings.[11]

Moreover, the process of modernisation and development has meant an increasing accretion of political power within the traditional social hierarchy re-inforced by new source of power thorough access to modern technology and increasing oppression of the traditionally deprived.

Rights cannot be understood in the framework of state versus individual or citizen for rights are asserted either in terms of caste, class or religious community in the third world. Similarly sources of injustice and exploitation basically lie in the socio-economic structure because civil society is yet to take a concrete shape in third world societies like India.

The implicit assumption of liberal discourse is the assumption of systemic equilibrium, structured stability and incremental changes. This does not help understand problems of third world societies like India which emanate from the path of development and the unjust and undemocratic social order — one reinforcing the other.

Social development has to take cognisance of power relations in socially powerful groups to play a leading role in management of polity and economy.

An attempt is made to capture the processes at work in politics which are responsible for the crisis of human rights. We try to construct a theme linking the class rule, exploitation and skewed development with growing unrest and state repression. The dominance, inequality and exploitation which permit the society dominated by partisan politics are articulated in the form of contradictions among various classes. These social contradictions and the failure to resolve them are responsible for human rights violation at multiple levels in our society. On the one hand, Indian State is endowed with many responsibilities like protection of rights and improving people's standards of living and protecting democratic values[12] while on the other hand, we see declining credibility and increasing ineffectiveness of the Indian state.

An answer to the main question- what are the underlying contradictions in society which generally limit prospects for implementing human rights—requires us to move from general to particular. It is also one, broadly speaking, that emanates from cultural diversity approach to the issue of human rights. Growing social unrest, including class conflict direct attention to the interactions between the state and social forces that help explain India's growing problems of governability.[13]

The answer runs roughly along the following lines:

a) Rights discourse within the third world emphasises to redefine rights.

b) Rights cannot be understood in the framework of State versus individual or citizen for rights are asserted either in terms of caste, class or religious community in the third world.

c) Sources of injustice and exploitation lie in the socio-economic structure. This is because civil society is yet to take concrete shape in the third world societies.

d) State-centric view of rights ignores the problems arising in the domain of civil society.

e) Understanding rights in a society specific context becomes necessary because of peculiar problem we face in our society.

'Individualistic notion of rights as understood in the west which presumes social cohesion can not be applied to plural communitarian Indian society.[14] The segmental view of the liberal discourse understands the violation of rights of women, minorities and ethnic groups as specific to them. This understanding ignores that the sources of these violations is located at a far deeper level in the 'socio-economic structure' of society.[15]

A CASE STUDY: POLITICAL-ECONOMIC CONTRADICTIONS GIVING RISE TO HUMAN RIGHTS VIOLATIONS IN THE METROPOLIS OF MUMBAI

This particular case focuses squarely on the contradictions between state-society and human rights, bringing it to life via concrete illustrations. It concentrates on the most important type of contradiction inherent in the political and economic process that affect society. It also considers an important question—how are human rights drawn into such processes.

The answer to the above question lies in the dual role played by politics in society. It reflects social forces and intervenes to transform the social structure. While performing the tasks of social development politics enters in a network of relationships with culture and history of society. The state in this context refers to aggregate power structure of society. It entails social basis of state power or social groups and classes who exercise power in society, and the way power is exercised and defended.

Economic processes can interact with politics in such a way as to seriously endanger the autonomy of individuals.

In independent India, Bombay continued as one state consisting of Maharashtra and Gujarat. This was an experiment in bilingualism.[16] Under the Bombay Re-organisation Act, 1960, Maharashtra and Gujarat were divided into separate states (w.e.f. 1.5.1960), with Maharashtra retaining the old capital, Bombay. Bombay was re-named as Mumbai by Shiv Sena Government in 1995, when it came into power.

Mumbai is a teeming metropolis accounting for 60% of the work force in the state of Maharashtra. It contributes nearly 25%

of the state net domestic product.[17] The stock exchange of Mumbai ranks third largest in the world with only USA and Japan preceding it.[18]

Mumbai until 1993 was often called an 'island of peace'[19] where local energies were mostly spent on monetary and business gains. This scenario has rapidly changed over a short span of four to five years. A spate of communal violence has emerged as a dark side of the growing contradiction within its social and political fabric—pursuit for political power has not excluded communal passions. Mumbai has come to be considered as commercially violent.[20] Communal violence particularly in Mumbai can be attributed to the emergence of modern capitalism because democratic politics and modern capitalism are essentially competitive in nature and it is this competition which gives rise to socio-economic contradictions. The rise and growth of Shiv Sena (an explicit communal organisation) is a reflection of the socio-economic dynamics in the region. The Congress party through its policies of accommodation like political patronage for its supporters, welfare schemes for the poor, reservation of seats in government jobs for the socially weaker sections, had successfully dominated state politics in Maharashtra. The policies meant to accommodate competitive groups though initially successful, could not sustained under conditions of proliferating claimants for patronage. In the long run this resulted in alienation of the dominant social groups from the Congress Party. The problems of the Congress were compounded by its image as a faction-ridden and corrupt party in the state. In order to save itself the party resorted to centralisation of power which only further eroded its credibility. Further more, the deteriorating socio-economic conditions led to widespread disillusionment with the Congress rule among the youth and middle classes.

It was under these circumstances that Shiv Sena under the charismatic leadership of Bal Thackeray raised a bid for political power. It came up with slogans of 'Hindu nationalist' and 'Maharastrian self-respect' alongside many other policies and programs to cover a diversity of social groups including weaker sections, minorities, women, workers and labourers. The 'free meals for the poor' schemes caught the people's imagination as it addressed the immediate needs of the survival of the poor. However this along with other schemes of urban resettlement and slum clearance were essentially populist in nature meant only to garner political support, and with no commitment to actual upliftment of the socially deprived.

Shiv Sena's electoral success saw the party reverting to the authoritarian style of functioning with a highly centralised decision-making system. Centralised power has always been a threat to democratic norms and institutions. It endangers people's rights as it relies mainly on the coercive apparatus to solute pressing social problems.[21] These bring us to an important point of distinction between state violence and social violence. Social violence has its roots in unfavourable social, political, and economic conditions, and generally results in violations of laws. But the state whose moral basis is the law cannot violate the law. State-violence tends to contradict the rationale for the basis of state. Another implication of this distinction is that there is no room for observance of human rights under autocratic dominant political systems. Such type of state aims at eliminating opposition while reducing the visibility of their excesses. It is awesome to note that Mumbai accounted for a very high percentage of detunes under the draconian Terrorist And Disruptive Activities Prevention Act (TADA) which has been cited as an examples of legislations which trample upon basic human rights and severely curtail civil liberties. (See Table)

Incidence and rate of cases reported under TADA

Year	Incidence of Crime	Crime rate	Persons arrested
1990	0	0.0	-
1991	40	0.3	62
1992	89	0.7	215
1993	108	0.8	493
1994	15	0.1	86

Source: *Crime in India*, New Delhi, National Crime Records, 1990-94.

Articulation of social tensions varies with the variations in political and economic power of the dominant castes on the one hand and the consciousness of the oppressed on the other. What is alarming is the involvement of men who are in power and the overt and covert collaboration óf police with them. This has a spill over effect on the rights of the poor. These unresolved existing and emerging contradictions in society cannot be tackled by a political change at the top. What needs to be done is to tackle the root of the problems and not use force to suppress its manifestations. Contrary to this logic the atrocities on the minorities were used by the ruling parties to discredit and defeat each other. The problem of poverty, unemployment and an overly coercive state continued un-addressed in the face of globalisation. Economic stratification in Mumbai broadly coincides with social stratification. Majority of the agricultural and industrial labourers are Muslims. The mutual reinforcement of one stratification by the other accentuated communal identity and blunted class polarisation.

The formidable unemployed youth force in Mumbai is one of the major sources of social polarisation. It has contributed to the riots and violence waves witnessed in Mumbai. Amongst the other strong reactions to the oppressive socio-economic order compounded by skewed politics is the rise of Dalit (downtrodden masses) consciousness. Here again systematic violence has been inflicted on them by the police to suppress the Dalit (Hindu low caste) movement.

It can be deduced from the crime data which shows not one but three trends:

(a) The minimal lowering of violence in 1991;
(b) An increase in 1992 during the upbeat of globalisation; and
(c) Peak rise in 1993 at the time of New Economic Policy of liberalisation and a substantive decline in 1994.

The Process of modernisation and development in the region enunciated by structural adjustments did nothing to solve the problems of the poor. The New Economic Policy (NEP) of the Congress Government with its thrust on privatisation and mercerisation had no comprehensive plan about welfare commitment on the part of the state from its welfare domain. This had an adverse impact on the standards of living of the already poor. Mumbai has witnessed a proliferation of slums where a majority of the population lives, largely neglected by the state. The response of the government to the slum problem has been to demolish them.

Furthermore in land disputes and urban housing problems in Mumbai the victims of police violence are mostly members of minorities or other group occupying the lowest rung in the social ladder.

The case study of Mumbai provides illustration of a number of concerns raised in the article. The transition from a more accommodative to a centralised state and its effect on autonomy of individuals is clearly evident. This happened because parties in power were controlled by economically dominant classes which related differently to the minorities and the poor sections in society. This also brought to light the fact that a change in regime or in managers of state apparatus does not necessarily imply a change in the nature of the State.

In Mumbai, though the population was politically mobilised on communal lines, there was not objective clash of interests between competing political elite. This gave rise to violation of democratic rights of marginal groups. The most striking thing about this case is the way it shows how economic processes can profoundly affect politics in society and lead to violation of human rights.

The article has outlined a number of suggestions, which need to be borne in mind while dealing with any general question related to the issue of human rights within the framework of state-society. There does seem to be evidence to suggest that status of human rights in relation to domestic social, economic and political forces may vary depending on the level of economic development and nature of political elite in power.

End Notes

[1] John Locke, *Two Treaties of Government*. Peter Laslett (ed.) Cambridge: Cambridge University Press 1960, s.6.
[2] See *Islamic Declaration of Human Rights*. 1981, London: Islamic Council.
[3] Wahiduddin, Moulana,Khan, *Indian Muslims: The Need for a Positive Outlook* New Delhi: Al-Risala Books, 1994, p.11.
[4] Henkin,Louis, *The Rights of Man Today*, Boulder: Westview Press, 1978, p. xiii.
[5] Lawson, Edward, *Encyclopedia of Human Rights*. Second Edition, United States of America: Taylor& Francis, 1996, p. 176
[6] Robert Nozick,. 1974, *Anarchy, State and Utopia*, Oxford: Basil Blackwell. Nozick, 1974, p.172.

[7] Rhoda Howard, and Jack.Donnelly, 1986, 'Human Dignity, Human Rights and Political Regimes, *American Political Science Review*, September. Howard & Donnelly, 1986, p.807.

[8] C.B. MacPherson, 1975, *Democratic Theory: Essay in Retrieval*, Oxford: Clarendon Press, 1975: 233-34

[9] J.S.Mill, 1910, *Utilitarian: Liberty and Representative Government*, London: Everyman, 1910, p. 74.

[10] Jeremy, Bentham, *The Works of Jeremy Bentham*, Jophn Bowring (ed.) New York: Russel & Russel, 1962, p. 501.

[11] Neera, Chandhoke, 'Of States and Civil Societies', in Chandhoke Neera, (ed.) *Understanding the Post-Colonial World*. New Delhi: Sterling, 1994, p. 197.

[12] Paul. R, Brass *The Politics of India since Independence*. New Delhi: Cambridge University Press, 1997.

[13] Atul, Kohli, *Democracy and Discontent: India's Growing Crisis of Governability*, Cambridge: Cambridge University Press, 1990, p. 19.

[14] See Rajni, Kothari, *State Against Democracy: In Search of Humane Governance*, Delhi: Ajanta Publications, 1989

[15] See A.R. Desai, 1986, 'Government Lawlessness', *Economic and Political Weekly*, Vol. 21, No. 23, June.

[16] Donald, Rosenthal, R. 1974, 'Making it in Maharashtra, *The Journal of Politics*, Vol.36, 1974, p. 413

[17] S.P. Gulahti, *Encyclopaedia of India: Maharashtra*, Vol VII, New Delhi: Rima Publishing House, 1992, p. 287

[18] *Ibid.*, p. 302

[19] Ashotosh Varshney, and Wilkinson, Steven, I. 1995, 'Hindu-Muslim Riots in India (1960-1993) What We Know, What We Don't', *Towards Secular India*, Vol1, No. 4, October-December, 1995, p. 45

[20] *Ibid*, p. 43

[21] See Gerard Henze,. 1992, 'Shiv Sena and National Hinduism', *Economic and Political Weekly*. 3rd October.

11

The Impact of Globalisation on Human Rights: A Case of India
MEHTAB MANZAR

> '...the tyrannical individual is even unhappier if he is not left to live as a private citizen, but has the misfortune to be thrust by circumstances to supreme power.'
>
> (Plato)

The phenomenon of Globalisation is the brain child of about a few American doctrinaire conservatives who drafted the 'Project for a New American Century' (PNAC). This think-tank has been the policy guru of George Bush who lured the best economic and political brains of the world to grab and initiate the process of adopting Globalisation. Apart from other major hazards, Globalisation has evolved into a world of poverty and hunger and denial of basic human rights to the common man. India is a great victim of Globalisation and the agricultural classes, the marginalised, dalits, minorities women, the aged, are all engulfed in poverty, starvation, ill health and lack of a decent standard of life. The UN, the state, and civil society - are silent spectators of their miseries. The question arises: Why Globalisation? At whose cost? For whom?

The post Cold-War era witnessed globalisation as the most dominating phenomenon in international relations which became more and more complex with diverse perspectives. Soon it captured the economies of the world and penetrated into social, political, ethical and other major areas of human relationships. Almost all aspects of human activities have come under its influence deliberately or vice-versa. Now international relations has turned into a more complex field of study and analysis because of the involvement of a large number of actors, agents and factors in inter-state and intra-state relations as well. Global market, global society, global village, global economy, and global culture are many such terms in usage today as familiar topics of discussion and debate.

Basically, globalisation is an economic phenomenon which expanded to other fields of human life later on. It denotes different meanings to different people. To economists, it is a concept which aims at the expansion of borderless economies in all parts of the world across countries and regimes, emphasising more economic freedom and concessions to economic enterprises. To political scientists, it is a theory of expansion of liberal democratisation to all corners of the globe emphasising essentially social, political, economic and cultural freedom. Likewise, it appeals to scientists, psychologists, doctors and other specialists as they interepret it in their own ways.

As a dominant force in the present context, globalisation has increased interaction among peoples and states, cultures, economies, groups and nations, media, political parties, pressure groups, interest groups, trade unions, specialists etc. The amazing revolution in the field of information technology has accelerated its pace of expansion. Now the world is literally transformed into a small entity- a global village, characterised by the immense power of access, availability and connectivity. Quick and faster connections, actions and reactions have contributed to a chain of co-related events.

The direct implications of this new economic phenomenon, called 'globalisation' is addressed to the economic policies of States and governments. It has also engaged them into economic debates of various nature at international, national, regional and even local levels. Those nation states were caught in a dilemma who could neither dare to exclude from the globalisation process, nor grab its benefits immediately and absorb them in respective economic strategies. The trend has been to give a serious thinking, discussion and debate at public and institutional levels to various aspects of globalisation and specially to particular national interests.

However, the Western powers, once again, proved their overwhelming political and economic domination which made globalisation, unavoidable and inescapable for the developing world. They also succeeded in their objective of overpowering the economies of the rest of the world and make the best out of the global resources for their own prosperity and sustainance.

Human Rights Yardstick

Since globalisation dominated international relations during the last decade of the twentieth century, it also influenced and motivated policy formulators in the corridors of diplomatic power. Soon, globalisation captured the issues of human rights and developed into a yardstick to be used by the advocates of globalisation. Economic aid, financial support, concessional loans etc. were clipped with the instruments of human rights, to gain political, economic and social supremacy over the developing states, in particular.

The political compromise between globalisation and the western yardstick has added to the woes of human kind. The developing and the undeveloped world are the worst sufferers of hunger, poverty, illness, backwardness, threat of deadly disease and all sorts of difficulties of life. These States, though largely benefited with/by globalisation, are undoubtedly the victims of the hidden interests of the developed world. If we review/study the UNDP Human Development Reports, it is easily understood that the overall situation of human life has not substantially changed. Neither the cooperation among nations spread over the last six decades nor the enthusiastic implementation of globalisation has transformed the condition of millions of the poor worldwide.

The United Nations, since its very inception has shown great concern for peace, security, justice, dignity and worth of the human kind. The journey towards realisation of human rights of all the peoples of the world started with the UN charter which 'reaffirmed faith in fundamental human rights, in the dignity and worth of the human person, in the equal rights of men and women and of nations large and small', and 'to promote social progress and better standards of life in larger freedom'. To achieve these noble objectives of the welfare of humanity, it was pledged, apart from other methods, 'to employ international machinery for the promotion of economic and social advancement of all peoples'.[1]

The UN Declaration of Human Rights was a follow up of the UN charter which declared that 'human beings are born equal in dignity and rights', therefore, entitled to all freedoms and rights as mentioned in the Declaration without any distinction of race, colour, sex, religion, gender etc. It was the first major international declaration on human rights which manifested the determination of the United Nations towards the achievement of human dignity, equality, liberty and prosperity of all nations. Later on, negotiations among the nations were arranged at the UN Platform. After massive exercises of debates, meetings, discussions, consultations and other techniques of exchanging ideas, two major covenants were framed, adopted by the General Assembly in 1966 under the titles 'International covenant on Civil and Political Rights, and, International covenant on Economic, Social and Cultural Rights.' These two significant UN documents on human rights set a landmark in the struggle towards human dignity and freedom.

Since then, a large number of covenants, regional and international conferences, meetings, debates have added billions of words to the UN documents on Human Rights which have brought almost all areas of human life under its umbrella. Problems of women, children, elderly persons, ethnic groups, war, affected persons, refugees, environment, development, population, health, education, sanitation, water, and many other issues have been of great concern to the United Nations.

The signatory States have accepted the norms set by the United Nations for the implementation of the UN human rights system and make all possible efforts to protect, promote the fundamental human rights in their respective states. India too is a prominent member state of the United Nations. Being second most populated and the seventh largest state (area-wise) in the world and by virtue of being one of the major states in Asia, its acceptance of the UN system for human rights implementation is equally significant. Accordingly, India is committed to eradicate poverty, to maintain minimum standards of human life, to provide elementary free education, primary health services along with food and shelter to the poorest. For the realisation, protection and promotion of human rights, India has developed its own administrative and legal mechanism. The initiative was taken by establishing the National Human Rights Commission in 1993, followed by Commissions on women, minorities, scheduled castes, scheduled tribes and now on children.

Human Rights and Globalisation

As globalisation has immensely influenced all aspects of human life, human rights is no exception. The most prominent development has been in the form of human rights as a diplomatic strategy of the developed world especially the US. This integration of human rights with global marketing and global enterprises has been of grave concern for the rest of the world vis-à-vis the dominant political powers. The fact is that globalisation has captured human rights as a hostage and therefore, exploiting the human rights' situation for the core purposes of economic prosperity of the dominant political group. Even the status of nations has gone major changes because of globalisation, making the latter more complex, multi-dimensional and too difficult to be interpreted fully. Its integration with social progress and justice has experienced serious jolts as far as the growth process in the developing world is concerned. Not only this, even local minor issues of socio-economic and political nature may be observed under the surveillance of globalisation. Therefore, even sovereignty and the extent of state authority seem to be under the threat of globalisation.

Now, the state is no more a central point of authority, as this authority has been eroded because of the negative impacts of globalisation, along with other factors. No doubt, the United Nations is the true champion of human rights but in a global village, human life has been shattered because of the inflow of MNCs into the state. We do not here underscore the benefits of the phenomenon but we can't ignore that this has been one of the major causes of the violation of human rights all over the world, especially in developing and undeveloped World. Now human rights have become victims of trade bargaining by developed states in the name of worldwide connectivity among the peoples and states. Leading to the formulation of public policies and legal arrangements, globalisation has made western values, norms, practices easily accessible to the developing world. Apparently, provisions of more economic freedom and opportunities have also been made. This phenomenon is very attractive but, in practice, the situation has emerged as contradictory in nature. The national economic systems, local trade activities, varieties of traditional economic transactions, production, consumption and distribution of various local commodities have been badly affected. The competitive framework of globalisation has immensely disturbed, disintegrated the national values of various societies.

India Embraces Globalisation

The financial crisis faced by India in the late 80s and the accelerating pressures of international institutions such as World Bank, IMF etc. to introduce economic reforms, consequently, led India to accept the phenomenon of globalisation and gradually absorb its norms into public policies. In fact, these proposed economic reforms were clipped with certain economic and political strings which brain washed the Indian top economists who got impressed by the concepts developed by Western economists and political strategists. The policy opened the floodgates of international capital into the country and very soon, multi-national companies were overwhelmingly welcomed by the elite, industrial class and dominant political groups who were fascinated by the flow of wealth. But the reality turned out to be quite the reverse as upcoming days unfolded itself.

According to Chunkara, 'After a stringent regime of 'autarky and command and controlled economy, from 1956 to 1975, India started a slow path of reintegration into the world economy, albeit in nascent form...' But this reintegration could not resolve the economic problems of the common man. The concept of globalisation was too complex and fashioned on the lines of Western interests, their norms, mind sets and so on. Even the United Nations realised the grim aspects in these words: 'While the globalisation of world economy has provided new opportunities for development, it has also created new risks. There is a risk of marginalisation of countries, groups and individuals that are unable to compete, as well as the increased possibility of economic or financial instability and social discontent'.[2]

It is true that India is competent enough to compete with other states, because of its vast resources – natural as well as human. India has been benefited by the UN bodies like UNICEF, UNESCO, WHO, World Bank etc. With their help, there have been tremendous achievements in areas like primary education, basic health facilities, extinction of some diseases, health and sanitation. Therefore, the mortality rate has gone down. Improvements have been noticed in the fields of safe drinking water to some villages, job opportunities in urban areas, land and credits accessible by the poor. These human rights indicators show an improved social picture of the country but the ground realties are harsh and bitter. A recent UN Report has urged Asian nations including India to refocus on agriculture, because migration to urban areas on a large scale has been adding to the governance problems. Instead of uprooting a huge population from their grass roots system to improving their living standards they must be relieved of the stresses of social and economic stagnation to come out of extreme poverty within the regions themselves.

According to Social Development Report, '...the distribution of poverty in India's hierarchical society remains skewed against traditionally disadvantaged sections of the population, including indigenous peoples and dalits. These disadvantaged sections accounted for 75% of the total number of poor people in India in 1999-2000'.[3]

To remove social and economic inequalities, a comprehensive policy dwelling on all aspects of the miseries of the poor and disadvantaged, must be taken into account. According to World Development Report, 2000-2001, poverty is characterised by the lack of assets, security and power. Being the largest democracy in the world, India has to concentrate on its art of governance – to make it devoid of corruption, discrimination, red tapism and bias against the poor.

Accountability:

Eradication of poverty and elimination of all socio-economic evils are the basic requirements leading towards development which is the ultimate goal of globalisation. The states, the civil society, NGOs and all groups and individuals are collectively responsible to carry on this objective. Of course, the most responsible role has to be played by the state only, which again is an embodiment of coercion and power. Instead of yielding positive results, the poor and the disadvantaged are neglected by the bureaucracy. Therefore, accountability of the state is the most significant pre-condition to eradicate poverty. 'There are often anti-poor biases built into the mechanisms through which disadvantaged people are entitled to use accountability mechanisms directly, such as the access restrictions that face litigants who might wish to seek judicial remedies against powerful state or non-state actors'.[4] In its report submitted to the UN Human Rights Commission, and then to the UN Economic and Social Council, the third working group suggested to the states to adopt economic and social measures to avoid exclusion of groups marginalised by extreme poverty.

o The Disadvantaged and Marginalised Groups: Minorities, dalits, Scheduled tribes, women, children, farmers in some parts of Andhra Pradesh, Maharashtra, Orrisa, Jharkhand, Chattisgarh, Madhya Pradesh, etc. and a greater number of rural people are most disadvantaged groups deprived of even the basic necessities of a dignified human life. Hunger, non-employment, debt, poor sanitation, lack of health facilities, social exclusion in the name of caste, religion, etc are important features of their lives. This does not thereby imply that the urban life and especially that of the middle and lower middle class is not free of difficulties. A study by WHO finds nearly half of India suffers from anxiety, depression, memory disorders and other signs of distress.[5] According to National Crime Records Bureau (NCRB), 1.13 lakh people committed suicide in the country in 2004.[6]

Sufferings of Rural India:

According to the Planning Commission's figures over 260 million Indians still live below the poverty line, 75% of these are living in rural areas. Various schemes have been launched recently to overcome this malaise of hunger – poverty in rural areas, notable among these is the National Rural Employment Guarantee Act. But poverty alleviation is still a dream to come true. However India is committed to achieve Millennium Development Goals by 2015 which has linked peace and security with social justice, human rights with fundamental freedoms and the right to development.

All sorts of miseries are experienced by rural Indians. Some states of the Indian Union have a grave situation as socio-economic disparities vary from state to state, district to district. The pain of poverty is realised by the farmers who with all physical hardships are unable to yield so much as to earn sufficient livelihood for their families. The burden of debt plus interest rates keeps them under severe stress. In the absence of health facilities, the farmers are unable to maintain their health and keep the wheel of life and work in motion. Their families too feel the deprivation – children, instead of joining schools, are compelled to work, women with many health, food problems face great difficulties to perform their household duties/work efficiently. The elders are worst victims of poverty.

Though, the Indian economy is receiving unprecedented global attention and it is being perceived as one of the major economic powers in the near future, the situation in rural India raises doubts over such prospects. Under globalisation, the Indian economy undoubtedly got a great boost. But the beneficiaries of globalisation are not traceable in most of the rural areas. India's GDP may be shining, economists are compiling volumes on India's growing economy, but this is just a paper tiger. Has the spate of starvation deaths shaken the rich and the powerful? Who thinks that the responsibility of looking after the poor lies with the state as the most organised and legally powerful institution. The Panchayati Raj institutions empowered by the 73rd and 74th Amendments have hardly achieved the aim of democratisation of power to villages. The census of India, 2001 recorded 12.66 million working children in the age group of 5-14 years of which 90% child labourers belong to rural areas.

The state, with the support and aid from the United Nations, ILO, UNICEF, NGOs and individuals has been trying hard to bring the children to school and not to work, but the targets are still far to be under the control of the State. Poverty and social ignorance still remains two powerful currents driving the children to work. These deprived child labourers when grown up, become uneducated, backward, ignorant, starved parents giving birth to the next generation of their own kind.

Why Globalisation?

This phenomena is not new, it is deeply rooted into the economic domination of the world by Europe, manifested in the policy of colonisation of Asia, Africa and Latin America. Though defeated by the nationalist waves, colonialism remerged as an economic threat to the developing nations in the name of a free, post world war humanity. Then the demise of the cold war helped the emergence of a new aggressive competitive global economic order. The officials at the United Nations realise that globalisation and liberalisation are posing new challenges to social development. There is a growing concern with achieving a more equitable sharing of the benefits of globalisation. Many governments, which have made great sacrifices in economic reforms and liberalisation, feel that they are yet to reap the anticipated benefits of globalisation. These benefits, moreover, have not been equally distributed, not even in the developed counties. For more than half of the world's population who have not benefited from it, the new global economy has often deepened the feeling of despair that the weak will never be able to compete with the already strong and powerful. 'There is a need to better direct the benefits of liberalised trade and investment towards reducing poverty, increasing employment and promoting social integration.'[7]

Globalisation has definitely increased the number of millionaires in India along with the number of starving farmers, small traders, common men whose number is much greater than the rich people. The sequence of industrial development may be going high on economic graphs, the number of medical tourists is multiplying but 70% of the population in India is still dreaming of basic medical facilities. Malnutrition is high among Indian children, women and aged people. Does it connote the glorious term of Globalisation? The Central Government has realised that armed forces in tough terrain desire high scales of allowances as much as Rs. 5600 p.m. rather than what is given to them, at present, i.e. Rs. 3734.00[8] p.m. Is the state really concerned about the feelings of these jawans who are committing suicides for just a few thousand or even few hundred rupees' debts? To quote V.R. Krishna Iyer, 'Poverty alleviation programmes are abounding in print and are propagandised hypocritically by every Party in State Power, the Left not excepted, and the United Front is truly guilty as it loyally, but ironically, follows the 'irreversible progress' of the IMF commandants. It is the comatose opium of the huge have-nots and the glow of life of the top glitterati. Privatisation and Globalisation are but Orwellian newspeak and this pro-MNC world order is forced by the North on the South...'[9]

Truly the words are bitter and harsh, but express the real ground realities in India. The failure of the poverty alleviation policy of the Indian state can be understood in the light of what Neil Smith put into words: 'In the US, and to a lesser extent throughout the advanced capitalist world, with the wealth of the upper classes now so disproportionately dependent on remittances from the global economy and from the sweat of the workers around the world, this elevation of free trade to the most human of human rights was not only a brazen apology for global looting, but it eloquently marks the victory of a new liberalised ideology in which market forces attain the stature of natural laws, and habitual winners in the capitalist jackpot defend their piles of booty as the product of natural right.'[10]

Conclusion:

Our foremost concern is: Why the human rights system developed by the United Nations, hasn't been successful in restoring dignity, worth, social justice equality and freedom to human kind? Why could not the whole world be in a position to combat the manifesto for the 'Project for a New American Century' (PNAC)? Why only two dozen doctrinaire American conservatives have been allowed to put billions of people on distress and misery?

We are stunned by the glitterati of Globalisation and yet observe bloodshed in Sri Lanka, Afghanistan, Palestine, Iraq, Botswana with relative indifference? The hidden agenda of Globalisation is not and can't be exposed for the cause of humanity? The states of the developing world are mesmerised, who'll speak on behalf of their peoples? Why the civilisation – the culture, the values of so many lands be allowed to crush under the bulldozer of Globalisation? Have the concepts of 'Nation-State, 'National Sovereignty', 'Self-determination' enriched by the sacrifices of millions of freedom fighters, meaningless and their sacrifices forgotten? The brain washing of ruling classes and elites have benefited the developed world, the US in particular. The truth is far from the reality: Globalisation has been more destructive than the two world wars and more hazardous than the Hiroshima and Nagasaki episodes. We, as a living nation, have to decide either to combat West's monopoly or keep our heads high in grace.

End Notes

[1] Basic facts about the United Nations. UN Department of Public Information, New York, 2000, p.5
[2] The Right to Development : UN Department of Public Information, New York, 1998, p.3
[3] Social Development Report. Chief Editor: Amitabh Kundan released on World Website.
[4] R.C. Mishra : Governance of Human Rights: Challenges in the Age of Globalisation. Authorspress, New Delhi, 2003, p.53
[5] For more details, see WHO Report on Health Survey of India, January, 2007
[6] The latest reports on the subject are under analysis.
[7] Basic Facts about the United Nations. Pp 157-158
[8] Hindustan Times, August 3, 2007
[9] V.R. Krishna Iyer: Globalisation Threatens Humanism
[10] Neil Smith: The Endgame of Globalisation. Routledge, New York 2005, p.145

12

Human Rights Education in the Age of Globalisation: Role of UGC

SYED MEHARTAJ BEGUM

One of the major concerns of the world today is centered on human rights. Human rights are generally defined as the rights which every human being is entitled to enjoy and to have protected. But the protection of human rights is the greatest challenge before every country particularly in the underdeveloped and developing countries. In India, even after completion of sixty years of Independence, an atmosphere for a life of human dignity has not been created.

One of the major concerns of the world today is centred on human rights. Human rights are generally defined as the rights which every human being is entitled to enjoy and to have protected. These include the first generation rights which are mainly concerned with the civil and political rights of the individual; the second generation rights which can be said to be security-oriented and provide for social, economic and cultural security; and the third generation rights are environmental, cultural and developmental rights. The protection of human rights is the greatest challenge before every country, particularly in the underdeveloped and developing countries. In India, even after completion of six decades of Independence, an atmosphere of a life of human dignity has not been created.

The Universal Declaration of Human Rights 1948 consists of a preamble and 30 articles recording the basic human rights and fundamental freedoms to which all men and women in the world are entitled to without any discrimination. In March 1993, UNESCO International Congress on Education for Human Rights and Democracy held at Montreal adopted human rights as a precondition for sustainable development, the civil society and democracy. It also accepted that Human Rights Education provides protection from discrimination, unfair treatment, undemocratic attitude, deterioration of cultural values, unawareness of society and environment, exploitation, bondage and abuses of human rights at any level. In June 1993, the U.N. World Conference on Human Rights held at Vienna drafted a Declaration ultimately inspiring the U.N. Decade for Human Rights Education 1995-2004. The Vienna Declaration stated that 'human rights education, training and public information are essential for the promotion and achievement of stable and harmonious relations among communities and for fostering mutual understanding, tolerance and peace'.

It is universally accepted that education is the best source of social mobility, equality and empowerment, both at the individual and collective levels. Education is necessary for people to know and understand their rights. Without knowing your rights, you cannot stand up for them. It is more important for women, who enjoy unequal status in many societies. For knowing our rights properly, it is utmost important that there should be human rights experts who are capable of challenging human rights violations whenever and wherever it takes place. Human Rights Education has begun to gather tremendous momentum in the new world order as a panacea of globalisation, liberalisation and privatisation because it is considered an important tool which can do both for the promotion and progressive realisation of human rights and for the protection and prevention of human rights violations in the process of development.

Objective of the Study:

Education is a powerful means of influencing people and changing their attitudes. The universities and colleges can play a vital role in developing people's awareness on human rights and attitudes appropriate to implement human rights concepts. Unfortunately, the Indian Education System has only recently begun to promote Human Rights Education. In India, the University Grants Commission (UGC) is a major national partner in the promotion of human rights culture. This article tends to highlight the significance of Human Rights Education and to make an assessment of the role of UGC in promoting it in India. In addition, few suggestions have also been laid out to further strengthen the Human Rights Education.

Significance of Human Rights Education:

In India, where majority of the people are not yet aware about their own rights the ideals of social justice, equality, fairness etc. may be reduced to mere day dreaming. In order to protect human rights, people must be aware about their rights and possible violations. Therefore, there is urgent need of Human Rights Education which develops the human rights and other related concepts properly. It is a tool for peaceful societal transformation with a gender perspective and framework for social development. It helps in empowering and building of capabilities of women, men, youth and children through critical thinking, understanding, applying and claiming all human rights. It contributes to strengthening the rule of law and capacity building for democratic governance, accountability and global governmental stability.

Human Rights Education is a lifelong process for the development of harmonious personality to comprehend the ever widening and deepening sphere of human endeavours. It is regarded as a weapon for the struggle against exploitation and removal of impediments to the growth of individual and socio-economic and political development of the country. Human Rights Education not only raises awareness about the human rights, but also protects from any form of discrimination; provide democratic structure, values as well as individual freedom. It protects from infringement of rights of racial, ethnic and religious groups in any country or area through inculcations of global awareness and mutual understanding among the citizens.

In the Indian context, Human Rights Education becomes more important as increasing violations of human rights, cases of custodial violence, mass detentions without trial, bonded and child labour and environmental degradation etc. are being brought daily to the public's attention by NGOs, media and public interest litigators. Moreover, Human Rights Education is essential for the revival of human values ingrained in the composite Indian culture and bring back the lost glory of our country.

UGC's Role in promoting Human Rights Education:

The UGC has been proactive in promoting Human Rights Education. In 1980, the UGC set up the Justice S.M. Sikri Committee on Human Rights Education. Justice Sikri Committee came up with a 'Blueprint for Promotion of Human Rights Education in India at All Levels' in 1983. This led to some restructuring of courses of study in some universities but chiefly limited to Law Schools. In 1985, the UGC prepared a blueprint for promotion of human rights teaching and research at all levels of education which also contained proposals for restructuring of existing syllabi and introduction of new human rights courses for students of all disciplines at the undergraduate and postgraduate levels for both professional and non-professional education.

However, the golden moment for Human Rights Education in India came when in pursuance of the United Nations General Assembly Resolution of December 23, 1994, declaring the period 1995-2004 as the UN Decade for Human Rights Education and the Programme of Action finalised in October 1995, 'Action Plan – Human Rights Education' was approved by the Government of India. In addition to others, the Action Plan included the need for introducing of human rights courses at the undergraduate and postgraduate levels; starting short-term/long term courses on human rights through the distance mode by the Indira Gandhi National Open University and other universities which should be encouraged by the UGC to take up these courses by liberal funding; and universities and colleges should be encouraged to hold seminars/symposia/workshops on issues of human rights.

In view of the above, the UGC started taking initiatives to promote Human Rights Education by providing financial assistance for introducing courses and organising seminars, symposia and workshops on human rights in universities and colleges. In the year 1997, the UGC framed guidelines 'UGC IX Plan Approach for the Promotion of Human Rights Education in Universities and Colleges' with an objective to promote Human Rights Education amongst the teachers and students. The scheme for introduction of Human Rights Education Programme at the Postgraduate/Certificate levels in universities and colleges was implemented in 1997 which was the beginning of the 9th Plan Period.

For the first time during the year 1997-98, the UGC sanctioned Rs. 7.43 lakhs to eight universities (three Central Universities – Aligarh Muslim University, Jamia Millia Islamia & Jawaharlal Nehru University and five State Universities – Cochin University, Andhra University, Saurashtra University, Nagpur University and Mumbai University) for starting human rights courses. Hence, the academic year 1997-98 became a beginning for introduction of full-fledged human rights courses in Indian Universities. Earlier, human rights were part of a small component of the syllabus of few courses in social sciences. In addition, an amount of Rs. 24.58 lakhs was sanctioned to twenty-six universities and fifty-one colleges for organising seminars/ symposia/workshops in the area of human rights.

During the year 1998-99, the UGC did not approve any new course in human rights but an amount of Rs. 24.59 lakhs for holding symposia, workshops and seminars on human rights was given to twenty six universities and fifty colleges.

In the academic year 1999-2000, on the recommendation of the Hon'ble Justice J.S. Verma Committee on 'Operationalisation of the suggestions to teach Fundamental Duties to the citizens of the Country', the UGC re-designated Human Rights Education Scheme as Human Rights and Duties Education. The main objectives of the Scheme were defined as follows:

- to develop interaction between society and educational institutions;
- to sensitise the citizens so that the norms and values of Human Rights and Duties Education Programme are realised;

- to encourage research activities; and
- to encourage research studies concerning the relationship between Human Rights and Duties Education and International Humanitarian Law.

In the same academic year, the UGC identified ten more universities for introduction of Human Rights and Duties Education Courses. Out of ten universities, three were given two year degree courses four were given one year diploma course and three were permitted to start certificate course. In addition, sixteen universities and nineteen colleges were financed for organising seminar/symposia/ workshops. For starting human rights courses in universities and organising seminars/symposia/workshop in both universities & colleges, an amount of Rs. 21.67 lakhs was given under the Scheme of Human Rights and Duties Education.

In the year 2000-2001, five universities were considered for introduction of Human Rights and Duties Education Programme. Out of five universities, one was given two year degree course, one was given one year diploma course and three were granted certificate course. In the same year, four colleges were given financial assistance for organising seminars and symposia. For this purpose, an amount of Rs. 5.73 lakhs was given to universities and colleges.

During the year 2001-2002, a total of twelve universities and colleges were given financial assistance for starting Human Rights and Duties Education Courses which include three universities and one college for two year degree course, five universities for one year diploma course and one university and two colleges for certificate course. In addition, five universities were also given financial assistance for organising seminars and workshops on human rights. An amount of Rs. 8.92 lakhs was paid to universities and colleges for introducing courses and organising seminars/workshops.

It is clear that during the 9th Plan period covering the 1.4.1997 to 31.3.2002, the UGC sanctioned a total grant of Rs. 92.92 lakhs to universities and colleges under the Human Rights and Duties Education Programme which include thirty-one universities and three colleges for introduction of degree, diploma and certificate courses and 48 universities and seventy-three colleges for organising seminars/symposia/workshops.

In the year 2002-2003 which was the first year of the 10th Plan, no permission was given to introduce human rights courses but nine universities and twenty-one colleges were considered for organising seminars/symposia/workshops and an amount of Rs. 19.47 lakhs was paid to these universities and colleges.

In the year 2003-2004, the UGC did not approve any proposal for human rights courses but it gave an amount of Rs. 12.93 lakhs for universities and colleges for the on-going activities under the Human Rights and Duties Education Programme.

In the year 2004-2005, a total of thirty-five institutions were given permission to start Human Rights and Duties Education Courses which included two universities and eighteen colleges for introducing foundation course; one university and eleven colleges to start certificate course; one college for undergraduate course and two universities for starting postgraduate course. For this purpose, an amount of Rs. 13.10 lakhs was sanctioned. In this year, the UGC also gave Rs. 14.10 lakhs for organising seminar/symposia/workshop/conference/moot court to twenty-four universities.

In the year 2005-2006, a total of forty-nine institutions were given financial assistance to start Human Rights and Duties Education Courses which included thirteen colleges for foundation course; two universities and twenty-five colleges for certificate course; one university for undergraduate course and six universities and two colleges for postgraduate course. For this purpose, an amount of Rs. 15.42 lakhs was sanctioned. In this year, the UGC also provided funds of Rs. 23.75 lakhs for organising seminar/symposia/workshop/conference/moot court to 06 universities and fifty-four colleges.

In the year 2006-2007, a total of 114 institutions were given financial assistance for introducing Human Rights and Duties Education Courses which included four universities and forty-eight colleges for foundation course; four universities and forty-four colleges for certificate course; one university and ten colleges for undergraduate course, three universities and eight colleges for postgraduate diploma course and five universities and four colleges for postgraduate degree course. In this year, the UGC also provided funds for organising seminar/symposia/ workshop related to human rights issues which included twenty-four universities and sixty-nine colleges for organising seminar, five colleges for organising symposia and four universities and twelve colleges for organising workshops. For this purpose, an amount of Rs. 92.94 lakhs was sanctioned by the UGC.

During the 10th Plan Period (from 1.4.2002 to 31.3.2007), the UGC released a total grant of Rs. 191.71 lakhs to universities and colleges under the Human Rights and Duties Education Programme which include thirty-one universities and 184 colleges for introducing degree, diploma and certificate courses and also sixty-seven universities and 167 colleges for organising seminar/symposia/workshops.

It is clear from the above that during the 9th and 10th Plan periods (from 1997-08 to 2006-07), the UGC distributed a total grant of Rs. 284.63 lakhs among the universities and colleges for different activities related to human rights education.

The UGC has not only been providing financial assistance to universities and colleges for introducing courses and organising symposia/workshops but it also took the following other important academic initiatives for upgradation of Human Rights and Duties Education:

1. In the academic year 1998-99, the UGC in collaboration with the British Council, organised two Workshops at Bangalore and Delhi respectively for the promotion of Human Rights Education in universities and colleges. Eminent experts in the field of Human Rights Education throughout India and the United Kingdom were invited to attend these workshops.
2. In the year 1999, the UGC appointed a part-time National Consultant on Human Rights to advice on various aspects of Human Rights Education.
3. In 1999, the Commission constituted a Curriculum Development Committee under the Chairmanship of Hon'ble Justice V.S. Malimath to develop the model curricula for P.G. Degree Course, Diploma Course, Certificate Course and Foundation Course at undergraduate level. The UGC Model curricula on Human Rights and Duties Education developed by the Curriculum Development Committee were sent to all universities and colleges in 2001 where the Human Rights and Duties Education Courses are conducted. The curriculum developed by the Committee are as follows:
    - Foundation Course in Human Rights and Duties,

- Certificate Course in Human Rights and Duties,
- Undergraduate Degree Course in Human Rights and Duties,
- Postgraduate Diploma Course in Human Rights and Duties; and
- Postgraduate Degree (MA/LLM) Course in Human Rights and Duties.

Conclusion and Suggestions:

Human Rights Education is a powerful tool to sensitise students, awaken their conscience and encourage them to respect human rights. India has to gain a lot from Human Rights Education, both for the promotion and progressive realisation to protection and preserving of human rights. Therefore, it needs to be spread throughout India through all possible manner such as introducing courses, organising seminars/symposia/workshops/group discussions/debates, arranging street plays etc. Though the UGC is making sincere efforts for promoting Human Rights Education in India it seems that these are not sufficient in keeping in view the size of the population of our country. Further, the number of universities and colleges offering human rights courses are still less compared to the total number of universities and colleges in the country. In view of this, there is an urgent need to allot more human rights courses to those other universities and colleges which wish to offer so that the numbers of students in these courses are increased. The UGC is required to make necessary efforts to get more funds from government for promoting Human Rights Education fast. In order to provide popularity of human rights courses among students, there is a need to link up these courses with the jobs so that the youth can join these courses in large number. The UGC should make some recommendations to the government for providing jobs to human rights students after receiving their degree.

Human Rights Education is a complex but vibrant concern for an age in which universities and colleges have also to contribute significantly in order to change the complexion of our society. It promotes tolerance and fosters peace and understanding among the people as well as different social, religious and ethnic groups and therefore, students need to be sensitised as to how the observance of human rights in their day-to-day life enhances quality of life in society. For this purpose, the syllabi of the human rights courses need to be updated on regular basis keeping in view the fast changing environment in the world. Human Rights Education implies the learning and practice of human rights. It should not only be taught theoretically in universities and colleges but should be imparted on the basis of the field work. It is important to provide practical oriented teaching by taking students to community for field experiences. In order to give Human Rights Education a grass-roots orientation, there is an urgent need to build up strong linkages and networking between universities and colleges and various NGOs and other groups working in the field. The students who join National Service Scheme (NSS) in universities and colleges can also significantly contribute in promotion of Human Rights Education.

References

1. Human Rights – A Source Book, National Council of Educational Research and Training, 1996.
2. Human Rights Education: Genesis and Policy Initiatives by K. Sudha Rao & Mithilesh Singh in Human Rights in Education: Perspectives and Imperatives, NIEPA, 2001.
3. Human Rights Education (A Volume of Selections of articles on human rights from University News) published by the Association of Indian Universities, New Delhi in 2005.
4. Annual Reports 2001-2002 & 2005-2006 of the Ministry of Human Resource Development, Government of India.
5. Annual Reports 1997-98 to 2005-06 of the University Grants Commission, New Delhi.
6. Website of the University Grants Commission: www.ugc.ac.in
7. Website of the National Human Rights Commission: www.nhrc.nic.in
8. Website of the UNESCO: www.unesco.org

GLOBALISATION AND INDIAN POLITICS/ADMINISTRATION

13

Power Sharing in the Federal Project in Post Globalised India: Governance and Fiscal Reforms

RUMKI BASU

Independent India's federal project was a constitutional arrangement of power sharing between the Central government and the states in the legislative, administrative and fiscal realms. The Centre and the states were never meant to be equal in the constitutional scheme in India and it was with this understanding that Centre state relations have been actually played out in practice from the 1950's to the 1990's. It was the intersection of both economic and political forces that made the change in Centre state relations foundational from the 1990's onward. Since the National Election in 1989 to the present Manmohan Singh era, coalitional governments at the centre have given ample federal inclusiveness to regional political parties. Economic and political decentralisation happened to overlap and coincide and Structural Adjustment Policies drove both governance and fiscal reforms since the 1990's. However this article surmises that a new model of Centre state relations is perhaps emerging beyond the horizon of a liberalised political economy. With the offloading of the Centre's powers and functions in many spheres, the states in India may come to enjoy more economic and political space to draw their own destinies in the federal common market economy where the centre can merely be a regulator or at best a facilitator of the developmental efforts of states.

Introduction

Independent India's federal project was a constitutional arrangement of power sharing between the central government and the states in the legislative, administrative and fiscal realms. The model of a centralised federation was as much a product of our highly centralised colonial administration as of a response to the exigencies of nation building after independence. The heterogeneity of cultures, socio economic disparities, regional diversities and the territorial vastness of India necessitated two sets of governance. But the horrors of Partition and the fear of fissiparous tendencies prompted caution and as a pre-emptive strike the centre's overriding powers of legislation, administration and taxation were written into the constitutional arrangement by its Founding Fathers. The Centre and states were never meant to be equals in the constitutional scheme and it was with this understanding that Centre state relations have been actually played out in practice.

Indian federalism in practice has devised several answers to the demands confronting it from time to time but if we have to periodise according to characteristics on the whole, then it can be said that India's federal governance has taken India from the 'benign centralism' of the Nehruvian era (1950-64) through the troubled period of 'excessive centralism' (1965-89), to the new 'negotiatory federalism' of the post liberalised era of Indian politics (1989-to the present)

Let us look at the constitutional power sharing arrangement in the legislative, administrative and fiscal areas. The number of items in the Central List is far more than the State List and in case of a conflict between the two sets of laws, the centre's will prevails. The residuary powers of legislation belonged to the centre. Through items in the concurrent list, the centre can exercise uniformity in centre state legislation as it has done recently in the case of electricity and education[1].

In administrative matters, the centre exercises control through the All India Civil Services (e.g. in matters of enforcing compliance to Central laws), which work in States but are controlled by the centre. The centre has the right to dismiss state governments (Act 356) and the governor can reserve any state Bill for the consent of the President. In fiscal matters, states have greater developmental responsibilities with less powers of taxation. The centre has all the elastic sources of revenue like income tax, customs, excise and corporate income tax while states have to rest content with mainly inelastic sources. There were other sources of central government transfers like Plan transfers from the Planning Commission, Finance Commission grants or through centrally sponsored schemes.

During the period 1950 to 1967 Centre State disputes were negotiated through the mechanism of the Congress Party framework, which was in power both in the centre and majority of states. From 1967 to the nineties, the centre state dialogue became more cacophonous with one state after another demanding more powers, more autonomy to correct what may be called the 'inequities' in the constitutional power sharing scheme and to make the constitution truly 'federal'. From the Rajamannar Committee Report way back in the fifties to the Anandpur Sahib Resolution in the seventies, the underlying note was similar – that the power sharing arrangement in the constitutional scheme was unequal and unfair and needed to be amended in favour of the states. However the final dig to state ambitions in the matter was given by the Sarkaria Commission Report '98, which stated unequivocally of the lack of need to make any radical changes in the constitutional scheme.

From the 50's to the 80's, the heyday of India's five-year plans, the Indian State came to occupy the commanding heights of the economy. As the new millennium opened, images of a centralised planned command economy had become a fading memory. In the 1990's India took the big leap towards a globalised market economy when state chief ministers came to play leading roles in the emerging federal economy. It was the conditions created by economic liberalisation that necessitated a shift from a centralised command economy to a federal market economy. Its raison d'etre was the displacement of public investment by private investment as the engine of economic growth. From the decade of the nineties, the states have become the principal arena for private investment[2]. Post nineties, the states command a larger share of economic sovereignty than they did under the conditions of a centrally planned economy. Their growth or decline depends a lot on their own initiative now. Despite structural constraints the states' arena of economic freedom has certainly increased, since the union government is transforming itself from the interventionist tutelary state of a centrally planned economy and the license permit raj to that of a regulatory state of a federal market economy that tries to enforce fiscal discipline and to ensure transparency and accountability in market and federal processes[3].

In recent years, there is an increased intensity among states for attracting domestic and foreign investment with the need to provide the parameters of good governance in order to attract aid from multilateral agencies[4]. In the eighties and beyond there was a marked decline in public investment and as a consequence the centre's financial leverage over the states gradually decreased. Capital expenditure of both centre and states as a ratio of total government expenditure also climbed down. The centre's deficits and the interest payments it entailed, made it increasingly difficult for the centre to help the states with investment funds or bail-outs for their fiscal deficits.

But it was the intersection of both economic and political forces that made the change in centre state relations foundational from the 1990's onward. Independent causal claims may have resulted in economic liberalisation and the transformation of the party system during the 1990's, but once in place, the two phenomena began to interact in ways that proved mutually reinforcing. The dominant congress party system of the 50's, 60's, 70's and 80's which enabled the centre to engage in centralised planned investment gave way from 1989 onwards to a regionalised multi-party system and coalition governments in which state parties played a major role.

Since the IXth national election in 1989 to the present Manmohan Singh era, coalitional governments at the centre have given ample federal inclusiveness to regional parties. Economic and political decentralisation happened to overlap and coincide at the same historical moment in India's destiny. Both the centre and the states had to undergo fiscal and governance reforms driven by economic bankruptcy and financial collapse since the 1990's.

Power sharing in governance – 1989 onwards

A growing assertion of state and regional identities expressed in demands for more state autonomy and restructuring of centre state relations was witnessed from the eighties onwards in the spheres of government and politics in India. Two trends emerged during the eighties in the party system in India, which had significant impact on the politics of power sharing between the centre and the states.

First, most of the regional parties particularly in south India came to power in the states with marked regional identities like Telugu Desam in Andhra Pradesh, Janata Dal in Karnataka along with DMK/AIDMK in Tamil Nadu, Pondicherry etc.

Secondly, a convergence occurred of opposition political forces along with regional parties in the form of conclave politics. The Bangalore Conclave (1983) of four southern state chief ministers, the Vijayawada conference (1983) of opposition leaders of fourteen parties, the Srinagar conclave (1983) of eighteen opposition political parties focused the attention of the country on the issues of state autonomy and restructuring of centre state relations.

The period between1989-2004 could be characterised as an era of 'Regionalisation of electoral federalism'[5] because of the assertion of regional parties on national politics and their increased strength in Lok Sabha elections. Since in successive Lok Sabha elections (from 1989-2004) no single political party received a majority to rule at the centre, minority/coalition governments brought into 'electoral federalism' heralding an era of coalitional governance (power sharing between national and regional parties) which continues to this day.

The emergence of coalition governments at the centre in 1989, 1996, 1998, 1999, and 2004 has reconfirmed the growing regionalisation of Indian politics at the national level. What began as a trend in the provinces in the post 1967 era with the capture of power by state based political parties came to be followed later in national politics. Although there is no set pattern, voters seems to have favoured a coalition government at the centre endorsing the multiplicity of interests that can seldom be articulated by a single party. This is exemplified by the major coalition of parties brought under one umbrella, where ideology appears to be insignificant.

Regional parties contributed almost 42% of the seats to the 13th Lok Sabha, which was reflective in the NDA composition. There were twenty-four parties that came together to form a stable coalition.[6] Also the NDA led by BJP was unique in providing stability to governance.

There is not an iota of doubt that the growing importance of regional parties in the formation of coalition governments since 1989 has accelerated the process of federalisation and power sharing between centre and states in India's parliamentary system of governance, which during the 'congress system', bordered on the centre's hegemony disregarding regional interest to a large extent.

The national parties on the other hand (whether the Congress or BJP) have become increasingly regionalised. Given the centralising trends under the Congress governments, the growing de-centering of power is certainly a corrective step to restore the vitality of democratic institutions and federal character of the Indian constitution.[7] There is now a highly regionalised and fragmented multi-party system, truly reflective of the diversities in India and the need for power sharing between different political groups, parties and levels of governance.

In recent years since 1989 the growing importance of regionalism and coalition politics has redefined the emerging contours of India's federalism by emphasising that a combination of parties/alliances will continue to rule at the centre. Both, the all India and the regional parties have accepted this changed political reality and its implications for governance.

Power sharing through 3-tiers of local governance

The 73rd and 74th Amendments of our Constitution have given a new meaning to Indian federalism. A third tier of governance has come into existence in India since 1992. Consequently, a separate list of 29 functions for rural local bodies and 18 items for urban local bodies were placed in the 11th and 12th schedules respectively for rural and urban local governments to implement concurrently with the states.

After the 73rd and 74th Amendments, India has now more that three million people's representatives in Panchayat bodies.

This is an unique experiment in power sharing through decentralisation. There are nearly 600 district Panchayats, about, 6000 block Panchayats, at the intermediate level and 2,50,000 gram Panchayats in rural India where 72.2 per cent of India's population lives. Urban India, with 27.8 per cent of India's population, has 101 city corporations, 1430 town municipalities and about 1,900 Nagar Panchayats. Women head about 200 district Panchayats, more than 2,000 block Panchayats at the intermediate level and about 85,000 gram Panchayats. Likewise, more than Thirty city corporations and about 500 town municipalities have women chairpersons. A large number of hitherto excluded groups and communities are now included in the local and governing bodies. As the Indian population has 14.3 per cent Schedule Castes (SCs) and 8 per cent Scheduled Tribes (STs), about 800,000 elected members – nearly 23 per cent of total membership in the rural and urban bodies – will be from Scheduled Castes and Tribes. This marks a profound change in the democratic and federal character of the Indian Union. Each state has become a federating unit with three layers following it – district, block and village. An organic link in the democratic process has been established from Gram Sabha (village assembly) to Lok Sabha (Parliament). India has moved from administrative federalism to multilevel federalism.[8]

Another important point of departure in recent years in that the new states like Jharkhand, Uttaranchal & Chattisgarh were proposed on the ground of administrative efficiency rather than on the language basis, the very reason which has ostensibly, guided state formation in the past. This also marks a shift in India's federal ideology, as regional identity, culture and geographical differences would not appear to be recognised as a valid basis for administrative division and political reorganisation. There has undoubtedly been a qualitative shift in the attitude towards new states amongst the large political parties at the centre.

Therefore the post '91 period in Indian politics is broadly marked by liberalisation of the economy, the rise of Hindutva and a shift from single party dominance at the centre to the emergence of a relatively stable system of coalition governments. Related to this is the 'regionalisation of politics', whereby smaller regional and state specific parties have come to exert more power not just in the states themselves (in government or as partners of national parties), but also in the national parliament itself. Recent national level debates and decisions about territorial reorganisation provides an opportunity of exploring these shifts.

Coalition governance in India needs to be viewed as an important forum of articulation of diverse concerns, mirroring the voice of articulate and combative regional forces or people marginalised both socio-economically and in terms of representation in the polity. Coalitions, especially minority coalitions have emanated the culture of power sharing. Under such circumstances, regional allied parties have been given power as never before in Indian politics. Thus coalitions have fostered consensus-seeking capability and the fact that a political culture of matured accommodation has been ingrained in a country of India's size and formidable diversities is no mean achievement.

Indian politics is undergoing a dramatic transformation. Its democratic ethic is acquiring a mass character and vibrancy. Its government and politics has emerged as a creative experiment of combining 'democratic responsiveness to cultural differences with a federal conciliation of regional community, identity and autonomy claims and a nationally concerted promotion of regional capability'.[9] The predominant 'Congress system' has given way to a multi-party system and coalition governments. In this process the terms of political dominance and political discourse has changed at the regional and national levels, quite different from the 'centralised power brokering and cooption and towards a more complex mechanism of negotiation, alliance and coalition-building'.[10]

Alongside such important indicators of political change, very significant social movements have grown over the years. These 'new social movements' are aggregating around supposedly non-class issues, and occupy diverse spaces such as civil rights for dispossessed groups, minorities and the marginalised, consumer rights, electoral reforms, common civil code, gender and ecological issues, education, environmental strategies etc. These are issues that are noticeably often avoided or neglected by mainstream political parties of all hues.

Coalitional pressures have forced parties to shift their policies and attention from merely seat adjustments to a new realisation that focuses on an inclusive agenda, one that includes electoral alliances, common agendas, all party meetings, chief ministers' conferences, multiple level coordination committees, interministerial groups and even agencies outside the sphere of conventional politics. Committees have acted as safety valves and as negotiating channels. The NAG (National Agenda for Governance) and now the NCMP (National Common Minimum Programme) went beyond the purpose of internal utility and have become public reference points.

The tenor of my argument is to demonstrate that the forging of political coalitions in India have led to simultaneous federal, social and consensual forms of power sharing into a schema whereby tolerance and accommodation, managing and organising of various incongruous diversities have been made possible.

Emerging issues in Centre-State fiscal relations

The Indian constitutional scheme provides for a demarcation of functions and finances between the central government and the sub-national governments (states). The federation is spread over twenty-eight states and six centrally administered territories. The Constitution requires the President of India to appoint a Finance Commission every five years or earlier to review the finances of the Centre and the states and recommend intergovernmental transfers for the next five years.

In the Indian context, even though economic planning[11] has been implemented in a mixed economy and democratic framework, the strategy of a public sector dominated, heavy industry based import substituting model of industrialisation necessarily implied a centralisation of both economic and administrative powers. Although the immediate cause of the unprecedented economic crisis of 1991 was the persisting fiscal imbalance through the eighties, it also helped to underline the fiscal unsustainability of the earlier development strategy. Market oriented economic reforms have been initiated sine 1991 with a view to imparting competitiveness to the Indian economy and integrating it with the world market.[12]

Structural adjustment has had repercussions on Central finances only since mid-1991, while in the case of the states, expenditure compression started much earlier, during the mid-eighties. The initiative of 'adjustment' at the Central level has further aggravated their problem on the fiscal front.

One of the important measures taken by the Central government in pursuit of 'liberalisation' relates to cut in tax rates. Since the states have a major share in revenue from certain taxes, this measure has led to a deceleration in the growth of tax revenues accruing to them. There has also been deceleration in plan and non-plan grants from the Centre in post '91 years.

The reduced rate of devolution in current transfers has been accompanied by a decline in the revenue receipts of states and a rise in the rate of growth of revenue expenditure. The imbalance between rates of growth in revenue receipts and expenditures resulted in large and rising revenue deficits, implying that the states have resorted to borrowing even to meet current expenditures. Since, states also have to borrow to finance capital expenditure, there has been a rise in the overall borrowing requirements of state governments.

The increase in borrowings by state governments, both from the Centre and the market, has coincided with a rising trend in interest rates, thus imposing a heavy burden on state finances. Interest payments, along with expenditure on administrative services, have largely contributed to the surge in non-developmental expenditure and the consequent rise in revenue deficits. The revenue deficit and the gross fiscal deficit seem to mutually reinforce one another, leading to a large debt burden for the states.

High fiscal deficits increase the risk premia that a country faces, and translate into higher financing costs, which may deter investment particularly in the infrastructure sectors where borrowing needs are generally huge. The level of public debt would be unsustainable if the interest rate on debt is higher than the growth rate of the economy. Public debt and associated interest burden on the central budget need to be stabilised as a share of GDP and then to be gradually reduced. For putting the economy on a sustainable fiscal path determined efforts will be required to mobilise tax revenues as well as strict containment and prioritisation of public expenditure. In addition to the factors just mentioned, in must be recognised that some states have benefited to a greater extent in terms of fiscal transfers from the Centre. External aid has also been concentrated in a few states and a few sectors. Within this holistic scenario, there are substantial differences across the states in terms of financial performance as well as efforts to raise additional resources. With the advent of New Economic policies a review of federal fiscal arrangements in India has become necessary. A pre-requisite to evolving a system of cooperative federalism is to analyze the existing federal fiscal arrangements from an economic perspective, identify the weakness in them and indicate the directions of reform.

The two main economic arguments in favour of fiscal federalism are fairly compelling and well known. First, there can be substantial efficiency and welfare gains from decentralisation of spending responsibilities. Second, decentralisation can act as a surrogate for market discipline in ensuring efficiency in the production of public goods.

As opposed to this, fiscal federalism has its economic problems as well. First resource endowments and levels of economic development differ across regions and in a federation, this regional disparity may be reflected in the ability of sub-national (State) governments to provide goods to the residents under their jurisdiction.[13] Decentralisation can, therefore, compromise the attainment of redistributional equity objectives by their uneven implementation throughout the country. Expenditure control is considerably more difficult under a federal set up with expenditure devolution than under an unitary system. The spending decisions of not only the central government but also of the lower level governments affect macro-economic equilibrium. Finally, fiscal federalism-particularly with the devolution of tax raising power can lead to tax exportation among states and tax wars through exemptions and tax concessions. This can impair the development of a common market and retard growth.

The Constitution of the Republic of India has been described as 'quasi-federal' for providing strong unitary features in both political and economic spheres. The states do enjoy a substantial degree of autonomy within the areas of responsibility granted to them by the Constitution. The Constitution devolves to the states several major responsibilities relating not merely to the basic functions of government such as the maintenance of law and order but also other wide-ranging functions closely connected to the social sectors, agriculture, industrial infrastructure and the overall development of the economy.

The Indian Constitution provides three lists of subjects- the Union List; the State List and the Concurrent List. Briefly all matters relating to currency, banking finance, defence, foreign affairs, including economic relations with foreign entities, matters affecting the country as a whole and those relating to interstate relations are placed in the exclusive domain of the Centre. On the other hand, matters closely concerned with the life and welfare of the population, such as local government, public health, agriculture and water management, are placed on the State List. The Concurrent List covers three important areas: education, planning and industries.

The assignment of tax powers in the Indian Constitution seems to have been based on two fundamental principles. The first is that the assignments should avoid giving concurrent tax to the Centre and States. The second is that the Centre takes on the most important taxes which have economy-wide implications or which can be collected most efficiently and economically by the Centre. Based on the second criterion, the Centre was given the power to levy income tax on non-agricultural income (individual as well as corporate), customs duties and all excise taxes on production, except those on liquor. This meant that the Centre had within its jurisdiction the most productive sources of revenue with a broad tax base. The states have been assigned tax revenues related to land and agriculture (land revenue, agricultural income tax and other duties on agricultural land), sales taxes except those on inter-state trade, excise on liquor, taxation of inland transport except railways, property tax and the entry tax.

The shares of the Central and State governments in revenues and expenditures may now be analysed. It is seen that the states on an average raise about 39 per cent of total revenues and incur 57 per cent of expenditure. The revenue derived from exclusive central taxes constitutes about 32 per cent; those from exclusive state taxes 35 per cent, and the remaining 33 per cent from sharable sources. The major taxes levied exclusively by the Centre consist of customs duty (22 per cent of total tax revenue) and corporation tax (8 per cent). Among the state taxes, revenue from sales tax constitutes almost 20 per cent. Other state taxes individually contribute less than 6 per cent of total tax revenue. Although on an average 55 per cent of the states total expenditures, is incurred on the central sector and centrally sponsored schemes, which are essentially in the nature of shared cost programmes.[14]

The Central government plays a major role in defence and industrial promotion, as indicated by the pattern of expenditure. The states, on the other hand, have a predominant share of expenditure in internal security, law and order, social services, like education, health, family welfare, housing, social security and in economic services like agriculture, animal husbandry, forestry, fishing, irrigation and power, and public works. The states' share in total government expenditure on administrative services is about two-thirds; on social services they spend over 86 per cent and on economic services their share is almost 60 per cent.

The Constitution demonstrates a clear centripetal bias in the distribution of tax and regulatory powers. In addition to the expenditure functions assigned, the Centre can also influence the expenditure decisions of the States. The assignment of most of the broad-based taxes and residuary tax powers to the Centre, its overriding powers in regard to the functions in the Concurrent List, and domination through economic planning and control over virtually the entire financial sector are only some instances of its dominance in the economic sphere.

In fiscal terms, 'imbalance' refers to the mismatch between revenue raising capacity and the expenditure needs of different governmental units. Such imbalances can arise vertically between different levels of the government or horizontally between different jurisdictions. In most federations, given that the Central Government has a comparative advantage in raising revenues and the states are relatively better placed to deliver public services, vertical imbalance is implicit in the assignment itself. The interjurisdictional difference in income due to various historical and institutional factors, besides variations in resource endowments, create horizontal imbalance. The consequence of constitutional assignment and fiscal developments over the years has been to create a high degree of fiscal centralisation and vertical fiscal imbalance in India.

The trend in fiscal centralisation in India shows that, while the states' share in total expenditure broadly remained constant (or showed a marginal decline), their shares in both aggregate current revenues and total expenditure showed a decline. Fiscal dependence of the states or the degree of vertical fiscal imbalance increased over time. Actually, the share of specific purpose grants for the central sector and centrally sponsored schemes in total transfers increased from 12 per cent during the Fifth Plan (1969-74) to over 18 per cent during the Tenth Plan. As most specific purpose transfers also have conditionalities attached, the intrusion of central authority over states' expenditure decisions has also correspondingly increased.[15]

An important feature of Indian fiscal federalism is the wide inter-state differences in the capability to raise revenue and per capita expenditure. There are 17 relatively more homogenous general category states, but even those have wide differences in revenue raising efforts, expenditure levels and fiscal dependence on the Centre. In addition, in terms of economic characteristics and endowments, the eleven mountainous states of the north and the north-east differ markedly from the rest and are, therefore, considered 'special category' states.

Statistics have shown wide variations in revenue among different states, both in per capita terms and as a revenue-income ratio. These variations indicate both inter-state differences in revenue capacity and, partly, differences in revenue among different states in per capita terms as well as revenue-income efforts put in by them. The special category states are characterised by low revenue bases even though their per capita incomes are not very low because in these states, much of the income generated is in the service sector, particularly government administration. Although the revenue bases in this category of states is very low, partly due to the higher unit cost of providing public services, their per capita expenditures is significantly higher than the all-India average. In regard to general category states, the fiscal dependence of the states on the Centre is not only high but also varies inversely with per capita income. At the same time, even after equalising transfers through the Finance Commission over the years, the per capita expenditure in high income states was higher than the average by 35 per cent and that of low income states was lower by 25 per cent. This shows that the equalisation mechanism has not been able to adequately offset the fiscal disabling of the poorer states. The inter-state disparities in India, even among the relatively more homogenous general category states, are not only high but also have also shown an increasing trend.

The trends in the relative share of the central transfers to states highlights several interesting features. First, the share of gross and net transfers as per cent of Centre's total receipts declined considerably from 1991 onwards. Second, the proportion of formula based transfers given by the Finance Commission and the Planning Commission has declined, and that of discretionary transfers has increased over the years. Third, within the Finance Commission, the proportion of tax devolution has increased.

Finance Commission Transfers:

The financial position of the States has deteriorated over the years and the states were making continuous demands for further increases in their percentage shares. The nexus between expenditure decisions and the related one of raising of tax revenues had seriously weakened. As the Constitution does not lays down any guidelines for the Commission, the approaches of the different Commissions have varied and have not led to the evolution of a set of principles firmly grounded in economic analysis or empirical research. The States' share of Central taxes was raised from 50 per cent of income tax in 1950-51 to 85 per cent of Union excise duties between 1985-86 and 1989-90. For the years 1995 to 2000, income tax share has been reduced to 77.5 per cent and Union excise duties raised to 47.5 per cent. Presently Finance Commission transfers constitute about 60 per cent of the total transfers.

Plan Transfers:

In all the major states, the resources available for plan investments from the states' resources, before any central transfers were given, were negative. It is also found that the deficits were higher in the poorer states. As the richer states had access to larger non-plan loans and as they could not get higher central plan assistance, per capita plan outlays in the high-income states were almost twice those in the middle and low income ones. The mild equalising trend in statutory transfers was hardly adequate to offset the regressive bias imparted by other forms of central assistance. Currently Plan transfers constitute about 20 per cent of total transfers.

Large federal transfers had to be made to cover the deficits of the States, which considerably weakened the finances of the Centre. Moreover, the loans granted by the Centre were to be invested in development projects such as irrigation work, electricity and transport undertakings or were to be lent for productive purposes. Actually portions of the loans were used to cover deficits and whatever was invested did not bring sufficient returns to cover interest and amortisation.

Assistance to the Central Sector and Centrally Sponsored Schemes:

The third component of transfer is given for specified purposes with or without matching provisions. These are called the central sector schemes that are initiated in regard to services falling within the states' jurisdiction to ensure that optimal levels of services are provided. These are shared cost programmes and the matching ratios vary from project to project, but are uniform across states. Indeed, the transfers given under the centrally sponsored schemes have attracted the sharpest criticism due to their discretionary nature and the conditionality attached to them. They formed about 40 per cent of the total plan assistance and 14 per cent of total current transfers in 2000-01.

Post liberalistion issues in fiscal federalism

The economic reforms since 1991-92 were occupied with problems of stabilisation, which pertain mainly to balancing the public sector income and expenditure. In India's quasi-federal structure, responsibility of the income and expenditure of the Governments at the Centre and the States are not evenly matched. India has now entered effectively the second phase of reform, the phase of structural adjustments. In this effort, the existing Centre-State relations, including the fiscal one, are coming into focus and likely to aggravate the problems already in hand. Structural adjustments involve areas which pertain not only to the Central prerogative in their assigned economic responsibilities but also largely to the domain of the States. Is the present framework of Centre-State relations congenial for and compatible with for such adjustments in the economic and fiscal spheres?

Resource transfers from the Centre to the States may take place in five ways : (i) States' shares in central taxes as per the Finance Commission award;(ii) non-plan grants under Article 275 of the Constitution as determined by the Finance Commission's;(iii) non-plan loans representing essentially ploughing back of the net small savings mobilised by the State plan comprising normal central assistance distributed across States according to the Gadgil formula; (iv) additional central assistance to cover externally aided projects; and (v) assistance for centrally sponsored schemes with a grant element of over 98 per cent.

Data shows that gross resource transfers from the Centre to the States as a proportion of Centre's total receipts (revenue+capital) have been coming down, dropping by as much as 5 percentage points between 1991-92 and 2001-02. The drop is even more significant in net terms.

The seventy five per cent of the net small savings mobilised by the States is transferred to the States as loan and has been an important source of finance for State plans. After a quantum jump in 1994-95, there has been near stagnation under this head which can be attributed to the unattractive interest rates on these instruments and the money, competing opportunities now available for saving, several of them with tax concessions.

There has been a substantial increase in external assistance flows to the States since 1991. However, a few relatively developed States have absorbed the major share of such flows. During the Eighth Plan to Tenth Plan period this has resulted in an increase in Central assistance to the more developed States, despite the weight in the 'Gadgil Formula' in favour of populous and low-income States.

Additional Central assistance for externally aided projects is skewed in favour of better-off States. External aid accounted for 40 per cent and above of Central Plan assistance while such contributions accounted for less than 20 per cent of the Central Plan assistance to most of the backward States. The role of private investment has acquired a special significance in the wake of economic reforms initiated in 1991. States are now in competition with one another to attract private investment, both domestic and foreign. Within states, the flow of investments tends to be skewed in favour of a few regions.

Maharashtra and Gujarat account for 37 per cent of total investment proposals, while Bihar, Madhya Pradesh, Orissa, Rajasthan and Uttar Pradesh, taken together, were able to attract only 26 per cent of investment proposals. During the decade from August 1991 to December 2001, the bulk of investment proposals were concentrated in States with a relatively high level of human development to the detriment of States, which have a low level of human development.

The cumulative share of financial assistance disbursed by national financial institutions during 1991-2001 indicates a big gulf between the less developed and more developed states. Maharashtra alone received almost as much financial assistance as Bihar, Madhya Pradesh, Orissa, Rajasthan, Uttar Pradesh and West Bengal put together. Bihar and Orissa have shares of financial assistance that are adversely disproportionate to their respective population shares. The southern and western States of India account for over 55 per cent of total bank deposits, while the comparatively backward States of central and eastern India account for a little over 31 per cent. Maharashtra alone accounts for over 20 per cent of the bank deposits.

Bank credit distribution is even more skewed than bank deposit distribution. A good portion of deposits mobilised in the backward states in central and eastern India supports advances to better off States in the south and the west. Again, Maharashtra (because of Mumbai) had a larger share of bank credit than the combined total of eight backward states. Likewise, Tamil Nadu's share exceeded that of six of these backward States (excepting Uttar Pradesh and West Bengal). The credit-deposit ratio captures the discrepancy in credit absorption vis-à-vis deposit mobilisation. Exceptions apart, credit-deposit ratios are much more favourable to the group of forward States as compared to the backward States.

Locating externally assisted programmes and projects in low human development States and regions could leverage a greater share of central assistance and help accelerate human development. However, problems of governance and widespread corruption at all levels of government in these States have discouraged some international development partners from locating projects in those States. Therefore, a substantial increase in technical assistance is needed to improve governance and institutional capacity in those States. If externally assisted projects are located in such States, international scrutiny and standards of accountability may stimulate public attention regarding the need for reforms.

If the present revenue sharing scheme remains unchanged, it could result in an increasing problem of 'gap filler' and likely aggravation of the dependence of the States on the Centre in the structural adjustment process. The basic premise of market economy has with it a large in-built decentralisation to make structural adjustment possible and introduces initiative and competition between States. Therefore, a decentralised revenue sharing scheme along with a sense of fiscal discipline and cost accountability in the State finance needs to be encouraged.

The Sarkaria Commission set up by the Government to review Centre State relations in its report also examined this issue at length. It favoured bringing the corporate tax into the divisible pool as part of permissive participation like the Union excise duties. It suggested that this might be accomplished by a suitable Constitutional amendment. The recommendation that the taxes form part of the pool is guided by the consideration that this will induce the Centre to exploit these tax bases, which are currently not being tapped. States will also benefit from such an exercise. While under Article 268 in the Constitution taxes may be kept out of the arrangement of fixing a common share for all central taxes, under Article 269 taxes except Central sales tax and consignment tax should be brought within the purview of these arrangements. There have been occasions in the past when the Centre had to augment its revenue for meeting emergent but temporary needs. Under such circumstances, a surcharge on income and corporation tax was imposed. Such occasions may arise in future also. The Centre should, therefore, continue to have the power to levy surcharges for the purposes of the Union and these should be excluded from the sharing arrangements with the States, which have been recommended. The Tenth Finance Commission (TFC) recommended the share of States in

Income tax, Union excise duties, additional excise duties and grants in lieu of tax on railway passenger fares.

All finance commissions so far have attempted to eliminate the States' non-plan revenue deficits through their devolution packages. Naturally, therefore, going by their estimates and calculations, the overall revenue and fiscal deficits of States would also stand reduced. The problem always has been that the estimates of the finance commissions have never turned out to be realistic.

It is in the above context that the award of the 12th Finance Commission assumes importance for all the States. They are bound to be sensitive to the changes made in the share of central revenues fixed for the States as a whole and even more to the inter-state distribution of the total amount to be devolved including both tax-share and grants-in-aid. For this purpose, inter-state distribution under Finance Commission award of one is bound to be compared with that of preceding commissions. Thus, if a state's share of the total devolution to the states has fixed by Eleventh Finance Commission (EFC) at a level which is lower than what was fixed by the earlier one the new award would naturally be found disappointing, especially if the state thus affected is not among those with particularly high per capita incomes and has, in fact, been arguing its case to be rewarded for high performance in socio-economic achievements. Andhra Pradesh and Kerala have raised the banner of revolt against EFC's award precisely on these grounds. Andhra Pradesh's share has been brought down from 7.98 per cent under EFC award to 7.13 per cent and Kerala's from 3.4 to 2.83 per cent. On the other hand, the share of an economically advanced state such as West Bengal has been raised from 6.61 to 8.1 per cent. Both Andhra Pradesh and Kerala feel aggrieved that instead of being rewarded for their progressive achievements, they have been penalised.

In defence of the EFC's award, it can be argued that the inter-state allocation of the total amount falling to the share of the States under the Commission's award has been decided on the basis of certain objective criteria. This raises the question of the choice of criteria which evidently penalises good programme performers vis-a-vis States not performing well nor can the larger evaluation about the choice of criteria and the relative weightages on economic and distributional grounds be avoided. One of the most striking features of Indian public finance at the sub-national level has been the crowding out of capital and other essential expenditure - including developmental and operation and maintenance expenditures by increasing revenue expenditure mainly owing to higher interest payments and wages. The salary bill both at the level of Centre and the State governments has been constantly on the rise. The Government's wage bill in the States as a per cent of the respective state GDPs has gone up by 2 to 4 percentage points during the current decade. Persistent deficits have resulted in a cautious increase in states' debt, and increasing debt has led to a growing proportion of the states' revenue resources getting spent on interest payments.

Although there appears to be near unanimity about the need for eliminating non-merit subsidies and targeting groups in a more accurate manner, concrete measures for such programme are yet to be drawn up. Though there is some evidence that subsidies as a proportion of GDP may be coming down over the years the reduction is not fast enough to make a significant dent in the fiscal deficit of the Centre and States as yet.

Expenditure management through appropriate prioritisation and control in providing adequate outlays for the relevant heads makes expenditure prioritisation an even more important issue in India than what it is in many other countries. There is need for more schools, hospitals, roads, hydro-electric and irrigation projects etc. on the one hand and adherence to fiscal prudence on the other.

In August, 1995, a committee of state finance ministers had recommended the expansion of the tax base by keeping the exemptions to a minimum, rationalisation of the rate structure by reducing the number of applicable tax rates, and horizontal harmonisation of the rates. In a significant move, after a meeting of the Chief Ministers on November 16, 1999, there was an announcement that floor rates would be implemented in every State and sales tax incentives would be abolished by January 1, 2000. Furthermore, according to the announcement, the States agreed to replace the sales tax by the value added tax from April 1, 2001.

The Centre needs to provide a leadership role in fiscal reform, particularly in an era of intensely competitive politics and coalition governments. While the hard budget constraint at the state level will continue to provide some safeguard, a Fiscal Responsibility Act at the central level, which was proposed by some, can bolster such a safeguard. It may be useful for States too to enact such legislation for containing debt and interest payments, and to impose ceilings on guarantees. Finally, it is also essential to move away from the 'gap filling approach' in fiscal devolution and devise stronger incentives for States to mobilise additional reserves, reprioritise expenditure and reduce deficits.

Speaking more generally, under the new economic regime and in the new political context of coalition government, the Central government should act in such a way as to promote cooperative federalism. At the same time, it is incumbent on the States to observe rules, which are expected to be followed by constituent units in a federation. The most important among them are: (a) they should agree that policies that militate against the common market and against the export efforts of the country must be eschewed; (b) tax exportation must be minimised; (c) there should be competition only of the welfare increasing type; and (d) the better off states should recognise and accept that the Central government must have a surplus in order to perform the 'equalisation' function (which should, of course, be performed without promoting any fiscal indiscipline on the part of the weaker states). The meetings of the Inter-State Council should be used as a forum not only for a dialogue between the Centre and the States but also for dialogue among the States themselves on communications for freer flow of trade.

It is desirable that the larger part of grants from the Central government to the States flows through the Finance Commission. To make this possible, the first concrete step will be doing away with the distinction between plan and non-plan revenue expenditure. That is to say, the Planning Commission's assistance for the state plans should only be in the form of loans to finance capital expenditure, and grants should ordinarily flow through the Finance Commission. If all the Centrally sponsored schemes cannot be given up, they should be at least pruned to the extent of 50 per cent. If this reform is brought about, the Finance

Commission will be able to recommend larger grants without increasing the revenue deficit at the Centre and the proportion of grants for devolution could increase in the transfers from the Finance Commission.

The distribution of the divisible pool of taxes would be largely based on the criterion of population. It is suggested that the grants given by the Finance Commission should not be aimed at gap-filling but at equalisation of fiscal capacity. The fiscal capacity of each major state should be measured through the application of average tax rates to potential bases. The difference between average fiscal capacity and the fiscal capacity of a given state should be sought to be matched by an equalisation grant, if the latter is smaller than the former. Equalisation could also in the form of specific grants extended to raise standards of key services in those States where the standards are low.

The federal constitutional scheme has passed the test of time. However, several loopholes are noticeable in the system. The distribution of revenue of power is tilted in favour of the Central Government disregarding the number of expanding developmental functions to be performed by the States. In the total transfers received by the States, the statutory portion on which the States have claim and can use independently, have been falling over the years and the share of Plan transfers is increasing. The State transfers on grant (excepting special category states) have become a factor of fiscal subordination of the States on the Centre. Discretionary grants come to the States in so many different routes and are given by the Central Government on judging the project content, which sometimes causes friction between Centre and the States.

In the perspective of the TFC schemes of pooling Central taxes a better source of action would be to give more powers and autonomy to the States in matters concerning taxation. Whether to devolve the powers of taxation to the States or to devolve share in Central taxes is a fundamental issue. There are two considerations that favour the latter approach. The first is the issue of harmonisation and the second is the basic constitutional scheme of protecting the interests of the weaker States. Though the scheme appears reasonable, its efficiency in establishing optimum Central-State fiscal relations in the present context of economic reforms is questionable.

Without making a complete overhaul of the present system, we should make some changes in the distribution of responsibilities between the Centre and the States. The functions of lesser importance concerning social and economic activities may be shifted to State governments along with the required financial support either through more devolution of funds or relaxation of control of the Central Government in raising funds from the market. The States' resources may be improved if they can collect revenue through taxation of agricultural income, which has so long been overlooked.

Taking into account major recommendations for a balanced and acceptable policy, the present constitutional arrangement need not be fully restructured. However, adjustments in policies, procedures and regulatory measures are necessary to remove the irritants between the States and the Centre. For liberalisation to succeed co-operation between the Centre and States is absolutely necessary and national as well as state priorities should be the focal points of joint effort, The issue is to be tackled very carefully in view of the existence of multiple party regimes in the states. Reforms in Centre-State fiscal relations should provide a proper blend of the criteria of autonomy, fiscal discipline and inter-state equity, which are necessary inputs for a new and functional model of negotiatory federalism working within a liberalised environment.

However, despite the ideological backdrop of the 'roll back state' philosophy staying predominant, GDP figures zoomed during the entire liberalisation period. We maintained an average of 6% growth during the last fifteen years and in the eleventh plan we would like to aim at a target of 8-10% growth rate. This should not surprise any one because it is total investment which affects growth and almost three fourths of the gross fixed investment at the national level comes from the private sector, private corporate investment accounting for 38% and private household investment accounting for 33%[16].

Impact of liberalisation on Centre State relations

This brings us to our central argument regarding the impact of liberalisation on centre state relations: the decline of central public investment and growth of private investment gives the states of India (the immediate sites of private investment), a greatly expanded role in promoting investment and growth. They do so in various ways – policy initiatives, leadership, and good governance as well as inherited economic positions.

The two factors that lead to economic growth and human development are investment reliant. While human resource development - a low public priority in India so far remains primarily if not exclusively the domain of public investment, attracting private investment in infrastructure / industrialisation has become an arena of intense competition among states.

There are diversified impacts of globalisation on the Indian polity and three different responses of Indian federation, to these challenges are visible. First, the deregulation of the economy has led to an uneven impact on the economic development of the country. While the developed regions (the western and the southern) have rapidly taken off, the under developed and backward regions (the eastern and the central) have relatively lagged behind. Under such circumstances, if the Indian state is to pursue its goals of equality and balanced development and at the same time address poverty issues in the backward regions, it becomes necessary that the powers of the national government has to be increased. Almost all studies of centre state relations in recent years point that there is a vertical axis dividing India's forward and backward states with the forward states doing much better than the backward states in all developmental indicators, patterns of private investment and infrastructure expenditure. While 42% of the country's population lives in these states, the backward states account for 54% of the population. All states in the latter group with the exception of Andhra Pradesh, Karnataka and Kerala have a net state domestic product per capita much higher than the national average, and all states in the backward group have per capita income below the all India average. Similarly, in the manufacturing sector, all the backward states are below the national average whereas in the case of developed states four fare poorly and are below the national average. Among the forward states Gujarat, Haryana, Maharashtra and Tamil Nadu have a share of manufacturing higher than the all India average. Similarly, in the reduction of poverty, all developed states except Maharashtra have a percentage of poor much below the national average.

In the stint for attracting more private investment, a decentralising trend to be observed is that there is a shift in power to the state trade and industry ministries from their counter parts in the centre. But the problem is that this has also led to accentuating original imbalances. e.g a study by Kurien has demonstrated that 40% of the all India value added in manufacturing has been grabbed by the 3 states of Maharashtra, Gujarat and Tamil Nadu. Out of a total of 7.5 crore worth of private investment proposals received by all Indian states from 91-2000 the developed states accounted for two thirds. Even the current debates on creation of Special Economic Zones fully highlighted the inequitable impact of such zones on the backward states of India[17]. In 2001-02, the five high income states having 19 per cent of country's population and contributing 28 per cent of GDP accounted for 27 per cent of central government investments, the five low income states 44 per cent of population contributing 28 per cent of GDP accounted for only 26 per cent of central investments.

Without some sort of redistributive agenda, where the goals of economic growth are reconciled with those of equity, poverty in the backward regions will remain a severe handicap in the economic development of the country. If the Indian state is committed to growth with equity, it should on the one hand allow the developed states to make extensive development initiatives, while retaining the power to make centrally managed corrective interventions in the economy of laggard states wherever necessary. *It is a citizen's right in this country to get a minimum of social and economic entitlements irrespective of which state he may be born into. It is ultimately the centre which should stand as a guarantor to a citizen's entitlement which sometimes in this country becomes state specific.* Without the intervention of the central government, the trend of increasing regional disparities will continue and adversely affect the most essential purpose underlying a federal project: the creation of a cohesive national identity keeping cultural and regional diversities (not to be read as disparities intact)[18]. The recently enacted Fiscal Responsibility and Budget Management Act attempts to set targets to phase out the revenue deficit by 2007-08 and limit Fiscal deficit at 2 per cent of GDP.

One of the underlying principles of any federalism in those unequal states should have equal powers. Regional disparities, it, is now well documented, do impact upon the bargaining power of the units via-a-vis – each other as well as vis-a-vis national and international actors. On the other hand they have negative effects, on the social and political participation of these units populations. While it is true that it was severe economic compulsion, (not choice) which was the reason, behind our liberalisation, the centre still has enough control in domestic policy matters to reassert its redistributive role since equity and balanced growth should remain a top priority in our internal agenda of development.

In coming years, the students of federalism will lay a careful look at the states and their evolving role. States have more political stability and certainly more political and economic space today than they ever did earlier. Incidence of President's Rule has also lessened dramatically. Since 1989 state regional parties have been partners in the coalition governments in the centre.

State Reform Efforts

A careful look at the states' sectoral success stories since the nineties is also necessary. They can learn a lot from each other. Economically savvy states don't wait for funds from the Centre, they are now raising funds from the market. The India States Reform Forum held from time to time since 2000 are helping us to look at fiscal and governance reforms they are initiating and implementing with success. Every state has started publishing Annual Human Development Reports, which map their efforts to improve their human development indicators. Several states have improved their tax revenues, widened their tax net base, implemented VAT, improved their human development and e-governance, records, introduced Citizen charters and enacted Right to Information Acts, since the nineties. Karnataka in August 2002 passed India's first Fiscal Responsibility Act – a clear case of the states leading the Central Government in the reform race.

23 states have issued more than 540 Citizens' Charters. Most of them relate to agriculture, finance, health, social welfare and urban development. Right to information acts have been passed in Goa, Tamil Nadu, Maharashtra, Karnataka and Rajasthan. Lokayukta Acts have been passed in several states. Orissa has

privatised its power sector. Andhra Pradesh has set up user groups across the states to manage the distribution of canal irrigation schemes. E-governance has progressed in maintaining records and delivery systems in several states. States have also recorded considerable reduction in poverty levels, literacy and improvement in delivery systems during the liberalisation period[19].

Fiscal reforms are those undertaken in part or in whole to restore fiscal sustainability or less prosaically to avert bankruptcy. Governance reforms relate to reforms in processes and institutions intended to improve the efficiency and transparency of government operations. Governance and fiscal reforms are not one and the same, yet they are in extricably linked. States will be able neither to end the fiscal deficits they face nor to improve growth, unless they address problems of governance. Whether the issue is tax compliance or the investment climate for the private sector, physical and social infrastructure, economic growth will be impossible without a significant redirection and improvement in the way these states run their administration.

Projections for the future:

On most of the economic problems India faces today, both Central and state action will be necessary to find a solution. There are many states looking for independent solutions, and there are lots of avenues they can follow in this search. Fiscal adjustment needs to be part of a much broader programme directed at revitalising government, accelerating growth and reducing poverty. In addition to key sectoral reforms, in both infrastructure and human development, core fiscal and governance reforms will be needed to achieve these goals.

Major states may be divided into 3 categories, based on the growth and human development indicators. The six fastest growing states (Gujarat, Haryana, Kerala, Maharashtra, Punjab and Tamil Nadu) during the liberalisation period need to focus attention on two main areas: first ensuring that growth is coterminus with sustainable development and, second, take a lead in initiating and supporting cooperative action between the states toward the creation of a common market and the elimination of unfair competition among them.

Second, the states which have not done well in terms of human development, but whose economic performance have been satisfactory (all states except those included in first and third category) seem to have succeeded in overcoming obstacles to growth but given their non-satisfactory record in human development, have to reorient their policies to channelise a sizeable portion of the benefits of growth of literacy, primary education, shelter, health, nutrition and access to safe water. If efforts towards these objectives succeed, these states will improve their growth rate too.

The main focus of change in the policies of the five states in the most backward category (Bihar, Orissa, U.P., M.P. and Rajasthan) will also need to be similar. The growth performance of two of them (M.P. & Rajasthan) has improved. The centre should extend substantial, additional and conditional assistance to the most backward states for carrying out certain major development projects. There has been some heartburn in the more advanced states on the ground that the centre has always pampered the backward states at the expense of the forward states. This was largely due to the 'gap filling approach' of the Finance Commission whose scheme of devolution and grants is geared to filling in projected deficits (on the non-plan revenue account). This obviously puts a premium on showing a larger deficit. There is a lot of talk about restructuring the Planning Commission today. Under the changed policy framework, the Central Plan assistance by way of loans and grants to the various states should be fixed according to a stipulated formula. Given that, a state should be free to formulate its own plan and to fix its size without the Planning Commission. Going through a detailed consideration of every plan, the Planning Commission (on behalf of the Centre) should rather concentrate on providing help to bring about the transformation of the backward states. This should be done by devising special development programmes for these states in consultation with the concerned state governments.

Here we may conclude by stating that a new model of Centre state relations[20] is perhaps emerging beyond the horizon of a liberalised political economy. Perhaps almost imperceptibly an informal amendment of the constitution is taking place over the last decade, a change that is likely to be irreversible given the trends in our emergent federal market political economy. With the off loading of the Centre's functions and powers in many spheres, the states feel less 'controlled' or 'suffocated', and have come to enjoy more 'economic' and thereby 'political space' to draw their own destinies in the federal common market, where the Centre can merely be a regulator and at best a facilitator in the developmental efforts of states.

End Notes

[1] With a view to improving, the performance of the State Electricity Boards, the Government of India promulgated the Electricity Regulatory Commission ordinance in April 1998, under which state electricity commissions have been set up in states. Uniformity in educational matters is enforced through the National Education Policies proclaimed from time to time. There are many Central initiatives in the field of education e.g. Sarva Shiksha Abhiyan, to be implemented in States.

[2] Economic liberalisation, the dismantling of the permit-licence raj, an increasing reliance on markets and a marked decline in central aid to states were the major reasons / incentives for some states to pursue private investment. The centre's gross assistance to states capital formation declined from 27% of the centre's revenue expenditure in 1990-91 to 12% in 1998-99. (Economic Survey, GOI 1999-2000 Appendixs 38)

[3] See L.Rudolph & S.Rudolph 'Sharing sovereignty in India's federal market economy' in EPW, May 5, 2001, p.1541 and Reeta Tremblay 'Globalisation and Indian federalism' in IJPA, vol. XLVII No. 2, April-June 2001, p 208-220.

[4] Aid from multilateral agencies have become conditional on providing an environment of good governance marked by rule of law, economic and social pluralism, sound development, management and political stability.

[5] S.K. Jain, Party Politics and Centre State Relations, Abhinav Publications, New Delhi, 1994.

[6] For the 1989 and 1991 election results, Subrata K. Mitra and James Chiriyankandth, Electoral Politics in India, Segment, New Delhi, 1992, and Election Commission Reports, 1996, 1998, and 1999. For 2004 figures, National Election Study, Economic and Political weekly, vol.39 (51), 18 December 2004, pp.5539-43.

[7] M.P. Singh and Douglas V. Verney, 'Challenges to India's Centralised Federalism', Publics, The Journal of Federalism, Fall 2003.

[8] See Indian Social Institute Papers pertaining to elections of Panchayat bodies post 73rd & 74th Amendments.

[9] J Dasgupta, 'India's federal Design and Multicultural national Construction' in Atul Kohli (ed.), The Success of India's Democracy, Cambridge, p.49

[10] T B Hansen & C Jaffrelot (eds.) The BJP and the compulsions of Politics in India, N. Delhi : OUP, 1998, p.7

[11] Plans in India were meant to lay out macro goals, objectives, directives and directions which allowed its sub-systems to be implemented through the

market. In the Indian context, therefore, planning was not necessarily an expression of a socialist model of growth or alternative to a market system. Planning in India began as an attempt to convert a poor, relatively static, primarily agricultural and traditional economy into a richer, dynamic, modern industrial nation. The three major objectives of a planned development strategy were poverty removal, adoption of a socialist pattern of development, self reliant industrial growth with equity and justice for its citizens.

[12] India's economic policies had been defined by the Industrial Policy Resolution, 1956 with minor changes over the years. This Resolution clearly defined the primary role of the public sector in India's economic development. The mixed economy model of growth spawned a huge bureaucratic-industrial network, with regulatory controls over the private sector. It was only to tide over the fiscal crisis of 1991 that India had to comply with IMF loan conditions, and introduce Structural Adjustment Policies which freed trade restrictions, dismantled the stifling bureaucratic-regulatory regime to a great extent by opening up opportunities for foreign investment, free enterprise and the market to play a role in the Indian economy.

[13] Additionally, like many private goods, some public goods are also subject to economies of scale. There can be diseconomies of scale when expenditures are devolved to small local governments. Given the size of the Indian states, in terms of population as well as area, this problem is likely to be of limited relevance for India.

[14] Amaresh Bagchi, Tax Assignment in the Indian Federation' in India's Economic Reforms and Development : Essays for Man Mohan Singh (Isher Judge Ahluwalia and I.M.D. Little, eds). Delhi : Oxford University Press, 1998.

[15] Govinda M Rao and Tapas K Sen Fiscal Federalism in India, Theory and Practice, New Delhi : Macmillan, 1996.

[16] Public sector investment at the national level is only about 28% of total investment and this includes both the centre and the states. Three fourths of national level gross fixed investment comes from the private sector, and 38% from private corporate household investment. At 28% of total investment, public investment by the centre and the states accounts for about 6.8% of GDP, of which state plans account for only one third. See Ahluwalia's essay in Sachs, Bajpai and Varshney (eds) Era of Economic Reforms OUP, 2000.

[17] N.J. Kurien 'Widening regional disparities in India : Some indicators' in EPW, Feb,12, 2000, pp 538-50 and Govinda M. Rao, Richard T. Shand and K.P. Kalirajan 'Convergence of Incomes in Indian States : A divergent view' EPW, Vol.XXXIV no. 13, March, 27, 1999.

[18] See Amaresh Bagchi 'Rethinking-federalism : overview of current debates with some reflections in the Indian context' EPW, Aug 19, 2000 p.3025 and C Rangarajan 'Fiscal Federalism : Some current concerns' in Indian Journal of Federal Studies, Center for Federal Studies, New Delhi, Jan. 2004.

[19] States which had 6% growth per annum and very little poverty were Gujarat, Haryana, Kerala, Maharashtra, Punjab and Tamil Nadu during the Tenth Plan Period. Among the poor states, Rajasthan and Madhya Pradesh made dramatic reductions in poverty. In the Education Guarantee Scheme of M.P. the community partnered with the state to make possible 26,000 schools in 2 years. Mizoram and Himachal Pradesh have recorded 99% literacy rates.

Delivery systems have improved with public/private/voluntary sector partnerships in the last 10 years in most states.

[20] The new model has been given new names – such as 'cooperative-competitive' or 'cooperative-negotiatory' model of federalism with reference to the emerging trends in Centre-State relations in the post globalised period.

14

Democracy and Development: The Indian Experience

FURQAN AHMED

The present article is an attempt to examine the role of Panchayati Raj Institutions in the Socio-Political development of the Rural Community. In this context various institutional parameters of rural development have been discussed. No doubt, as viable democratic institutions the panchayat bodies can play a significant role but the present system of Panchayati Raj is beset with built-in conflict and confusion of responsibility and does not encourage local initiative and enterprise. It encourages politics where it is unnecessary and harmful and denies politics where it is necessary and useful. Due to these reasons, it is not coming up to the expectations of the people. In order to make them more viable and useful as instruments of rural development, a drastic change in the functions and powers of the Panchayati Raj institutions is outlined.

One of the major questions facing developing countries has been the problem of achieving social and economic development through democratic processes. In India, the commitment to democratic processes is as great as the concern for economic development. At grass-roots level, Panchayati Raj institutions were set up to associate village leaders with the administration of planning and development. One of the major issues in Panchayati Raj is decentralisation and the degree of autonomy to be enjoyed by Panchayat bodies.

Parameters of Institutional Structure:

The basic factors in creation of suitable institutional structures are the people, the leadership and the bureaucracy. With regard to people there have been focal views about qualities of citizens in a democratic set up. Inkles. A. has summaried the acts in these lines:

The citizens of a democracy should be accepting the others rather than alienating and harshly rejecting; open to new experiences, to ideas and impulses rather than excessively timid, fearful, or extremely conventional with regard to new ideas and ways of acting, able to be responsible with constituted authority even though always watchful, rather than blindly submissive or hostilely rejecting of all authority; tolerant of differences and of ambiguity, rather than rigid and inflexible; able to recognise, control and channel his emotions rather than immaturely projecting hostility and other impulses on to others[1].

The parameters of qualities of citizens are basically related with traditional social and political institutions, national character and the level of basic need satisfaction. 'The idea of community participation, of sharing good- will and friendship, and of rational decision- making based on an objective assessment of social reality would appear psychological. It is. Therefore, not surprising that the participation of the public in the Panchayat Raj institutions has created such problems as the misappropriation of public funds, nepotism and favoritism and pressures on the official agency to serve private interests, all of which reflect personal fears regarding economics and social deprivation.[2]

It may, however, be argued that the peoples representatives in democratic institutions need not be typically the citizens at large. The question, however, is how different the leaders can be from the masses in terms of interests, orientations and values and whether the leadership role makes it possible for them to preserve their self-identity as distinguished from that of the masses. Even if it is conceded that the public leadership is by and large liberated from the satisfaction of elemental needs and therefore, predisposed toward flexibility, objectivity and other-orientation, whether it is able to express these qualities in practice depends upon its ability to assert its individuality in a role that makes it incumbent upon the leader to be relevant to the electorate. It is difficult to conceive how the leadership can preserve its independent identity and role when its own status depends upon the support of the masses. The leader, therefore, leads to a large extent by articulating the needs and interests of his constituency. Although the concept of leadership implies a following, it is not a one way relationship, and, in a democratic political system, the constituency is as important as the leaders.

Some political scientists have emphasised the role of the leadership in generating value congruence between the elites and the masses, and in bringing about popular consensus around policies evolved at the higher levels of the government. While the importance of this function in the context of a democratic political system is obvious, it is not at all certain how in a country like India the leaders will bring about consensus among the masses and how far the needs and ideas of the masses determine the nature and scope of political consensus. For example, all political parties in India, regardless of their ideological differences, have supported the cause of the landless and the small farmers, advocated reduction in income disparity and in the size of large holdings and have promised various kinds of concessions to the rural sector. In practice the efforts of local leaders are generally directed at securing benefits for small groups of their own through construction of tube wells, roads, schools or programmes of industrial development. It is also observed that the success in elections is not usually a matter of ideological commitment or personal integrity but depends upon the leaders' ability to win over the support of critical individuals and groups, and to sustain their loyalty by being personally useful to them.

It is important to comment on the nature of political orientation of the rural community and its leadership. The rural community, which still provides the home for the over-whelming majority of the population, is characterised by face-to-face gemenienshaft relationship. Personal contacts and group affiliations are common in arriving at decision relevant for the community. As the discussion on values has indicated, the rural population considers the preservation of community harmony and integrity more important than community development[3]. There is considerable acceptance of authority, hierarchy and status. These values of the rural population, even of the rural elites, are bound to restrict the full flowering of democratic processes and to foster a climate of factionalism and particularism. Such a climate and consequent modes of solving problems through rigid social divisions are not conducive to the effective functioning of the formal democratic institutions. Thus, in addition to the fact that the leadership is not quite free to assert its identity even though it may be potentially capable of doing so, it is also hampered by the lack of such skills and attitude as are required for the participation in formal decision-making processes of the Panchayati institutions.

As a third variable, the bureaucracy is a stable, organised and competent segment of the administrative system. Its role in development is to implement policies and programmes formulated at the higher level and to act as an instrument of the government for the achievement of development targets. Given the characteristics of the leadership and the political environment commented upon earlier, the role of the bureaucracy in development assumes an important place. The bureaucracy gets directly involved in the process of policy formulation as well as in the details of programme implementation. By its very nature, however, the bureaucratic system is based on formal rules and tends to be impersonal. The Indian bureaucratic tradition, dating from the time of the colonial rule, has lent the government bureaucracy a highly authoritarian and caste status not necessarily characteristic of other bureaucratic systems. The current responsibilities of the bureaucracy for development, however, require it to be radically different from its past self-image. It now needs to be innovative and flexible. It is to be problem rather than procedure oriented. It must function as the guardian of the people's interests and not merely as an impersonal arm of the government. In its approach to problems, it is required to be receptive to external inputs and situations.

A close association between the public leadership and the bureaucracy in the planning process creates certain anomalies and also makes incompatible demands. First, the bureaucracy has to reckon with the demands and pressures of the public leadership, which has very different ideas about the tasks of government and the needs of the people. Second, it is expected to strengthen those very institutions and systems, as for example, Panchayati Raj, to which it is subordinated, and which apply standards of conduct and efficiency that are different from theirs. Third, it is required to work through public leadership, which is not necessarily receptive to innovations, is motivated by particularistic considerations and pulls of political strings at the highest level to subvert administrative decisions. Fourth, it is made to give a good account of itself in terms of performance under conditions that are difficult and perhaps unrewarding. Under such circumstances the bureaucracy might resist innovations that seem to undercut its own influence or become apathetic, demoralised or undisciplined on account of conflicting demands made on it by the public. As individuals, the civil servants and the technical personnel are as vulnerable as the public in general to temptations such as opportunism, nepotism or graft. The social environment, instead of helping to curb such deviance may even encourage it. The efforts of the bureaucratic system to discipline deviants may be frustrated by internal cliques and external political pressures. The organisational cohesiveness of the bureaucracy and its ability to function as an effective organ of the government are obviously undermined.

In addition to the characteristics and shortcomings peculiar to the political leadership and the bureaucracy, the institutional organisation of the Panchayati Raj brings together divergent elements without successfully resolving their mutual conflicts. As it has already been pointed out earlier, the very diversity of political and bureaucratic cultures makes it difficult for both the political and bureaucratic elements to work together harmoniously. The attempt to yoke these two elements together breeds organisational conflicts because the system is based on divided authority and precludes a clear focus of responsibility. As a result, one blames the other for the defects and failures of planning and development. None of the students of Panchayati Raj can avoid being struck by the cleavages and grievances that divided the bureaucratic and the political wings of the administration. It would be naive to expect that a little of sweet reasonableness would help to resolve these differences and conflicts. These differences arise not from the perversity of the leaders or the officials but from their different perceptions, interests and values. The plight of bureaucrats is worse because they ultimately bear the burden of implementation and are called upon to serve two masters- their bureaucratic bosses and the people.

Perspectives for Reforms:

The problem of effective institution building calls for devising a machinery to reduce the areas of conflicts and to generate a capability for self-sustaining growth. The present system of Panchayati Raj is beset with built in conflicts and confusion of responsibility, and does not encourage local initiative and enterprises[4]. It encourages 'politics' where it is unnecessary and harmful, and denies 'politics' where it is necessary and useful. A correct perspective on administrative reform must devise various institutions and entrust functions appropriate to each of them.

It may be argued that the local political system should be vested with complete authority not only in policy- making but also in policy implementation and financial mobilisation. At present the Panchayat Raj institutions are assigned some functions but they lack autonomy and finances almost depending entirely upon grants from the state government. Lack of financial independence destroys not only local autonomy in planning according to local needs and circumstances, but also destroys a sense of administrative responsibility for whatever they do or do not do. Current planning is nominally from below, but in effect allocation of resources and formulation of policies and targets are determined by the state government. No system of modern local government can dispense with grants-in-aid from higher authorities, but grants cannot be a complete substitute for local resources without destroying the local initiative, flexibility and responsibility in planning. For purposes of planning, therefore, it is necessary that full authority in making administrative and fiscal policies and decisions should be assigned to these local political institutions.

This proposal, however, must take into account a number of difficulties. First, there is a general reluctance on the part of local bodies to levy taxes and collect them efficiently. Secondly, the local bodies may not afford all the technical expertise, which is required for a comprehensive planning of rural development. Thirdly, the task of rural development cannot be undertaken piecemeal, and must include responsibilities in three major fields: (1) Building the infrastructure of economic development; (2) Provision of technological inputs; and (3) Provision of civic and social amenities. Keeping in view the massive requirement of these tasks, it would be obviously beyond the means and capacity of local political systems to undertake planning and development on their own.

Another path leading to reform would be to entrust all the aforesaid responsibilities to government administration. This, however, not only violates the political values of democratic decentralisation but also would make planning itself more difficult and less fruitful. As pointed out above, the state government and its agents in the district will be unable to take into consideration the local needs and thus plans would tend to be uniform and rigid and in all likelihood utterly unrealistic. Also the task of development involves in many cases active association and participation of people. The most important task of development administration is to improve the adaptive qualities of the people so that they may be easily induced to accept changes. Greater participation of the people in the process of planning and development is likely to ensure that the interests, orientations and values of the people should be in harmony with the objects of planned development.

The way to break through the horns of this dilemma between local authority and bureaucracy may be found by clearly identifying various areas of planning process and examining it in order to assign the areas viz. Political, bureaucratic or a mixed system[5]. In this connection, differences between the district and the block levels are suggestive. Interaction between the people and officials are closer at the block level than at the district level. People come to the block officials more as clients in need of services and suppliers. At the district level, public leaders approach the officials for protection or promotion of particular interest not related directly to development purposes. This leads to an important conclusion that if the relationship between officials and people is one of supplier and client, then there is possibility of relatively closer and better interaction. The most important requisites from the viewpoint of agricultural development are the building of the necessary infrastructure such as power, irrigation facilities, roads, etc. and specific agricultural production activities such as provision of seeds and fertilisers. There is no reason why such requisites cannot be achieved by government agencies without the direct involvement of political institutions. The most urgent task in agricultural development is the creation of such conditions and provision of such facilities to ensure regular, adequate and timely supply of input factors. It should be the duty of government to guarantee such overheads and inputs through its administrative agencies. Popular participation, if necessary, can be achieved through advisory committees consisting of both government servants and the nominees of political institutions.

Besides the economic overheads and the supply of technological inputs, there is another large area of activities, which includes area development and other social and civic functions such as water supply, sanitation, village health and primary education. In these areas, the local political system should be encouraged to develop their own initiative and responsibility. The state should ofcourse offer grants-in-aid even in these areas, but the main administrative authority and financial responsibility for such functions should rest with the local political system. It should be realised that the primary purpose of Panchayat Raj institutions is to ensure the social and political development of rural communities that would be capable of collective and cooperative efforts for community improvement. It is indeed more likely that popular participation under the social conditions prevailing in villages do not produce the desired results. However, the purpose of political participation is to encourage popular education and interest in community matters. If government undertakes to take care of basic requisites for economic development, the responsibility for providing and augmenting the social and civic services can be fully entrusted to Panchayat institutions without much damage. The elimination of poverty and unemployment is a sine qua non of community development in any other sphere of life. Let the government take full responsitibility for economic overheads and inputs and let the people have full authority to manage their own local government.

This clear demarcation of economic and civic functions and the separation of institutional responsibility for each of these is necessary to remove the present confusion and fragmentation of authority between the bureaucracy and the Panchayat institutions. Indeed the present system failed to ensure either full responsibility of the bureaucracy or full initiative and enterprise of the Panchayat Institutions. The solution lies in making both the bureaucracy and the panchayats fully responsible for functions that should belong exclusively to one or the other.

The last point that needs stressing is the inadequacy of the village as a viable unit of development. An average village in terms of its population and resources is unfit to be used for area planning. The ultimate test of rural development must lie in the high degree of its environmental improvement marked by the presence of such civic amenities as are sought to be made available in towns and cities. A single village can hardly attain a high standard of all-round development that is not merely economic, but also civic and social in its scope. Even from the viewpoint of total economic development, the village is fast becoming inadequate, as agricultural development has to be supplemented by agro-industrial development in order to absorb the landless and other unemployed people. It is, therefore, imperative that new and bigger areas of growth and development be designed. These areas need not be uniform in size. The craze of uniformity in administrative reorganisation does not help local development, which must be related to the contiguity of habited areas, their interactions, size and character of the population, the nature of transport and communication.

Thus, in our scheme there should be government bureaucracy in charge of mostly economic overheads and the supply of all inputs. For civic services and the need of environmental development, the local political systems should have complete authority of policy formulation and implementation. There should also be a coordination committee consisting of representatives of both the government bureaucracy and the local political systems. Thus there would be need for drastic reforms in the organisation, functions and powers of the present Panchayati Raj institutions. At the same time the emphasis should be on strengthening, streamlining and improving the process as well as the personnel of the government bureaucracy apart from institutional restructuring. Indeed even in areas where local political systems have full authority, political leadership would need technical and administrative personnel. Thus ultimately the role of the bureaucracy remains crucial. The aim should be to ensure not only bureaucratic responsibility to the political leadership, but also bureaucratic independence and competence. Problems arise where functions and powers are confused and one does not know or does not have a chance to do what is his task.

End Notes

[1] For details see A Inkeles, National character and Modern Political system. In F.L.K. Hsu (Ed.), Psychological Anthropology: Approaches to culture And Personality, Homewood, III The Dorsey Press, 1961, pp. 172-208

[2] K.K. Singh and A. Ashraf, Bureaucracy, Leadership and Development. 1971, pp. 84-90, (Project report submitted to the ICSSR), N. Delhi.

[3] *Ibid* pp 204-208

[4] Douglas Ensminger, Panchayati Raj and Decentralisation, The Indian Express Bangalore, March, 1979

[5] G. Ram Reddy, 'Panchayati Raj Proposal' Seminar No 234 New Delhi, February 1979

15

Public Administration in the Age of Globalisation: An Alternative Paradigm*

RUMKI BASU

In contrast to the traditional model and the new public management paradigm – the two mainstream models that are rooted in the idea of rational choice – an alternative model of public administration has been advocated by Janet V. Denhardt and Robert B. Denhardt in their book. In this article, the relevance of this model for India is carefully examined in the backdrop of a search for excellence in public services and the ongoing administrative reforms. In today's changing India, a question of overwhelming importance is regarding the criteria of successful administration. The article attempts to outline some answers.

Introduction

The traditional model of public administration advocated by writers such as Woodrow Wilson, Henri Fayol, Frederick Taylor, Max Weber, Luther Gullick and Lyndall Urwick gave way to

---

* Reprinted with the permission of the Editor, from the Indian Journal of Public Administration, Vol. LII No.3 July-Sept. 2006. The article was titled 'The New Public Service Revisited : Relevance for India' in the IJPA.

other models only towards the end of the 20th century[1]. This model professed political neutrality as a behavioural imperative of hierarchical bureaucracies, called for routine of office work according to codified rules and opted for efficiency (as opposed to responsiveness) as the primary criterion for evaluating the work of public agencies which were looked upon as closed systems of organisation.

The first serious opposition to this model came from the New Public Management paradigm[2], which started unfolding during the last two decades of the 20th century, presenting itself as an alternative to the traditional model. According to New Public Management theorists, the government should be the monopoly service provider only in areas, which cannot be privatised or contracted out, and rest of the services should be provided to citizens by private or voluntary agencies regulated by the government. This will enable greater competition among delivery systems and the citizens can be ensured greater choice. New Public Management would suggest that public managers "steer, rather than row" (Osborne & Gaebler, 1992) and are given greater freedom to improve efficiency and productivity, on condition that they remain responsive and accountable to public needs and demands. The theoretical roots of New Public Management lies in public choice theory, agency theory and in the use of economic models in the making of public policy.

In contrast to these two mainstream models that are rooted in the idea of "rational choice", Janet V. Denhardt and Robert B. Denhardt have advocated an alternative model of public administration in their book the *New Public Service* (New York, H.E. Sharpe, 2003). In this book, the writers trace the intellectual heritage of the New Public Service first and then outline the main tenets of the normative model. The contemporary precursors of the New Public Service include 1) theories of democratic citizenship; 2) models of community and civil society; 3) organisational humanism. Let us now carefully examine these, accordingly.

The need for people's participation and a more proactive citizenry as a desirable input in democratic decision making processes is being increasingly called for in recent political theory. In the New Public Management model, the relationship between state and citizens is based on the idea that government exists to ensure that citizens make choices consistent with their self-interest by guaranteeing certain legal procedures and individual rights. Obviously underlying this perspective is the "public choice economics" based on rational choice.

Others have argued that civic morality or the public spirit plays an important role in the process of democratic governance. Michael Sandel, (1996) for example, states that citizens have the capacity to look beyond their self-interest to the larger public interest, adopting a broader and long-term perspective that requires knowledge of civic affairs and also a sense of bonding with the community at large. Others advocates that, public spiritedness need to be encouraged and maintained by revoking the principles of justice, public participation and deliberation. This alternative view of citizenship however does not suggest the elimination of self-interest, but it does suggest a balancing of these two kinds of public behaviour (selfish and altruistic) as the ideal in a democratic society. This really calls for a restoration of a view of citizenship based on civic interests rather than self-interest. In two recent books Government is Us (King and Stivers 1998) and Citizen Governance (Box, 1998), both writers have asserted that administrators should view citizens as citizens (rather than merely voters, clients or customers), should share authority with them and repose trust in the efficiency of a citizen – centered government.

The roots of the New Public Service in the widespread current revival of interest in community and civil society by both the Left and Right wing thinkers can be traced out. The Left advocate community as an antidote to the unrestrained greed and self interest that marks modern society. The Right views community as an instrument for the restoration of basic communitarian values, which are perceived to be under threat in modern society. John Gardner (1991) holds that a sense of community, which might be derived from many different levels of human association from the neighbourhood to the work group, might provide a helpful mediating structure between the individual and society. Beyond these features, according to Gardner, a community is based on caring, trust and teamwork, bound together by a strong and effective system of communication and conflict resolution. As Robert Putnam (2000) argues, America's democratic tradition is dependent on the existence of civically engaged citizens, who collectively constitute a "civil society". Where strong networks of citizen interaction and high levels of social trust and cohesion among citizens exist, public administrators can count on these to build even stronger networks of social capital, to open new avenues of dialogue and debate, and can further educate citizens on matters of democratic governance.

Organisational humanism is the next important theoretical root of the New Public Service. Since the 1960's, many organisational theorists have put forth the view that traditional hierarchical bureaucratic approaches to organisations are restrictive in their view of human behaviour and have explored alternative ways of designing organisations less dominated by principles of hierarchy, authority and control. Chris Argyris and Robert Golembiewski explored these concerns in their books through the last part of the twentieth century.[3] Argyris maintained that standard management practices seemed to inhibit the development of employees rather than enhance it. For example, in most organisations, people have relatively little control over their work and organisation rules do not necessary enhance the personality development of people in organisations. Argyris sought an approach to management in which managers would develop and employ *skills in self awareness, in effective diagnosing, in helping individuals grow and become more creative* (Argyris 1964). In the field of public administration, the organisation development (OD) perspective has been explored most thoroughly by Robert Golembiewski who sought a way to enlarge the area of discretion in organising avenues of individual freedom (Golembiewski 1967). Following an OD perspective, Golembiewski urged managers to create an open problem-solving climate through the organisation, so that, members can confront problems rather than fight about or flee from them. He said the idea was to maximise collaboration between individual and units whose work is interdependent and to develop reward systems that recognise both the achievement of the organisation's mission and the growth and development of the organisation's members. He said, Managers should work to increase self-control and self-direction for people within the organisation to create conditions under which conflict is surfaced and managed appropriately, to increase awareness of group process and its consequences for performance (Golembiewski 1977, 1992).

Other important contributions to constructing more humanistic organisations in the public sector were made by a group of scholars collectively known as the New Public Administration theorists, essentially the public administration counterpart to the late sixties / early seventies radical movements in social science[4]. The New Public Administration (NPA) movement that started at Minnow brook has been criticised as anti-theoretic, anti positivist and anti bureaucratic. NPA displays an intense concern for relevant social problems, stressing ethics and values, innovation and social equality. It lays great emphasis on human relations and a creative approach to administration and social change. Theorists of citizenship, community and civil society, organisational humanism and the New Public Administration movement have helped to establish a climate in which it makes sense today to talk about a New Public Service. We do acknowledge that though substantial differences exist in these various viewpoints there are also similarities that distinguish the cluster of ideas we call the New Public Service from those associated with the New Public Management and the Old Public Administration Among these the following are relevant[5]:

1. Serve Citizens, Not Customers: The public interest is the result of a dialogue about shared values rather than the aggregation of individual self-interests. Therefore, public servants do not merely respond to the demands of "customers" but rather focus on building relationships of trust and collaboration among citizens.

2. Seek the Public Interest: Public administrators must contribute towards building a collective, shared notion of the public interest. The goal is not to find quick solutions driven by individual choices. Rather, it is the creation of shared interests and shared responsibility.

3. Value citizenship over entrepreneurship: Public interest is better advanced by public servants and citizens committed to making meaningful contribution to society than by entrepreneurial managers acting as if public money were their own.

4. Think strategically, act democratically : Policies and programmes meeting public needs can be most effectively and responsibly achieved through collective efforts and collaborative processes.

5. Recognise that accountability is not simple : Public servants should be attentive to more than the market ; they should also attend to statutory and constitutional law, community values, political norms, professional standards and citizen interests.
6. Serve rather than steer: It is increasingly important for public servants to use shared, value based leadership in helping citizens articulate and meet their shared interest rather than attempting to control or steer society in a new direction.
7. Value people, not just productivity: Public organisations and the networks in which they participate are more likely to be successful in the long run if they are operated through processes of collaboration and shared leadership based on respect for all people.

In the preceding paragraphs, we have presented a theoretical framework that gives full priority to democracy, citizenship and service in the public interest. Janet V and Robert B. Denhardt have called this framework as the "New Public Service". They have argued that the New Public Service offers an important and viable alternative to both the traditional and the now dominant models of public management. It is an alternative that has been built on the basis of theoretical exploration and practical innovations in public agencies.

The New Public Service : Relevance for India

The good governance debate in the context of globalisation and liberalisation is an ongoing debate in India since the 1990's[6]. Indian administration is responding to the challenges of managing the largest democracy in the world through a framework of socio-economic planning, negotiating with the needs of a changing federal structure and evolving appropriate policy interventions. The administrators are increasingly becoming facilitators in this transformational process of empowerment through conscious policies of civil service reform.

Looking at the Indian scenario, a classification of reforms undertaken can be attempted as below listed:-

i) The first category of reforms pertains to the legal basis of government action. Instruments to review administrative laws, the constitutional amendments to impart stability to the rural and urban local self governing institutions and legislation for an effective set of vigilance bodies belong to this category.

ii) Comprehensive or specific reforms of administrative structure, size and design – allocation of work, status and hierarchy, etc. and administrative procedures. The application of Total Quality Management (TQM) concepts would clearly be within this reform category. Procedural reforms in financial decentralisation and delegation of powers, personnel management, vigilance, machinery etc. are essentially meant to speed up internal or inter departmental operations.

iii) Initiatives essentially aimed at the creation of a better system of human resource management. Reference may be made here at the efforts to develop and enforce a system of a professional code of ethics in central government over and above the prescribed conduct rules and updating practices through training and dissemination of good habits in the work place.

iv) Reforms for more active partnerships between the government, private/voluntary sectors and citizens. These include the all-important interface with citizens (Right to information, Redress of grievances, Citizen's Charters etc.), with local self-governance institutions (the municipalities and panchayats), with NGOs, registered associations (for instance of residents of urban localities, or societies), with elected and other public representatives.

Governments today and of the future in India will undergo enormous social and economic transformations, profoundly affecting the work of public administration. Innovative ways of steering society will require us to consider new standards of assessing administrative performance, including not only the traditional legal and political standards, but also the market and economic criteria and finally the democratic and social criteria associated with the proposed New Public Service. *While it is imperative to maintain a concern for legal, political, and economic criteria, it is of overwhelming importance that we place at the center of our work a concept of the public service based on and fully integrated with citizen discourse and the public interest.* (Janet & Robert Denhardt 2003.)

Today public administration in India relates to the who[1] of society and to the changed political economy after liberalisation. Thus assuming its overwhelming importance, the question may now be asked – In today's changing India, what are the criteria of successful administration?[7] The norms of an administrative system are both old and new. Traditional norms – efficacy, economy, good management and public interest – are well-established measures of judging the success of any administrative system. To these, can be added, continuing socio-economic progress, maintenance of good delivery systems, economic regulation and striving for equity and justice. Inequality is still a big political and human rights issue in India. Widespread inequalities provide the breeding ground for social ferment, dissent and alienation. The effective public administrator will continue to be the 'rational calculator' of different ways of implementing public policies. He will have to learn to satisfy conflicting public demands and understand the continual need of improving public services with fixed resources. With the increasing diversification of tasks of the civil services, there is no room for the amateur in administration at present. What is needed is a specialist or a professional civil servant who has acquired the requisite professional training and is truly dedicated and committed to the goals and objectives of this service.

Public administration in India will have to face a host of challenges and pressures that will put its adaptability and performance capacity to a severe test. If man is to survive in the face of nuclear threats, overpopulation, environmental pollution, rapid technological change coupled with increasing societal turbulence, public administration will also have to learn to decentralise, democratise and humanise itself. To be a good and effective civil servant in the New Public Service mould, he will need to be more responsive and responsible. The key to responsiveness is organisational adaptability to change. The process of social, economic and political change will continue to accelerate making it vitally important that organsations adapt. Organisation leaders must learn to anticipate social, economic and political change and to creatively work on it. There will be conditions under which the patterns of change will require organisational growth. But there will be equally as many and perhaps more situations (in today's age of 'roll back of the state') in which these change processes will require organisational decline, cut back and devolution. The good administrator will be adept at scanning the political, economic and social horizons and leading the processes of adaptation to growth or decline. Change in the 21st Century is more likely to be the result of imaginative policies and complex economic political and social choices rather than the mere application of technological solutions to administrative problems.

End Notes

[1] The works of Wilson, Fayol, Taylor, Weber, Gullick and Urwick have been variously termed as 'classical', 'structural', 'mechanistic', 'formal', 'engineering' and 'empirical' approaches. Their writings were labelled so differently because they attempted to propound simple principles of general application and possessing characteristics of formality, symmetry and rigidity. Their theories emphasise the importance of the structure and subsume the amenability of humans to work to meet the administrative demands. The underlying premise is that the patterns of behaviour and relationships can be deliberately planned for the members of the administration.

[2] The new conceptualisations in the discipline of public administration coinciding with the remarkable changes in the practice of governments and public agencies world wide since the eighties have been termed as a paradigmatic shift and given the generic name of New Public Management.

[3] Chris Argyris and Robert Golembiewski attach great significance to human behaviour in organisations and the psychological character of such groupings form the foundations of their theories. The concern is primarily with the process by which the individual and the organisation adapt to the needs of each other.

[4] For details of the New Public Administration school that came into being following the Minnowbrook Conference in 1968, see Frank Marini (ed) Toward a New Public Administration, Chandler, 1971.

[5] Quoted from The New Public Service by Janet V Denhardt and Robert B. Denhardt, New York M. E Sharpe. P. 43

[6] The 'governance' perspective provides a reference point which challenges many of the assumptions of traditional Public Administration, See Gerry Stoker 'Governance as Theory : Five Propositions' in International Social Science Journal no. 155, March 1998 pp13-28. For the 'good governance' perspective as spelt out by the World Bank and its implications see Niraja Gopal Jayal 'The Governance Agenda' EPW, 22 Feb. 1977.

[7] There is a huge volume of literature on ongoing administrative reforms in India. For a look at the rationale and theoretical issues involved in the debate on administrative reforms see the articles in Part III of B. Chakravarty and Mohit Bhattacharya (ed) Public Administration A Reader, OUP, New Delhi, 2003.

16

Role of Non-governmental Organisations in Public Policy in the Era of Globalisation

SREEPATI RAMUDU

Globalisation has ushered in a change in the meaning and context of NGOs in terms of their increased role as service delivery institutions as well as implementation agencies of public policy. While there is a gradual shrinking of the public sector, NGOs are stepping in to fill up the gaps that have been retreated by the withdrawal of the state. Interestingly, the whole process of transformation of the NGO sector has on the one hand accelerated the state's retreat and on the other it has contributed to the wide spread socio-economic exclusion of the poor, marginalised and disadvantaged sections from the development framework in the developing, as well as, developed countries. In view of this, a number of questions are raised in the development discourse about the credibility, accountability, capability and transparency of the NGOs.

Non-governmental organisation (NGOs) have come to occupy a significant place in the development discourse all over the world, particularly in the contemporary era of globalisation. The rapid penetration of the globalisation forces has resulted in the retreat of the governments from social welfare arenas in many developing countries including India. The withdrawal of state from social welfare has created a vacuum in society, paving the way for a number of non-governmental actors to occupy the space. Meanwhile, the World Bank's emphasis on governance reforms has also accorded prominence to civil society organisations in the developmental process, as a part of its Structural Adjustment Programme (SAP). This provided a fertile ground for the NGOs to sprout and play a vital role in the public policy of a country. In view of their growing importance and changing nature, this article makes an attempt to present different dimensions of the NGOs with a special focus on their role in influencing public policy formulation.

In the last two decades, the developing world has undergone a process of economic reforms in the form of liberalisation, privatisation and globalisation. While the reforms have adversely affected a majority of the population, the poor and marginalised groups, a small section has gained advantage and multiplied its wealth in myriad forms.

The reforms forced the governments to withdraw investments and subsides from social service and agricultural sectors in order to reduce the fiscal deficit in their budgets. Such focus has resulted in an unprecedented growth of poverty, discrimination, environmental degradation and socio-economic exclusion of a large section of masses. As a response to the situation, anger and frustration of the masses has consistently surfaced in the form of protests and agitations all over the world. To address such issues, the protagonists of the economic reforms and the international financial institutions came out with a concept termed as 'governance reforms' that openly acknowledged and encouraged civil society organisations to take a direct part in the development process. Taking this opportunity a number of NGOs mushroomed in a variety of areas with diverse objectives. Subsequently the rise of NGOs following the neo-liberal agenda increased spectacularly since the 1980s. On many occasions, the NGOs have stepped in to fill the vacuum in the social sectors, vacated by the state. In some instances, the growth of NGOs further accelerated the state's withdrawal from social services.[1]

Though, the term NGO is used interchangeably to denote grassroots organisations, social movements, civil society organisations and major groups, etc., they are however not the same as any one of them.² NGOs are commonly defined as non-profit organisations that are independent of the government.³ According to the World Bank, NGOs are "private organisations that pursue activities to relieve suffering, promote interest and provide basic social services or undertake community development.⁴ NGOs are therefore not homogeneous groups and based on their nature and scope of activities they have been categorised into different types, such as, INGOs (International NGOs), BINGOs (Business International NGOs), RINGOs (Religious International NGOs), GONGOs (Government operated NGOs), and QUANGOs (Quasi-Non governmental organisations), etc.⁵ According to the Ministry of Home Affairs, their numbers have been growing at a faster rate and around 20,000 NGOs were registered under the Foreign Contribution and Regulation Act (FCRA) by the end of 2000 in India.

NGOs take up a variety of issues, which generally include poverty, human rights, literacy, environment, child labour, racial, caste and gender discrimination, etc., at the local, national and international level. India had a wide variety of NGOs that work on different issues. Prof. T.K. Oommen characterised NGOs on the basis of their functional specialisation into three categories. First, there are NGOs, which plays a techno-managerial role to accelerate the development process greared to reinforce the system stability. Second, there are NGOs, which are involved in conscientisation and are reformist in orientation. These are inclined towards bringing about incremental change. Finally, there are NGOs that mobilise the deprived sections of society into collective action.⁶ Broadly speaking the functions of NGOs can be divided into two categories: viz., a) service provisions and b) policy functions. While the former perspective includes social welfare functions such as health, education, nutrition to women and children and capacity building through training, the latter consists of a different set of activities to influence policies and bring about desired changes in them.

NGOs claim to make an important contribution to realise development goals in view of their in-depth knowledge of developmental issues, intimate connections with target populations and low operational costs, etc. However, the activities of NGOs related to public policy have been considered to be pivotal and proved to be quite effective in the last few decades. For the important role that the NGOs play in the development processes of a society they have been considered as the 'Third Sector', the first and second sector being government and market respectively.

In view of the significant role played by the NGOs, it would be appropriate to discuss their contribution in policy formulation. To begin with, it has been widely recognised that the presence of NGOs is indispensable and unavoidable in the entire exercise of "Agenda Setting". Agenda setting is a process by which, a collection of problems and their understanding gains the attention of public as well as, different actors involved in public policy making. The identification of a problem or its prioritisation takes place in the agenda setting process. The policy related activities of the NGOs initiate with agenda setting, when they bring a number of social and economic issues to the notice of policy makers, in order to bring them in the realm of the policy process. This target may be solely undertaken by a single NGO or a group of NGOs. Through campaigns, protests, seminars and media, etc., the NGOs try to get their issues in the public domain. Further they also lobby with the policy makers for achieving their ends.

Once their issue gets priority, the NGOs shift their attention to the next stage, i.e., policy formulation. At this stage, they present the policy makers with all possible choices and alternatives to address the issue. They also prepare innovative and inexpensive strategies to deal with problems so as to widen the choices available to the policymakers. In this process, the NGOs rigorously work as policy makers in their own style, as far as they attempt to incorporate their views and perspectives into the policy domain.

After a policy is formulated, they join the officers concerned for its execution. They work towards enhancing responsiveness of the delivery system, so as to make it more effective in achieving goals of the concerned policy. They also educate and guide the target groups for the optimum utilisation of resources. In this process they simplify and demystify the technology to generate interest among the target sections and ensure their full participation in the implementation process of a policy. They also mobilise experts to clear the doubts of the people when and where they are required. They also monitor implementation processes and register difficulties, if any and report them to the experts from time to time. Such cooperation and coordination make the target sections a part of the decision making process which proves the relevance of the NGOs beyond doubt.

Thus, NGOs study the whole process of implementation, gather essential data and present it to policy makers to highlight as to why a particular policy could not achieve its desired goals or otherwise, during the process of policy evaluation. They use evidence to substantiate their arguments and draw the attention of policy mechanisms to bring about necessary changes in public policies. Such feedback provided by the NGOs enables the policy makers in developing suitable policies and at the same time evaluating the impact of existing ones.

NGOs mostly use the advocacy method to influence the public policy process. In this approach the NGOs make recommendations to the government on policy matters with respect to a variety of issues. But the final authority lies with the policymakers whether to accept their recommendations or not. The NGOs enter policy advocacy by mobilising masses, organising protests, campaigns or by joining the policy networks. This method has proved to be quite successful in mobilising people to draw the attention of the policy makers.

The NGOs also undertake research in collaboration with research institutes that tend towards a more progressive policy outlook. The knowledge generated in this manner is shared between different NGOs and equips them with correct data on several issues. They also organise seminars and workshops and invite policy makers to look into their perspective in providing a solution to a particular problem. A best instance of such an initiative is the Indian Social Institute (ISI). The ISI's initiative to draft an Alternative National Rehabilitation Policy has attracted the attention of NGOs, scholars and policy networks. The database it has provided helped in sharing information and initiating deliberations among NGOs nation wide. With the help of this database the NGOs, activists, research institutions came out with a set of abstract principles to highlight the importance of the rehabilitation policy for internally displaced persons or refuges, as well as, strategies to achieve them.[7]

The contribution made by the NGOs in collaboration with research institutes had really enlarged the scope of public debates in searching for better policy alternatives. But it is unfortunate that the government does not pay adequate attention and has been half receptive to such alternative sources of policy research and action.

But on the other hand, there are a few instances where the government has responded positively. For instance a demand made by a network of women's groups for a more gender-based budget received healthy response from the Finance Minister in 2005.

The NGOs also mobilise people to establish alternative democratic orders. For instance, *Mazdoor Kisan Shakti Sangahatan (MKSS)* a peoples grassroots' movement led by Aruna Roy in Rajasthan organised a struggle to fight corruption and demanded government accountability and genuine decentralisation snowballed into a countrywide movement, which finally led to the formulation of the Right to Information Act in India. Thus, the NGOs work, not only to fill up the gaps left by the government, but also to establish a democratic environment in society through policy initiatives.[8]

Criticism:

In spite of their growing importance and popularity along with their increasing numbers the NGOs are not free from criticism. According to James Petras and HenryVoltmeyer the proliferation of the NGOs in the past few decades reflects the origin of a new social class with a petty bourgeoisie nature. They claim that the NGOs work like the earlier 'comprador' bourgeoisie to link imperial enterprises with the local petty commodity providers engaged in micro enterprises. Usually the NGOs are started and run by ex-Marxists and others who combine anti-Marxist and anti-statist appeal with populist rhetoric. Politically, they hold that the NGOs are designed to fit into the imperialist framework at the local level. They maintain that while the World Bank and International Monetary Fund are engaged in complimentary work at the top to pillage the economy, the NGOs work at the bottom to neutralise and deflect the discontent among the masses. They argue that the NGOs generally co-opt most of the "free floating" intellectuals and make them abandon their class origins which results in a temporary gap between profound crisis of capitalism and the absence of significant organised revolutionary movements.[9]

In many instances, the delivery of services by NGOs suffers from lack of professionalism. They work in a variety of fields, but in many cases without technical know-how. The absence of coordination between different NGOs obstructs the realisation of broader developmental impacts. Several NGOs are highly territorial, leading them to insist on communities working with them exclusively and their interventions are confined to only a few villages with good market access, a concentrated population and a reliable infrastructure.[10] They do not pay serious attention to remote villages where their services are badly required. They are perceived as institutions that are more concerned with building their own business empires, protecting their share of the aid market and cultivating relations with donor governments than helping the beneficiaries.[11]

The NGOs are also criticised, as they tend to be elitist and unaccountable except to their donors. They often control their clientele rather than representing it. They claim and presume to speak on behalf of those who cannot speak for themselves. But, the legitimacy of their status is always open to doubt.[12] It is a common feeling among many independent observers including those who are NGO friendly. In this context, transparency that many NGOs seek from others, needs to be extended to them as well.[13]

The loyalty of the NGOs to people also raises many doubts since the social movements they undertake and leaders which they project are generally not from the masses. The managers of the NGOs are paid officers who ultimately give a bureaucratic flavour to them. Under such circumstances, one cannot expect a serious social transformation to take place in a society, simply by the presence of NGOs. The NGOs are also criticised for their inability to act independently and their reliance on funding agencies. Therefore, their activities cannot cross the limits prescribed by their donors. This approach reinforces the belief to some extent that NGOs are concerned with accumulating funds rather than delivering social services.

In most of the developing countries, the NGOs face criticism for other reasons as well, i.e. they are mostly started and run by influential and elite classes only to amass huge amounts of funds under the safety valve of social service. Therefore, it certainly brings forth several doubts regarding their credibility and their analysis. It is also observed that a majority of the corporate houses open NGOs, only to evade taxes on the pretext that they contribute funds to the NGOs, which are exempted from taxes. Finally, people cannot automatically demand anything from the NGOs and what they receive from them is charity, making them unaccountable to the people.

Globalisation has brought about a transnational character to the NGOs. The fresh start of NGOs in the 1980s can be seen as part of the neo-liberal projects, through the Structural Adjustment Programme(SAP) that aimed at, by passing the state. Many NGOs came into existence as a response to the massive opening up of funding opportunities unleashed by the force of globalisation. According to an estimation, half of the United State foreign aid was channelised through the NGOs in 2000.[14] The recent information and communication technologies have also facilitated a rapid growth of the NGOs in terms of their internal and external expansion. Several similar characteristics of the new social movements all over the world have further brought the NGOs together.

Conclusion:

The economic reforms launched by the World Bank and the IMF have ruined the lives of a vast section of the population, the poor and marginalised all over the world and pushed them to a situation of suffocation that made them respond aggressively in the form of protests and agitations. It is in this context of discontent among the masses that the large-scale proliferation of the NGOs should be located. Several NGOs that were formed after the Second World War proved their credentials and stood up to their goals of social justice and equality. But a majority of them which came along with the advent of globalisation do not seem to be really concerned with the problems of the masses.

As criticised by several scholars, the present day NGOs do not appear to be democratic in their style of functioning. Further, they are also not accountable and transparent to any one except their donors. In many instances, they suffer from lack of professionalism. It has been established beyond doubt that several NGOs function as fund raising companies rather than as social service organisations.

However in view of their in-depth knowledge of developmental issues, their close proximity to the local people, their people-friendly approach and knowledge generating abilities they should not be under estimated and ignored. If the NGOs transform themselves as true social service organisations, they are capable of producing the desired results. They can strengthen their role in public policy formulation. Today, public policy formulation suffers from what Herbert Simon called "bounded rationality." With the help of the NGOs, the government can easily overcome this problem. The NGOs have the potential to shape and mobilise public opinion and bring in necessary changes in the public policy processes. A healthy relationship among the policy makers and the NGOs is needed to produce better policies. What is required at this juncture is a public mechanism to monitor and regulate the activities of the NGOs. They should not be allowed to escape from the principles of good governance, particularly, accountability and transparency. The Government should take necessary steps to achieve a proper coordination among the policy makers and the NGOs.

End Notes

[1] David Harvey, *A Brief History of Neo-Liberalism*, London, Oxford, 2007, p.177.
[2] Carolyn Stephenson, Non-governmental organisations (NGOs) <http://www.beyondintratabiliyt.org/essay/role ng/>
[3] Jagdish Bhagwati, *In Defence of Globalisation*, New Delhi, Oxford, 2004, p.37.
[4] Anup Shah, http://www.globalissues.org/trade related/ poverty/ NGOs, asp
[5] Carolyn Stephenson, Ibid.
[6] T.K. Oommen, *Nation, Civil Society and Social Movements*, New Delhi, Sage, 2004, p.15.
[7] Navdeep Mathur and Kuldeep Mathur; Policy Analysis in India: Research Bases and Discursive Practices in Frank Fischer, Gelaid.J.Miller, Mara S. Sidney (Ed) *A Handbook of Public Policy Analysis*, New Jersey, CRC Press, 2007, pp. 610-613.
[8] *Ibid*.

9. James Petras and Henry Veltmeyer, *Globalisation Unmasked*, New Delhi, Madhyam Books, 2001, p. 138.
10. Annelies Zoomers, Rural Development Policy in Latin America: The Future of Country Side, New Delhi, *Social Scientist*, Vol. NO-30, November-December 2002, p.72.
11. Vanessa Pupa Vac, The Demoralised subject of Global Civil Society, in Gideon Barker and David Chandhy (Ed) *Global Civil Society: Contested Features*, New York, Routledge, 2005, p.58.
12. David Harvey, *op cit*. p.177.
13. Jagdish Bhagwati, *op. cit*. p. 44.
14. Howards H. Lentner, *Power and Politics in Globalisation*, New York, Routledge, 2004 p. 57.

Contributors

Rumki Basu, editor of this book is a Professor of Public Administration and currently the Chairperson of the Department. She has a B.A. and M.A. in Political Science from the University of Delhi, standing first from Lady Shri Ram College in graduation and completing her post graduation with a National Scholarship. She did her M.Phil and Ph.D. from Jawaharlal Nehru University and has 6 books and 25 published articles in leading national and international journals. Besides completing an UGC Project, she was awarded an ICSSR Teacher Fellowship for post doctoral research. She has presented papers in many national and international seminars/conferences.

Nisar-Ul-Haq is Professor in the Department and his main areas of interest are International Politics and South Asia. His Publications include Gulf Cooperation Council : An Introduction (1995), Regional Cooperation in South Asia (2003) besides several articles in Journals. As a member of UGC Televised video / Media project in Political Science, Prof. Haq designed and delivered lectures on International Politics. Prof. Haq has participated in many national and international conferences.

Mohammed Badrul Alam is Professor in the Department, earned his B.A. and M.A. degrees from Utkal University, Orissa; M. Phil. from Jawaharlal Nehru University, New Delhi and Ph.D. from Cornell University, New York, USA. He has taught for over two decades at various universities in India, USA and Japan. His most recent publication is Constructing Nuclear Strategic Discourse: The South Asian Scene (New Delhi: India Research Press, 2007). His research interests include: Nuclear issues in South Asia, Indo-US Relations, Indo-Japan Relations and the Study of Indian Elections.

Mehtab Manzar, Associate Professor in the Department was educated at Aligarh Muslim University and joined Jamia Millia Islamia in 1989, teaching Political Science and Human Rights.

S.A.M. Pasha, Associate Professor, teaches Political Science and Human Rights in the Department. Earlier, he taught at the University of Jammu, Aligarh Muslim University and North-Eastern Hill University, Shillong. Besides, he was till recently the Deputy Director (Hony.), Centre For West Asian Studies at Jamia. He specialises in Islamic Politics with reference to West Asia, Central Asia, and South Asia. He has to his credit, a published book on Pakistan and number of published articles in referred journals.

Furqan Ahmed, Associate Professor, has obtained his M.A. (Political Science) and Ph.D. (Public Administration) from Jamia Millia Islamia. He is associated with ISAC (Institute for Social Analysis and Communication) in an advisory capacity. He has written two books viz. Bureaucracy and Development Administration and Political Economy of Reforms in India (Co-author). Besides, he has contributed many articles and research papers in professional, journals and national seminars.

Muslim Khan is an Associate Professor in the Department with M.A. (Jamia Millia Islamia) M. Phil. (JNU) and Ph.D. (Jamia Millia). He has published 2 books and several articles in well known journals. He has lectured in UGC's countrywide Telecast Programmes and attended several seminars and conferences. His areas of specialisation are African studies and State politics in India.

Bulbul Dhar-James is an Associate Professor in the Department. Her doctoral research as a Commonwealth Scholar, on 'The Politics of Economic Liberalisation in Urban Tanzania' is submitted to the Department of Economics & Politics, School of Oriental and African Studies, University of London. A Post Doctoral Fulbright Fellow, she had published articles in national and international journals based on her presentations in national and international conferences.

Kadloor Savitri, Associate Professor in the Department, has obtained her Ph.D. in international organisation from Jawaharlal Nehru University, New Delhi. She was awarded British Chevening Scholarship (Foreign and Commonwealth Office) in

2002-2003 to pursue Masters in Human Rights at the University of Leicester, UK. She has many articles in edited books and referred journals to her credit.

Syed Mehartaj Begum, Assistant Professor in the Department, has been teaching for the last ten years. She has a M.A. and Ph.D. from Sri Venkateshwara University, Tirupati (A.P.). Her areas of specialisation are Police Administration, Crimes against Women and Role of Law Enforcement Agencies in India. She has 4 books (2 are co-authored) and 10 research papers to her credit. She is the recipient of UGC Research Award for post doctoral research.

S.R.T.P. Sugunakararaju, Assistant Professor in the Department, has post graduate and M. Phil. degrees from the Jawaharlal Nehru University, New Delhi and his area of specialisation is International Politics.

Amir Ali, Assistant Professor in the Department, has a Graduate Degree in Economics from the Aligarh Muslim University. He did his Masters Degree in Political Science from JNU. He also holds M.Phil. and Ph.D. degrees from JNU. He has published a number of articles on themes relating to Multiculturalism in the Economic and Political Weekly.

S. Ramudu, Assistant Professor in the Department, completed his M.A. and M. Phil. from the Central University of Hyderabad and is currently pursuing his Ph.D. from Jamia Millia Islamia.

Farah Naaz, Assistant Professor in the Department, has previously worked with the Institute for Defence Studies and Analyses as Associate Fellow. She has written extensively on West Asia particularly on India's relations with the countries of the region. She has published two monographs on 'Israel-Palestinian Relations: Road to Peace' and 'India-Israel Cooperation'. Her articles have been published in academic journals.

Naved Jamal, Assistant Professor in the Department, teaches Political Science, Public Administration and Human Rights in the Department. Earlier, he taught at the University of Delhi. He specialises in Urban and Local Politics, Indian Administration, Human Rights and West Asia. He has, to his credit, a number of published articles in referred journals. His academic pursuits took him to United Kingdom, Germany and Iran in recent years.